Thick Big Data

Doing Digital Social Sciences

DARIUSZ JEMIELNIAK

UNIVERSITY PRESS

OXFORD

UNIVERSITY PRESS

Great Clarendon Street, Oxford, OX2 6DP,
United Kingdom

Oxford University Press is a department of the University of Oxford.
It furthers the University's objective of excellence in research, scholarship,
and education by publishing worldwide. Oxford is a registered trade mark of
Oxford University Press in the UK and in certain other countries

© Dariusz Jemielniak 2020

The moral rights of the author have been asserted

First Edition published in 2020

Impression: 1

Published in the United States of America by Oxford University Press
198 Madison Avenue, New York, NY 10016, United States of America

British Library Cataloguing in Publication Data
Data available

Library of Congress Control Number: 2019954570

ISBN 978-0-19-883970-5 (hbk.)
ISBN 978-0-19-883971-2 (pbk.)

DOI: 10.1093/oso/9780198839705.001.0001

Printed and bound in Great Britain by
Clays Ltd, Elcograf S.p.A.

Thick Big Data

Preface

After conducting traditional and digital ethnographic research for more than a decade, my attention turned to quantitative studies and data science. In this book I combine my research background with my work as a free knowledge activist in the Wikimedia Foundation and as a member of the Board of Trustees.

This book is a concise, easy, and practical introduction to doing digital social sciences—the key new area of social change—and the tools to study them. It may serve as a reference book and a starting point for further exploration. It summarizes quantitative and qualitative research methodologies, and postulates that we should collect what I call Thick Big Data. In my view, Big Data not only can, but definitely should, be interpreted by *thick data*: the more quantified and powerful the datasets we use, the more important it is to use qualitative tools that improve our understanding of the outcomes. Unlike brick-and-mortar studies, quantitative digital research often raises more questions than answers, and without contextualization it does not reveal its full potential. Qualitative studies done alone are also much less rich in the digital world, since they are based on grounded intuition of cultures much more volatile and multifaceted than in the brick-and-mortar world, although we can add numerical facts with relative ease. I do not believe there is a one-size-fits-all approach to Thick Big Data, but all of the tools presented here, and many others can be combined. More importantly, combining quantitative and qualitative approaches significantly increases the value of outcome when studying digital phenomena, and with much less effort than in offline studies.

Each of the tools and methods described here deserves its own book. Many of the quantitative approaches are simply described, without detailed explanations on how to build models of the data or how to visualize it. Many of the qualitative methods are not presented in a way that will allow a quantitative researcher to undertake qualitative studies. However, the description opens some doors and windows for both quantitative and qualitative researchers, gives them a map of possibilities, encourages them to venture into the unknown, and to see the value of Thick Big Data.

I am deeply grateful to the team of the Management in Networked and Digital Societies (MINDS) department at Kozminski University for their support and constructive remarks during my work on this book. The advice of the following people has been especially stimulating: Tadeusz Chełkowski, Magdalena Kamińska, Paweł Krzyworzeka, Aleksandra Przegalińska, Agata Stasik, and Helena Chmielewska-Szlajfer. My doctoral student, Yaroslav Krempovych, assisted me with the section on the use of data scraping, for which I am most indebted. Wojciech Pędzich, another doctoral student, did the first draft of this manuscript's translation into English. My colleague, David Duenas-Cid helped me write the part about social network analysis, and made many useful remarks about the content. I am truly grateful for his input. I am equally grateful to Krzysztof Konecki and Kazimierz Krzysztofek, who reviewed the first final draft of the book and offered several useful suggestions. Many beneficial remarks and pieces of advice came from my colleagues at the Berkman-Klein Center for Internet and Society at Harvard University, especially from Francine Berman, Erhardt Graeff, and Momin M. Malik. Christine Hine's encouragement and constructive feedback made me realize some omissions I made in the earlier drafts. Naturally, none of these people are responsible for any faults and flaws in this book. Writing this book was possible partly thanks to a grant from Polish National Agency for Academic Exchange (PPN/BEK/2018/1/00009).

Without the patience and unceasing support of my beloved wife, Natalia, this book would not have seen the light of day. My daughter, Alicja, taught me that there are more important things in life than academic work. Maybe this book would have been completed sooner without those lessons but then I would never have known about the adventures of Peppa Pig, or about the deceitful Prince Hans. It is also quite possible that I would have built fewer Lego castles.

I sincerely hope that even if I do not convince all readers of my point of view, that academic researchers will find this book useful.

Welcome to the Internet. I will be your guide.[1]

---

[1] "Welcome to the Internet. Please, follow me," or "Welcome to the Internet. I will be your guide" have been popular Internet memes since 1998. I will devote a section of the book to memes as a research phenomenon. More details on this one may be found here: http://knowyourmeme.com/memes/welcome-to-the-internet

Contents

List of Figures

List of Tables

1

Introduction

Researching social phenomena online could, until quite recently, be perceived as a novelty. Nowadays, practically every research project in the social sciences needs to take online research into account. According to Bauman (2007), an important share of interpersonal interactions and social life has migrated into the online realm. This means that to maintain the current level of interest and detail of social analysis, the introduction of online research is increasingly necessary. As Bainbridge of the *National Science Foundation* warned in 1999:

> It is wrong to consider "cyberspace" an exotic, peripheral realm deserving of only occasional sociological scrutiny, because soon the Internet will become the primary environment where sociologists perform scientific research. [...] Sociology faces the choice of either innovating in the use of the new computerized media for research, or retreating into a narrow niche in the university curriculum while other disciplines become the social sciences of the future.
>
> (Bainbridge, 1999, p. 664)

We live in a "a world in which commercial forces predominate; a world in which we, as sociologists, are losing whatever jurisdiction we once had over the study of the 'social' as the generation, mobilization and analysis of social data become ubiquitous" (Savage & Burrows, 2009, p. 763). Facebook, Tesco, Google, or Mastercard know more about their users and know it sooner than classical sociological studies ever could. To survive, the social sciences need to engage more in the creation, development, and research of technology and the associated changes (Hynes, 2018).

Thick Big Data: Doing Digital Social Sciences. Dariusz Jemielniak, Oxford University Press (2020).
© Dariusz Jemielniak.
DOI: 10.1093/oso/9780198839705.001.0001

Online social sciences can be home to numerous research projects and are worth systematizing. There are at least three approaches to the topic:

Study subject
People while using Internet
Online communities
Online culture output

Areas of interest of online social sciences

We may be doing traditional research by observing people going online or talking with people about the experience. Such analyses are useful, especially when for whatever reason the participation in an online community or its observation could be difficult for the researcher. For instance, interesting research can be done in the online financial communities (Campbell, Fletcher, & Greenhill, 2009). However, without detailed knowledge of finances and high speed trading it will be difficult to conduct online observations (Preda, 2017). Moreover, it may turn out that we will learn more about the online culture of brokers or bankers by physically staying in the same room because first, we will be able to better understand the context of online behaviors and second, we may simply ask for their assistance in making sense. Such research, in its methodological part, often has much in common with classical ethnographical research or Science and Technology Studies (STS). Ethnographic research of people going online is a very interesting issue; however, it does not require a separate description, as observational studies are the subject of many books (Baker, 2006; Whyte & Whyte, 1984). Similarly, STS advances are large and abundantly described (Jasanoff, Markle, Peterson, & Pinch, 2001; Latour, 1987; Sismondo, 2010; Stasik, 2018; Woolgar, 1991). I have not applied any of the strategies in my academic work—this monograph will therefore focus on other areas of online social sciences.

Another possible understanding of online social sciences is the research of online communities—the relations, behaviors, dynamics. According to Howard Rheingold, an online community can be understood as "social aggregations that emerge from the Net when enough people carry on those public discussions long enough with sufficient human feeling to form webs of personal relationships in cyberspace"

(Rheingold, 1993, p. 4). A purely virtual research relies, naturally, on the observation of avatars (Williams, 2007), not people. This is apparently a nuance but an important one. When studying the behaviors of avatars, we need to keep in mind that seemingly different avatars may have been created by the same person or that one avatar may be under control of several people. Additionally, not all interactions are with people; bots are increasingly common (Ciechanowski, Przegalinska, Magnuski, & Gloor, 2019). This in itself is also an interesting research area for online social sciences, and one that gains extra value when we realize that machines are writing the messages.

For these reasons, research on avatars is often supplemented by research on people—through traditional interviews and observations, although the research of avatars can also be valuable in itself (Przegalińska, 2015a). This is the fundamental difference between pure virtual sociology (based strictly on online research) and digital sociology which also considers the human aspect and is supplemented with interviews, even via Internet messengers. Research into online communities naturally has an important quantitative dimension—we may go as far as to say that social sciences underwent an irreversible change once Big Data and modern online social analysis tools became available. In this book, I will describe how to use these approaches, starting with the most quantitative, including those related to Big Data, through qualitative ones from the virtual and digital ethnography. I will also encourage triangulation through the quantitative and qualitative methods of data gathering and analysis.[1]

The last possible understanding of online social sciences is the research on Internet culture. Such studies are important, as the digital revolution has led to a situation where the majority of consumers of culture can be creators and distributors of culture at the same time—and often they assume such roles, even if to a limited degree. In order to participate in the creation of cultural artifacts, a smartphone or a memes generator are often sufficient; there is also a growing trend of applications supporting cultural production, be it more traditional Instagram, or a

---

[1] This is an important distinction in that the collected quantitative data can be analyzed qualitatively and vice versa—for instance, on the basis of the conducted ethnographical interviews, one can do some quantitative operations, such as measuring the frequency of the occurrence of some words. In this book, I describe the selected methods of gathering and analyzing data—however, because this book is not related to general methodology, I do not make a detailed distinction in each case, assuming that the readers understand the methods.

bit more modern Tiktok. In consequence, even though in the pre-digital society researching cultural expression could be treated as a less important way of learning about social norms, values, and assumptions, in the online era it is much more crucial. This monograph attempts to present how to apply a research apparatus, so far typically used in narration and anthropological research, for online social sciences.

In my understanding, quantitative and qualitative analyses of online communities may and should intertwine with the research of products of digital culture. Applied together, in what I call Thick Big Data, they offer a coherent system, based on a variety of research tools and perspectives. Its use, in whole or in part, should enable a solid sociological analysis, setting foundations for constructing theories on people's behaviors online.

The last part of the book focuses on the issues of research ethics. Most of the readers will have the understanding of the ethical challenges in social sciences as such, however, online research opened the fields for a plethora of new ethical questions which need to be addressed. I briefly explain these issues, interpreting the state of knowledge in the area based on my own experience.

2

Online Revolution

The Internet has transformed human behavior. Methods of interacting, spending free time and time at work, making friends, and even the understanding of what constitutes intimacy have undergone rapid changes (Hobbs, Owen, & Gerber, 2017; Jinasena, 2014). New social phenomena have arisen, such as online communities composed of people who have never met face to face but who still have a strong connection.

Initial research has suggested that people who are deeply involved in online communities may be visibly more antisocial—this is the stereotype of the solitary computer geek in the basement (Nie & Hillygus, 2002). Because the use of social networks has become ubiquitous and participation in online communities brings undisputable social gains (Pendry & Salvatore, 2015; Raza, Qazi, & Umer, 2017), this stereotype has lost credibility. It is worth mentioning, though, that Facebook is more frequently used by people who claim to be lonely (Song et al., 2014). The addiction to social media has also become a growing social problem (Hawi & Samaha, 2017).

For most of the social sciences, there is a mirror field within online sociology, useful for exploration both as complementary research and as independent projects. Cybernationalism (Jiang, 2016), involvement in civil societies (Chmielewska-Szlajfer, 2019), relations of power in international trade (Jarrett, 2003), online social gender construction (Brickell, 2012), and a multitude of other issues whose sociological analysis has become possible only with the use of online research show that the Internet revolution has great potential for the social sciences. It may well be a defining moment for them (Possamai-Inesedy & Nixon, 2017).

This book serves as a methodological reference and may be useful to readers who are interested in these online-related social phenomena and those who work with the traditional research subjects but now need to be more attentive to account online elements.

Thick Big Data: Doing Digital Social Sciences. Dariusz Jemielniak, Oxford University Press (2020).
© Dariusz Jemielniak.
DOI: 10.1093/oso/9780198839705.001.0001

Social processes and phenomena that online media have brought to light are good examples of possible research topics. This monograph is not devoted to their detailed or systematic description; I will, however, provide a summary of three major socio-economic changes caused or intensified by technology. These three changes are new and important research subjects and they are worthy of further attention: online relations, expert knowledge crisis, and the development of sharing economy.

2.1 Online Relations

The widespread availability of online communication tools has created unprecedented possibilities to maintain old relationships and make new ones (T. Davis, 2010; Holmes, 2012). As Lee Rainie and Barry Wellman observe, we are experiencing a triple revolution of social contacts: by the increased use of the Internet, by mobile technologies, and by social media (Rainie & Wellman, 2012). This is the result of development of "online individualism." This phenomenon relies on an individual belonging to an online community, while acting autonomously and making his or her own highly customized composition of relations and networks, adjusting the community to which he or she belongs to his or her needs (Rainie & Wellman, 2012).

The use of social media reshapes private relations. We are faced with mediated online intimacy and interpersonal relations that are purely personal in some ways and quasi-public in others. In addition, the use of networked media allows for unprecedented semi-public disclosures of emotions, and of physical and mental health issues (Das & Hodkinson, 2019). Social networks allow for a major increase of involvement in the cultivation of weak ties and the formation of "personalized public networks" of contacts (Chambers, 2013). Even though keeping diaries or sharing photos with friends are nothing new, and as Lee Humphreys notes, describing one's meals was customary among eighteenth-century diarists, the use of technology widens the circle of recipients of life details that we wish to disclose (Humphreys, 2018).

The use of social networks occasionally assumes a pathological character, as children (Ihm, 2018) and adults often abuse these networks (Kuss &

Griffiths, 2017), frequently out of Fear of Missing Out (FOMO). Pervasive datafication leads to a digital colonization of human life: that is, appropriation of resources as a result of "free" connective technologies. There is also a correlation between the inclination to seek friendships online and Internet addiction, although it is hard to pinpoint the causation. It is possible that people who have a predilection to such addiction are more willing to search for relations in that medium; or that deep involvement with online acquaintances and friends leads to Internet addiction (Smahel, Brown, & Blinka, 2012). Some researchers have even concluded that an increased use of digital forms of contact leads to higher social involvement, face-to-face interactions, and local social ties (Chayko, 2014). The online and offline worlds also permeate each other; social exclusion in real life may be the consequence of exclusion in virtual life, not only the other way round (Marsh, 2016). Besides, the virtual-real dichotomy is not particularly useful. Perhaps we should juxtapose virtuality with actuality (Lévy, 1997), and apart from virtual reality we may also speak about real virtuality (Castells, 2000).

It is undisputable, though, that the observation of acquaintances' behaviors on social media affects our own behavior comparably to traditional reference groups. For instance, seeing their friends drinking alcohol or smoking will increase alcohol and tobacco use among teenagers (Huang et al., 2014). Some relations between technology and social inequalities are also hard to discern—for instance, refugees from Syria, despite limited means, use smartphones because the devices enable their survival under critically difficult conditions (Kaufmann, 2018; Narli, 2018). Of course, this can also be related to mobile services replacing traditional institutions and infrastructure, especially in Africa (Asongu, 2018).

Prominent sociologists differ as to whether the growing importance of technologically mediated relations has a positive or negative impact on social relations. Optimists like note that despite rapid changes in the social world, technology could tighten interpersonal relations as well as make them more democratic and cooperative, based on the partnership of equal but independent, individuals (Couldry, 2012; Giddens, 1991). Others, such as Beck, stress that we are facing an ongoing individualization which in the age of globalization is the only solution that retains some sort of social coherence (Beck, 2002). More pessimistically, Bauman claims that intimate relationships are becoming contingent and liquid; he warns against the commodification of interpersonal relations as the result of technology-initiated social changes (Bauman, 2007). The liquid character of relations is caused by an increasing imperative of change and perceived lack of attachment as freedom (Bauman, 2003); it is only partially the result of the mere increase in the number of distant acquaintances with whom we maintain contact. Liquidity is found in all spheres of private or professional life (Jemielniak & Raburski, 2014), and it changes typical behavior trajectories.

Close relations arguably underwent even more of a metamorphosis. Services and apps that enable social or intimate encounters with others are especially popular. The example of intimate ties is intriguing and I will use it in my discussion of online relations.

Between 2013 and 2016 the number of 18- to 24-year-olds in the US who used dating services nearly tripled (from 10 percent to 27 percent); in the whole adult population it was 15 percent, and 59 percent of Americans were of the opinion that it is a good way to make new contacts (A. Smith & Anderson, 2016). I do not have access to more recent data or detailed analyses for other countries, but we can safely assume that the popularity of dating services is still on the rise.

They are used by people of all ages, although, naturally, older and younger users of these apps have different expectations (Malta & Farquharson, 2014). The use of Internet dating sites solves a few social problems:

- they facilitate preselection, as users search people who are interested in making contact;

- they reduce rejection-related stress, because with services like Tinder or Bumble, contact is initiated after the other party has approved;

- they shorten the amount of time required to make the first decision, which results in the decision being based on the profile picture, rather than on some selection filters used by older apps. Even if some selection criteria for some users would be considered at least as important in real life as appearance, a simple and quick system of initiating contact is superior to the alternatives.

People who are more sensitive to rejection are more likely to use online dating services (Hance, Blackhart, & Dew, 2018). An even bigger change in the shaping of intimate relations was introduced by dating services for non-heteronormative people. Especially in conservative societies, their social space for meeting someone was limited—therefore, dating services offer a new quality and a transformation of the organization of social life (Wu & Ward, 2018).

Substantial changes to the forms of meeting new people are also relevant for people seeking extramarital affairs, which sometimes leads to atypical discoveries. Ashley Madison was a Web portal that enabled married strangers to contact each other for affairs. After a hacker attack, Ashley Madison refused to pay ransom. As a result, data on millions of users was leaked. Social scientists found that 80 percent of users of the website interacted with Ashley Madison bots (Cockayne, Leszczynski, & Zook, 2017). The bots were so convincing that they exchanged 20 million messages with users (Tsvetkova, García-Gavilanes, Floridi, & Yasseri, 2017). This is a practical example of romantic relations between people and bots. This should not even be a surprise, given relations with dolls and sexbots (Ciambrone, Phua, & Avery, 2017), which have led to bioethical concerns and that portend even larger social changes (Carvalho Nascimento, da Silva, & Siqueira-Batista, 2018; Cheok, Levy, & Karunanayaka, 2016).

Rituals of matching in interpersonal relationships also take online behaviors into account. For instance, the intensity of public Internet interactions, their type, frequency of commenting on pictures or tagging oneself in them are elements of social signaling of interest and involvement. For declared relationships, such behaviors can emphasize belonging while also marking one's territory and underlining a couple's independence (Mod, 2010). The success of a face-to-face date can be reliably forecast from online conversations, the first impression, and the exchange of social signals (Sharabi & Caughlin, 2017).

The intertwining of online and real interactions as well as the incorporation of online communication into the repertoire of symbolic social signals that lead to intimate relationships can be perceived within the categories of augmented reality. They have physical and real dimensions but they are also under the important influence of perceived digital and online identities, narratives, and self-creation (Newett, Churchill, & Robards, 2018). For these reasons, it is increasingly important to research the formation of close social ties online as well as their connections and changing modality in real life. Given the rising impact of technology on the shaping of interpersonal relationships and the limited research into the important effects of those technologies, it is a topic that requires recurring analyses and that constitutes a significant research field.

Finally, the analysis of offline friendships and other social relations can benefit from the rise of new technologies and network analysis. For instance, sensors worn by the research participants (which can be replaced with apps) have led to the collection of valuable data supplementing traditional diaries or questionnaires. I will explore these areas in later chapters (Mastrandrea, Fournet, & Barrat, 2015).

2.2 The Demise of Expert Knowledge

The online knowledge revolution has come to light at a time when universities and trust in academia are in crisis (Jemielniak & Greenwood, 2015). The fall of higher education system was spearheaded by the McDonaldization of the university (Hayes & Wynyard, 2016). McDonaldization is based on strict proceduralization and control of academics' worktime, setting of "production" short-term goals (Berg & Seeber, 2016), and other methods typical of corporate deprofessionalization (Hadley, 2014; Washburn, 2006). One symptom of the change is the introduction of strict measures of "academic excellence" (Vessuri, Guédon, & Cetto, 2014) and insistence on publication only in peer-reviewed journals from a bureaucrat-approved list. The need for control is so strong that the critique of journal ratings does not merit attention, regardless of whether it is done from the perspective of revealing the methodological errors or irremovable flaws of the rankings (Nkomo, 2009; Özbilgin, 2009; Sangster, 2015; Tourish & Willmott, 2015), by proving them to deepen the inequalities in the academic world (Beigel, 2014a, 2014b; Olssen, 2016) or showing their destructive impact on academic freedom (Tourish & Willmott, 2015). Bureaucrats "can't read, but they sure can count" (Gorman, 2008). This control of academic efforts is made possible by the development of information technology and through peer control, where scholars control each other, exerting pressure on others setting up ORCID, ResearchID or Google Scholar accounts. The research of these technological advancements as well as their impact on the changes of academic hierarchy (Putnam, 2009) or the perception of commodification of academia (Hogler & Gross, 2009) online is an interesting stream within social sciences, also worthy of wider quantitative research. The development of rankings and evaluation systems is a useful academic field. For instance, with two colleagues we conducted research (Jemielniak, Masukume, & Wilamowski, 2019) based on tens of thousands of bibliographic references, scraped with the use of dedicated bot scripts from English Wikipedia. We showed that some medical journals most often cited on Wikipedia also appear in traditional journal rankings but diverging trends can also be observed— Wikipedia favors open-access publications or review papers. This is a contribution to what is considered a valuable source of information in public opinion.

More importantly, the crisis of universities and the neoliberal takeover of academic institutions is characterized by the de facto questioning of the role of intellectual elites in social life (Giroux, 2015; Ritzer, 2006). Some scholars even speak of "the death of expertise" and a systematic campaign against scientific knowledge (Nichols, 2017). It is difficult to inquire into reasons and consequences but this social phenomenon is closely linked to the development of online communities, has great impact on life and, as such, deserves further consideration.

The authority of academia seems to have been permanently damaged and new models of knowledge creation and distribution are still being shaped (Bijker, Bal, & Hendriks, 2009). We can see the dissonance between the academic and expert worlds, solidified by the separation of theoretical from practical knowledge (Bok, 2009), with the debate on the role of technocracy in today's democracies adding to the sharp divisions within these two groups (F. Fischer, 2009). Moreover, through the coordination of modern tech platforms, new social movements focused on independent collection and interpretation of knowledge may organize themselves and influence political decisions, as with, for instance, fighting smog or the protests against the exploitation of shale gas (Lis & Stasik, 2017). Thus, expert authority is becoming distributed (Nowak, 2013).

The Internet has also slashed the costs of accessing knowledge, although the costs of sensible sorting and filtering of knowledge have increased. The online revolution revealed an interesting phenomenon: many people visibly prefer speed and ease of accessing information over its quality, verifiability, or reliability. This is especially visible in medical knowledge—related to health which is, literally, vital to all of us and where reliability of information is of colossal and often irreversible impact. Unquestionably, this area of expertise requires solid and systematic education—in most countries, medical studies take longer to complete than for other fields, and becoming a medical practitioner often requires additional vocational training, internships, and apprenticeships. Nevertheless, the Internet has become the primary source of health and medical information (Nettleton, Burrows, & O'Malley, 2005). This is due to the rapid democratization and decentralization of expert knowledge, and the revolution of the epistemological hierarchy (Brosnan & Kirby, 2016).

Sometimes, this can have a positive impact, even in medicine. For rare illnesses, "Doctor Google" can prove quite helpful (Bouwman, Teunissen, Wijburg, & Linthorst, 2010). Patients surely have an incentive to find out "what's wrong." They can also self-organize, compare doctors, and either rule out those who are less involved or encourage the less educated physicians to update their knowledge (Nicholl, Tracey, Begley, King, & Lynch, 2017). Moreover, decreasing the hierarchy and unidirectionality of the transfer of knowledge may improve the efficacy of medical treatment. In Detroit, the inclusion of patients as equal partners in medical research led to more valuable results (Lantz, Viruell-Fuentes, Israel, Softley, & Guzman, 2001). The involvement of parents in the exchange of information and in the search for therapy for their sick children also has positive results, although it may also cause shifts in authoritative knowledge (Prior, 2003; Schaffer, Kuczynski, & Skinner, 2008). Sick people are usually eager to share information on their symptoms with others diagnosed with the same disease, creating online communities of knowledge, whose existence has therapeutic and medical meaning—because in such cases, patients communicate differently with each other than with a doctor (Lupton, 2014). Nonetheless, there is a long history of discussions over the top-down model of decision-making and not supplying information to the patients in medicine and sociology of health (Emke, 1992; Henwood, Wyatt, Hart, & Smith, 2003). Perhaps it is time to redefine the role of medical professions (Tousijn, 2006)—however, this issue no longer generates much resistance from health professionals, and doctor–patient relations change dynamically (Petracci, Schwarz, Sánchez Antelo, & Mendes Diz, 2017).

Medical knowledge, in addition, has always been communicated and consolidated not only through contact with medical professionals, but also, even primarily, in the home (Dew et al., 2014) and in peer contacts. Simply, the same things are also happening online, and in contact with strangers, and because of the ease and simplicity of such contacts, they can prevail over other the types. The problem is that the trust and personal authority in knowledge exchange took years for local communities to build (McClean & Moore, 2016; Penner, 2015) and major social changes in trust occur over generations, not decades (Sztompka, 1993). Some elements of knowledge-related trust are located online, with no verification mechanisms, and online reputation control systems, far from solving the problem, exacerbate it (Kuwabara, 2015).

There is an important change in online social capital undergoing important transformations and being far from institutional stability (Julien, 2015). Technology is becoming a key lever: societies rich in social capital draw larger benefits from it as it assists in the growth of technological innovations. The trust is carried over to algorithms and machines, as a risesult of automation, have perceptible costs and limitations (Beverungen & Lange, 2018).

The extent to which people are ready to rely on unverified information that has a major impact on health and life is considerable. It is noticeable in medical knowledge, which shows the processes of knowledge hierarchy changes—it is related to a branch of knowledge requiring very specialist preparation, based on years of study and practice, it is also related to vital issues undergoing a revolution. I will use medicine as the example, stressing that the indications of similar phenomena also appear in other disciplines.

The use of Internet forums in relation to dietetics is ubiquitous, even though some of the advice given on the forums is harmful (Kimmerle, Gerbing, Cress, & Thiel, 2012). The communities of the sick can unite against this environment. For instance, anorexics set up online support groups that confirm their belief the rest of the world is mistaken, and they are healthy (N. Smith, Wickes, & Underwood, 2015; Wooldridge, 2014). Some of these people insist that anorexia is their desired lifestyle (Kamińska, 2013).

Similarly, knowledge of supplementary and alternative therapy is commonly acquired from the Internet (Sharma, Holmes, & Sarkar, 2016). Influenced by information found online, even medical professionals reach for alternative medicine (Eastwood, 2000). This gap, created by loss of public trust in academic knowledge, is immediately filled. The interpretation of medical knowledge is no longer the domain of specialists. There is an increasing number of health-related tests, presumably offered to consumers (Bowman, Woodbury, & Fisher, 2016). There is also a tendency towards self-use of measuring equipment (Cheung, Krahn, & Andrade, 2018; Piwek, Ellis, Andrews, & Joinson, 2016) as part of the Quantified Self movement. These changes are difficult to evaluate—although there is no doubt they can be conducive to pro-health behaviors.

Other changes are more disturbing. Witch doctors and fraudsters make millions. There is a rapid increase in the number of well-educated and privileged parents who refuse to vaccinate their children (Sharma et al., 2016). According to some studies, these parents may even be more inclined not to vaccinate (Yang, Delamater, Leslie, & Mello, 2016). This dismaying fact may be the consequence of false information about vaccines; like academic knowledge, it requires involvement and a will to acquire information, in addition to the perceptive skills for processing it. Such anti-knowledge and pseudotheories are spread largely through online communities (Kata, 2012). An interesting fact is that the testimonies of anti-vaxxers (*vel* pro-epidemics) are characterized by self-confidence but they are also symptomatic of analytical thinking (Faasse, Chatman, & Martin, 2016). Even people who insist that the earth is flat have managed to organize themselves online (Berghel, 2017) quite literally around the globe. We are experiencing what Stacey calls "virtual social sciences," the use of advanced communication technology to socially construct "truths" and alternative beliefs about the world (Stacey, 1999).

Social media and the Internet spread complex knowledge systems and mediate the contacts of their supporters (Delgado-López &

Corrales-García, 2018). This may reveal a specific social process—even a radical one, as rare ideas may serve as the axis for the organization of a group, and online communication platforms have enabled much more precise matching of people with similar beliefs and preferences, by adapting "the long tail" of demand, similarly to the strategy of global corporations retail chains. Beliefs that had been poorly circulated and whose isolated supporters were reluctant to voice them, found strong support in online communities. Support and knowledge exchange groups take on a tribal character, isolating themselves from these ideas that do not match their common denominator (Rusu, 2016), although there are some positive aspects of this phenomenon. For instance, people who are stigmatized in everyday social life because of their weight can create a safe online space for themselves in which they are accepted (Dickins, Browning, Feldman, & Thomas, 2016). As d'Ancona aptly shows, proepidemic communities—as anti-vaxxers should probably be called—show a very efficient synergy of anti-establishment tendencies, anti-information and anti-academic industries, fake news, and conspiracy theories (d'Ancona, 2017). They also benefit from strong individualistic attitudes, as well as from a general version to syringes and needles (Hornsey, Harris, & Fielding, 2018).

Academic authority is not sufficient in light of the proliferation of online communities—in other words, it is not enough to be right (Camargo Jr & Grant, 2015) because the radical changes were related not only to the ease of accessing information or the clarity of messages but also the fundamental trust in sources (Fotaki, 2014). What is interesting is that such changes do not mean that the personal authority of the author or the prestige of the publisher cease to matter but that ease of access and perceived non-existence of financial relations (such as no ads) are more important than ever (Sbaffi & Rowley, 2017). It is also crucial that medical and professional authority have eroded in recent decades, independently of the Internet (Cook, 2010). We may even talk about what Bauwens calls "anticredentialism": highly developed skepticism of formal authority (Bauwens, 2006), which, in addition, cannot be fought from modernist positions which are often assumed as opposed to those presented by pseudosciences.

There is also the impact of controversial research, experiments, or even unclear financial dependencies and conflicts of interest of some researchers on pharmaceutical, tobacco, or fuel companies.[1] In fact, large corporations were and are able to skew the results of professional research in ways that benefit them (Light, 2007). Hierarchic systems of knowledge and the domination of the expert system have contributed to people starting to prefer the democratization of knowledge in light of many violations of the public trust (G. Gray, 2007). In the public surface-level discourse it is also difficult to defend the fact that the scientific method is not the way to acquire unerring and sure knowledge, but merely the well-tried, repetitive method of building beliefs about the world which may lead to mistaken beliefs but in a way that maintains the complex system of knowledge as a coherent whole (Brickhouse, Dagher, Letts IV, & Shipman, 2000; Konieczny, 2016).

The prevailing model of knowledge distribution is therefore questioned, not only through the growth of knowledge within open collaboration models (Jemielniak & Aibar, 2016). New hierarchies of knowledge and legitimization systems are still far from equilibrium; the influence of corporations in the "democratic" online knowledge is in many cases equal to, if not larger, and there are still no control and verification mechanisms. For these reasons, phenomena such as the development of citizen science, networks of anti-science and alter-science movements, communities of open science, or fake news, are a priority and momentous for social sciences—with digital sociology in the lead.

2.3 Sharing Economy

Apart from a major reshuffling within the sources of social knowledge, the development of online societies revealed other interesting phenomena. One of them is the sharing economy, a concept both popular and overused, in popular belief associated with such radically different organizations as Uber and Wikipedia, Airbnb and Mozilla.

Categorizations associated with sharing economy are ambiguous (Jemielniak & Przegalinska, 2020; Rodak & Mikołajewska-Zając, 2017).

---

[1] Examples are the Miligram study of obedience and electric shocks, and the Tuskegee study, where black men with syphilis were denied access to treatment just so that the progress of the disease could be tracked (cf.: Derbyshire, 2008). Please, add: Derbyshire, S., 2008. The ethical dilemma of ethical committees. *Sociology Compass*, 2(5), pp.1506–1522.

Initially, researchers assumed that creating or copying zero-reproduction cost products, such as digital ones, can be their defining characteristics. Indeed, if we look at Internet piracy (M. Mason, 2009) or free/open source software, zero-cost replication was the major change introduced by sharing economy. The implications of peer-to-peer media sharing and the resulting changes to fairness and property perceptions are substantial (Hergueux & Jemielniak, 2019). Additionally, a new model of innovation emerged, the "private collective," thanks to which groups of strangers, dispersed around the world, produce works that had needed much better coordination and organizational structures, usually corporate (Von Hippel & Von Krogh, 2003).

At the same time, one can argue that the changes in organizational structures have even deeper consequences than the zero-replication costs. Internet communities, thanks to cooperation-enabling tools, seriously reduced the need of top-down process management. Raymond suggested a metaphor of a bazaar, as opposed to a cathedral (Raymond, 1999/2004)—the latter requiring an architectonic plan, a construction foreman, and division of tasks. In contrast, the bazaar, the reference point for open software projects, does not need a holistic vision and can be based on local coordination efforts so that it serves its function. The first researchers of the p2p economy and sharing saw, above all, the tremendous potential for systemic revolution, the replacement of a capitalist system and the elimination of the associated inequalities that are the result of asymmetry of knowledge and access to means (Bauwens, 2009).

The sharing economy is directly associated with the gift economy, based on the perception of the symbolic role of gifts and the ritual of making exchanges in many social institutions (Cheal, 2015; Mauss, 1954/2001), especially visible in open collaboration communities (Bergquist & Ljungberg, 2001). As it turns out, people are willing to support one another, even strangers, under specific conditions, and online contacts facilitate such behaviors. All the free/open-source movement,[2]

---

[2] The discussion of whether we should speak of "free software" or "open software" is heated. Richard Stallman, who wrote the 1985 GNU Manifesto in which he laid the foundations for a free operating system that eventually became Linux, claimed that only the former is right—because the essence of the revolutionary change lies in the freedom to copy, modify or use the code, not only its accessibility (Stallman, 2009; Stallman & Gay, 2009). However, open knowledge or open access movements indicate that the word "open" is already

or software development with the ideal of making source code reusable by others, including commercial competitors, has shown that even large-scale projects needing cooperation of thousands of professionals can be delivered in a model where many of the participants are not even paid (Benkler, 2002). The overwhelming success of Linux, the world's most popular server operating system and the base for Android, the world's most popular smartphone operating system is typical. It was developed by thousands of programmers who do not know one another personally, within a free/open-source project, and it is living proof that free/open collaboration models can compete against profit-driven companies. Other examples are the Firefox browser, developed by the Mozilla Foundation, or Wordpress, the most popular content management system (CMS)—they were at least as successful, if not more so, than their commercial counterparts. The free/open-source model is simply more effective and efficient in certain product categories, and encourages participation (Benkler, 2011; Weber, 2004).

Immaterial goods created through the use of information technology and open collaboration are not only characterized by zero or low copying cost but also often have a non-competitive character and can impact economic development. As Romer (Romer, 1990) states:

Nonrivalry has two important implications for the theory of growth. First, nonrival goods can be accumulated without bound on a per capita basis, whereas a piece of human capital such as the ability to add cannot. Each person has only a finite number of years that can be spent acquiring skills. When this person dies, the skills are lost, but any nonrival good that this person produces-a scientific law; a principle of mechanical, electrical, or chemical engineering; a mathematical result; software; a patent; a mechanical drawing; or a blueprint lives on after the person is gone.

Especially in reference to open licensed goods, this results in rapid growth of commons. For example, the social profits from Wikipedia are

well-understood, while the word "free" can be associated not only with freedom but also with "no cost" and can be abused by different business models such as adware or freemium. Cf.: https://perma.cc/T5AD-QPPE, https://perma.cc/MF3R-WLE9

estimated in the hundreds of billions of dollars per year (Band & Gerafi, 2013). Peer-to-peer generated commons-centric social systems, in the view of some authors, has the potential to revolutionize capitalism and make the emerging modes of production and goods exchange a new default (Bauwens, Kostakis, & Pazaitis, 2019).

However, the initial enthusiasm for online communities has significantly weakened—more reflexive and critical streams appeared, drawing attention to the important problems of abusing people with technology (Azzellini, 2018; M. L. Gray & Suri, 2019). Strict limitations on online collectives have been noticed, which seem to bear the characteristics of immanent organizational weaknesses (Kreiss, Finn, & Turner, 2011). It was also noticed that a visible axis of division, which explains the changes in the world, is not so much the focus on the cost of reproduction, or even the organizational structure per se, as rather the organization's business model: whether we are facing for-profit or non-profit activities. In this sense, we can see the sharing economy as the opposite of "information capitalism" (Zukerfeld, 2017), an alternative type of information society, founded on strict control of intellectual property rights, while exhibiting wide freedom of expression and online access (Haggart & Jablonski, 2017). Its example revealed a new type of modality, based on the logic of sharing in the areas that had been occupied by strictly entrepreneurial entities (Benkler, 2004). The other side of the story is the partial arrest of areas which had been left to non-economic exchange by businesses as well as the use of technology to deepen the commodification of the social world (Wittel, 2013).

A trait of modern businesses which are associated, at least in popular belief, with the sharing economy is deepening social inequality, using algorithms to exploit their employees and customers, or the progressing atomization of the recipients which makes use of information asymmetry and the power to generate higher profits (Schor & Attwood-Charles, 2017). It is characteristic of companies like Uber. They are de facto the opposite of sharing, through putting a price tag on services that had previously been evaluated financially. The absurd rhetorics of "sharing" in reference to Uber and similar platforms are clear in a simple example. If a hypothetical citizen has a hair dryer and allows their roommates to use it, this is sharing. If they expect monetary compensation for the use of the dryer, this is the opposite of sharing (Jemielniak & Przegalinska, 2020); the inclusion of goods that had not been fully utilized previously, into the capitalist system. Despite this obvious contradiction (Botsman & Rogers, 2010), many corporations use the "sharing" discourse, mainly for marketing and promotional reasons (Terranova, 2004). At this point, they privatize the results of group, cooperative efforts, with the parallel transfer of their own business problems into the public sphere with the avoidance of responsibility (Frenken & Schor, 2017). It is not a trait typical only of contemporary online corporations, as traditional ones undertake similar activities (Klein, 2000), but lack of a canon, legal frameworks, or the modern technology-related social norms which are still at their early stages of development, facilitate similar activities among technological companies. This gives rise to regulatory problems (Leshinsky & Schatz, 2018), new relations of power, and new forms of relation which are sociologically fascinating and worthy of further exploration (Hynes, 2018).

Corporate approaches to the possibilities offered by modern technologies of cooperation and online communities are described in terms of "platform capitalism" and the "gig economy." Platform capitalism, with examples such as Uber, Airbnb, Google, Apple, or Microsoft, relies on technological platforms that are closely controlled by the corporation but that also allow large groups of people to cooperate or to meet each other's everyday needs (Srnicek, 2017). Platform capitalism is therefore based on an intermediary, which—through strict regulation of information resources and rules of engagement—can utilize the work and resource contribution of individual people (Pasquale, 2016). This process noticeably changes the shape of social relations as such (Van Dijck, Poell, & de Waal, 2018), and results, among other things, in on-demand "ghost work," the invisible labor of thousands of people who actually make the platforms work (M. L. Gray & Suri, 2019).

Another view is the concept of gig economy, indirectly associated with the technological revolution. The gig economy is based on the precarization of professions and a trend towards not offering full-time work but rather favoring one-time orders, usually offered under the pretense of rhetoric of professionalization, entrepreneurship, and independence of contractors. Portals like Uber, UpWork or TaskRabbit found their business models on putting customers in contact with contractors

(Aloisi, 2015). People working in this model undergo commodification and through the use of information technologies, the profit margin on their work can be maximized, both on the side of the customer and the company's share in the profit, while avoiding the consequences related to the standard regulations of labor law (Steinberger, 2017). Under the pretext of greater freedom, workers in the gig economy are deprived of the protection characteristic of employer–employee relations (their services are paid for by accidental private individuals, and the platform pretends their only role is that of associating customers with contractors).

Table 2.1 Sharing economy-related terms

Term	Description
Platform capitalism	The emergence of technological platforms which present themselves as mere intermediaries between customers and contractors but in reality, through strict control of algorithms, regulations, access to information, and business model, may dominate the two groups.
Gig economy	The elimination of full-time employment through single-order work, often under the pretense of "professionalization," with the use of technological platforms that allow to associate customers and contractors. Related to "ghost work," the invisible labor exploited through technology.
Peer-to-peer economy	The elimination of intermediaries from economic relations, with the use of new technology and in the form of online cooperatives.
Collaborative society	The increase of the natural inclination to interpersonal cooperation with the use of new technologies, both in the economic and the social-cultural dimensions.
Gift economy	The establishment of social institutions based not only on economic exchange but also on symbolic exchange and within the rules of gift, especially in free/open-source environments.
Informational capitalism	The development of information technologies leading to the blurring of traditional class divisions between capital owners and the working class, creating new divisions associated with knowledge work and information access (Fuchs, 2010), resulting in changes within the system of values (Arvidsson & Colleoni, 2012).
Sharing economy	A concept related to new forms of activity and direct exchange between individuals but also generalized to describe business organizations and forming the basis for business models founded on the willingness to share (Stephany, 2015).

Since such exploitation of activity is sometimes linked to the sharing economy, the term that more accurately explains cooperation for common good, without focus on material gains of one side or another, is the "p2p economy" (Bauwens, 2012). It is based on online cooperatives (Pazaitis, Kostakis, & Bauwens, 2017) and fits communities like Wikipedia and Linux, which develop products of unquestionable social value spontaneously and for free. Bauwens, a fierce supporter of open collaboration, describes this process as the abandoning of capital communism at the gain of common goods capital (Bauwens & Kostakis, 2014).

These ideas emphasize the economic aspects of technological changes. It is apparent, however, that many of the social changes are not founded on the production or exchange of goods or services—these are sometimes a side-effect but rarely the driving force of the activity. This is, above all others, the drive towards sharing, as discussed by Aigraine (2012) or John (2017). Perhaps the main issue is more about different forms of cooperation than about sharing. For instance, the collaborative production and consumption of Internet memes at Imgur or 9gag, group discussions on 4chan, or all the chatrooms and Web forums can be seen as joint experience of culture or communication with no final product. A part of the Internet revolution is collective experience of culture, rather than just its co-production. For this reason, with Przegalińska, we use the term "collaborative society" to describe the processes based on the radical increase of collaborative tendencies as a result of new communication technologies and tools (Jemielniak & Przegalinska, 2020). These terms are presented in Table 2.1.

3

Methods of Researching
Online Communities

Some researchers of social phenomena consider the combination of qualitative and quantitative methods risky or at least problematic (Bryman, 2007; D. R. Buchanan, 1992). While taking their reservations into account, I believe that the advantages of using a variety of tools and approaches outweigh the disadvantages (Hammersley, 1992), although the whole needs to be situated in a single coherent paradigm. Although the use of qualitative and quantitative methods has a long history in traditional social research (Jick, 1979), in the digital world it presents an especially large number of advantages—because of much easier access to ordered quantified data with the parallel need of its deep interpretation which is complicated by the massive inflow of sources and their lack of ambiguity. Mixed methods fit Internet studies particularly well (Hine, 2015). In digital social science, I propose the use of Thick Big Data, the conscious, programmatic combination of Big Data (highly quantified datasets) with *thick data* (deeply qualitative fieldwork).

Especially with the research of online phenomena, quantitative studies of exploratory character are an excellent choice, unlike traditional social science research. It enables a problem to be sketched, then exposed and explained through qualitative research (Spillman, 2014), to identify people and communities that can be explored, and to select the subsets of text for narrative analysis. It needs to be noted, though, that the division of research into exploratory and explanatory is an artificial one (Stebbins, 2001), and many research projects are based on the pragmatic iterative approach, returning to the same questions and blurring the division.

The interpretation of large amounts of data through a deep qualitative project is an excellent way of positioning Big Data in social research

Thick Big Data: Doing Digital Social Sciences. Dariusz Jemielniak, Oxford University Press (2020).
© Dariusz Jemielniak.
DOI: 10.1093/oso/9780198839705.001.0001

(Curran, 2013), although it does not exclude the "anthropological frame of mind" (Czarniawska-Joerges, 1992) and reflection that are typical of qualitative research. The use of different research methods facilitates non-stereotyped thinking and increases the possibility of theorizing across micro and macro perspectives (J. Mason, 2006)—especially thanks to the Internet-enabling power of quantitative data, the use of such data to visualize problems that are explained in detail through a qualitative process makes sense. Of course, one cannot assume that the compilation of data with varying levels of detail and depth will always be problem-free— it is therefore of key importance to contextualize the results and the use of data to create a common, sensible, and consolidated interpretation (Brannen, 2005). Thick Big Data may similarly rely on the use of qualitative research for an initial pilot study, in order to identify the areas and sensible research questions for a Big Data problem. Naturally, there is no reason to strictly separate the pilot study from the full-fledged study because one needs to remember the fluidity of such divisions (Nadai & Maeder, 2005).

The sense of combining quantitative and qualitative research methods in social sciences was noted twenty years ago (Sudweeks & Simoff, 1999). Sociology and social sciences were adapting to the new reality, developing independent and mixed methods of online research. In the meantime, strong competition to those sciences arose. First, many social studies based on online data are being conducted by large corporations, using data which is not available to the public. Second, questions reserved for sociology started to be answered by academics specializing in data analysis, information sciences, mathematics, and widely understood computational methods (Newman et al., 2011). The social sciences have also been invaded by specialists from biology, medicine or physics (Barabási et al., 2002; Palla, Barabási, & Vicsek, 2007). There is also a significant rise in the digital humanities whose scope of interest has begun to encompass areas previously occupied by social sciences (Sayers, 2018). There has been a similar development in digital culture studies (Jenkins, Ford, & Green, 2018).

What is interesting is that because those researchers did not participate in decade-long discussions on the research methods and traditions, they initiate their discussions usually by ignoring the canon of good practices or the defined paradigm in social sciences, including fundamentals of research ethics (Frade, 2016). Access to vast amounts of data posed a great challenge to sociology as a discipline, making it necessary for the research identity to redefine and consolidate itself (Lazer & Radford, 2017; McCarthy, 2016). Without reacting to the developments and adjusting to the new possibilities, it is threatened with loss of importance, although the excess of data and home-grown sociologists may increase the need for more reflection and methodological rigor because the illusion in which the data speaks for itself will quickly dissipate (Dourish & Gómez Cruz, 2018).

As Wellman, a pioneer in online social research wrote in 2004 (Wellman, 2004), to write an online behavior-related article all one needed were some interesting thoughts and insights. Later, the era of the craze of data presentation dawned. Afterwards, the period of focusing on analysis and interpretation instead of merely reporting the observations came. It can be added that currently it is even more important to skillfully combine different tools—especially Big Data analysis and/or network analysis with ethnographic and qualitative studies. Big Data in this wide sense needs *thick data*—because with the use of quantitative methods based on large datasets it is so much more important to give them sense through qualitative analysis (Blok & Pedersen, 2014; T. Wang, 2013). Thick data allows interpretation of big data—data do not speak for themselves and that require contextualization. The opposite is also true—qualitative research increasingly needs IT support (Ducheneaut, Yee, & Bellotti, 2010), even for the reason of social life increasingly often permeates the virtual realm and the inevitability of excluding the digital part of everyday life.

Combining thick data and Big Data is also pragmatic. Big Data allows for immersion into unprecedented amounts of human behavior data. We may even speak of the "datafication" of sociology (Millington & Millington, 2015). At the same time, the use of research only from this area places sociology in an untenable position: Big Data analysis, as performed by professional data scientists is a serious competition. Naturally, the supposed plummeting demand for specialist social science knowledge is exaggerated, and the data in itself is of low value when disconnected from skillful analysis, but the wider audience and institutions that decide upon the financing of research do not need to understand this.

Interpretation, especially supplemented with deep qualitative research, allows a proper understanding of the results of Big Data (Halavais, 2015). It is a paradox, but the greater the inflow of quantitative data the greater the need for qualitative analyses (Babones, 2016). The interpretation of traditional quantitative studies on its own is possible, because such research is usually already quite well-contextualized through research questions, and the selection of input material. There is a lot less context in Big Data, though. Finally, the access to data ceases to be a problem, while making sense of the data becomes increasingly problematic. Naturally, the opening of social sciences to Big Data leads to the "wild interdisciplinary character" of research in which sociology meets anthropology, organization theory, or information sciences (Goulden et al., 2017), and in researching works of culture with media sciences, cultural studies, or even literary analysis, but it allows the delivery of really useful and rich social research. In this sense, we may speak of "symphonic social research projects" (Halford & Savage, 2017). In the analysis of large datasets, other disciplines are more advanced; however, sociology takes a unique privileged stance: having very high quantitative competences combined with long tradition of qualitative sociology, with the added benefit of purely ethnographic research (A. Goffman, 2014; Willis, 2013), and a deeply developed and proceduralized (Atkinson, 2013) canon of such approaches as grounded theory (Hodkinson, 2015; Konecki, 2008a), as well as developed interpretive standards within sociological theories. If you think about it, sociology is uniquely positioned to develop the canon for digital social research, as it has strong tradition of the use of qualitative and quantitative approaches, as well as of developing methodologies for human-subject research.

The use of Big Data ought not to be a goal in itself but rather a road to specific knowledge, a valid supplement for which can be found in qualitative data (Alles, 2014). Canons and ways of combining such approaches are still in the making (Huc-Hepher, 2015). For example, GPS geographical data and MySpace information helped contextualize and localize ethnographic data (Hsu, 2014). Bornakke and Due show (Bornakke & Due, 2018) how Big Data can be combined with ethnographic contextualization: using observations and interviews but also the data from 1000 hours of video footage used to record the most frequent trajectories of customers walking around a store, or combining the GPS data of 371 cyclists with observation and interviews. Similarly,

Table 3.1 Stages of Thick Big Data research

Quantitative data			
Widely understood Big Data	Online questionnaires		
↓			
Searching for regularities with the use of Big Data tools, including AI	Classic statistical analyses	Network analysis	Culturomics
↓			
Identification of key and most interesting areas for deep qualitative analysis. What phenomenon are we trying to explain? What phenomenon is it hard to explain? What data is surprising?			
↓			
Qualitative research			
Digital ethnography	Case analysis	Online interviews	Narrative analysis	Analysis of works of culture
↓			
Interpretation of the results of quantitative research through qualitative research			
↓			
Contextualization and assigning of meaning to quantitative data through a qualitative insight			

in a Danish research team large mobile phone datasets were combined with ethnographic insights (Blok et al., 2017).

Latzko-Toth, Bonneau, and Millette suggest that Big Data can be contextualized with thick description (Latzko-Toth, Bonneau, & Millettte, 2017), composed of:

- trace interviews: talking to selected people to whose quantitative data we have access and gathering their comments and common interpretation of the said data;
- manual data collection: collecting quantitative data but not with the use of automated tools but rather through purposeful selection, by creating a database of tweets not based on specific searches but through reading each tweet and conscious classification thereof to a

specific category. The next step can be a quantitative analysis of such a qualitatively identified network.

Table 3.1 presents a possible sequence of research stages, from quantitative research to qualitative. Naturally, within a specific research project one needs to choose the quantitative and the qualitative tools and methods of data collection. The opposite can also be applied, progressing from qualitative analysis and the generated theories to formulating hypotheses and verifying them within a quantitative project. It is important here to understand the power behind Big Data and thick data.

This part of the book is devoted to the researching of online communities, the behaviors, organization, and culture of people and avatars, starting with the description of the available arsenal of quantitative methods, and progressing to qualitative methods. Complex research of communities may also be later supplemented by the research of cultural artifacts, which is described in later in this volume.

3.1 Quantitative Research

3.1.1 Big Data

With billions of people using the Internet, we now have the possibility of tracing even the minute factors that would ordinarily be imperceptible—because of the small sample size. For instance, taking into account the changes in communication patterns, we are able to ascertain that a given person is unemployed (Llorente, Garcia-Herranz, Cebrian, & Moro, 2015). We may also observe hourly changes in a population's moods, compare habits of individual communities, and reactions to headaches or alcohol consumption just by analyzing public tweets (Golder & Macy, 2011).

Even raw data, if based on sufficiently large samples, may be a useful starting point for future research: for example, one of the most popular porn websites, and the world's 22nd most often visited page, Pornhub, publishes an annual report on its users. In 2016, there were 23 billion visits to the website, and the visitors watched more than 91 billion hours of video, making it a remarkably large database. The report indicated some interesting cultural differences—the longest visits came from the

Philippines and lasted an average of 12:45 minutes; the shortest were from Cuba, lasting an average of 4:57 minutes. The average visit from Mongolia lasted 5:23 minutes. This data, naturally, does not allow for interpretations or cultural generalizations, since only a fraction of the population visits pornographic sites, and in each country the visitors might come from a different cultural and demographic group. Nevertheless, the data is a treasure trove for social researchers of sexual behavior across the world. A piece of information from the report, that the word "teen" was among the most searched keywords, may be valuable for sexologists and criminologists attempting to research sexual interest in minors (A. Walker & Panfil, 2017).

There is also a proliferation of information sources. For instance, a sentiment analysis of online movie reviews allows an automatic assessment of their emotional load (Thet, Na, & Khoo, 2010), which can be especially interesting in cross-community research. Mountains of data on the various kinds of human activity are also growing—the Quantified Self movement (Swan, 2013), where people measure the parameters of their own activity (Lyall & Robards, 2018), often making them publicly available, relying on sport trackers like Fitbit or Garmin, reaching into the mass scale. Access to such data allows for better insight into the daily activity cycle, stress at work, and the influence of physical activity—issues that have long been the subject of interest of sociology of health (Pantzar, Ruckenstein, & Mustonen, 2017). The scope of biometric data is also increasing—simplified EEG measuring equipment has entered mass usage, even though it is most usable in lab conditions or during meditation (Przegalińska, Ciechanowski, Magnuski, & Gloor, 2018). Mood detection in elderly people allows for a dynamic adaptation of environment (Capodieci, Budner, Eirich, Gloor, & Mainetti, 2018). Availability of professional sensors is also increasing, inserted into the body of the research subject (Rich & Miah, 2017).

From yet another area, but still associated with the technological development, the expansion of IoT (Internet of Things) devices, which are all sorts of equipment that is constantly online and transmits data, also opens new fields for social analyses (Dale & Kyle, 2016; Ytre-Arne & Das, 2019). We can therefore predict the onset of computational social sciences (Lazer et al., 2009). As a counterweight, there have also been advancements in contemplative (Janesick, 2016) and humanist sociology (Giorgino, 2015).

Big Data may lead to the discovery of fascinating dependencies and intimate knowledge. In 2013, Kosiński, Stillwell, and Graepel published an article (Kosinski, Stillwell, & Graepel, 2013) on predicting some potentially private data, such as sexual orientation, ethnicity, age, gender, religion, political views, psychological features like life satisfaction, intelligence, personality, the tendency to use drugs, and marital status of parents just based on Facebook likes. The model is 88 percent accurate in assessing men's sexual orientation and the differentiation between African Americans and white Americans is as high as 95 percent accurate.

The research covered 58,000 individuals who needed to grant access to their Facebook profiles in exchange for taking a free psychological test. The researchers could access the results of all the tests and match them with the profiles, so they were able to pinpoint which likes were the best predictors of specific features or preferences on a large sample. Even though as many as 300 likes per person were taken into account, even singular occurrences could have a predictive value. As an example, liking the television show *The Colbert Report* was a good prognostic of high intelligence, while liking Harley Davidson could be an indicator of less intelligence. It is natural that some likes were directly related to the researched trait—obviously, liking the page "I love being gay" was a clear indicator of the person's sexual orientation. Some were, however, rather ambiguous, but still efficient, such as liking "Shaquille O'Neal's fanpage," which was a good prediction of male heterosexuality.

In a sample of over 86,000 individuals, Youyou, Kosiński, and Stillwell (2015) showed that computer predictions based on the analysis of likes may be more accurate than the assessment of the research subjects' friends. In some cases related to the use of psychoactive substances, political sympathies or health, prognoses may even be more accurate than the self-assessment of the researched person. A simplified version of a tool showing how a similar system may work can be found at applymagicsauce.com (for a limited number of Facebook likes and tweets) on the website run by the Psychometrics Center at the University of Cambridge, where Kosiński worked for a few years. For social researchers, the key message is clear: completely unrelated collections of large datasets may bring valuable, verifiable information.

This phenomenon is of immense value to marketing. Andrew Pole, the statistician for Target, an American hypermarket chain, asked an interesting research question in 2002: how, based on the data at the chain's disposal, can we guess that a customer is pregnant, even when she is reluctant to reveal this information? This is a crucial question for hypermarkets, because young parents are a gold mine, and their needs are easy to define. If they can be won at an early stage, by stabilizing their habit of buying diapers, they will most likely make it a habit to also make other purchases, staying with the chain for longer. This is why Amazon has offered the "Amazon Mom" for young parents since 2010. Members of the program can use Amazon Prime services, which costs about US$119 per year, for free for up to a year, as long as they meet certain purchasing criteria. Target used the data for this kind of prediction—and the dataset was quite rich, as Target keeps each customer's credit card information, demographic data, address, and email in its database. Knowing the email address allows to connects the chain data with the online databases of consumer behavior, which are often quite well-developed—and based on online customization systems. Additionally, the chain buys data on the secondary market; these often contain data on marital status, credit rating, education, and even typical subjects of online conversations. They analyzed the purchasing history of women who signed up for the baby registry. With sufficient amounts of data and research subjects, interesting patterns started to emerge. For instance, at the beginning of the second trimester a large group of pregnant women started to purchase odorless body balms. In the first 20 weeks of pregnancy, many of them started to stock on calcium, zinc, and magnesium. Finally, the research team limited the predictive model to 25 products, based on which they could safely assume whether or not a customer was pregnant, and predict the due date (Duhigg, 2012).

Based on the algorithm, the chain started to send discount coupons for baby products. In 2010, a man in the Minneapolis area complained about his daughter receiving these coupons. Target naturally apologized for the mistake; but as it turned out, that the man's daughter was indeed pregnant (K. Hill, 2012). Since then, Big Data analysis has made considerable progress. It is now combined with AI research, with the use of neural networks and machine learning. In 2017, Kosiński published the results of his research, according to which neural networks, following the analysis of over 35,000 images of people from a dating site, were able to state with quite high accuracy the sexual orientation of photo subjects. The accuracy was 91 percent for men, from which each had five photos analyzed, although accuracy is related to comparing pictures in pairs, rather than at random (Y. Wang & Kosinski, 2018). Still, it proved more accurate than human assessment.

Earlier research by Kosiński's team had been exploited by Cambridge Analytica, a private corporation established in 2013 to interfere in American political campaigns. The company became controversial because of its support for Brexit in Great Britain and Donald Trump's successful presidential campaign. Cambridge Analytica collects extensive data on voters. It uses all the possible sources, including "free" psychological tests and polls, datasets collected by market research agencies, and specially developed mobile applications, often without the consent and knowledge of the participants (H. Davies, 2015). The company prides itself on the use of "behavioral microtargeting," which, as they state, may forecast the needs of the research subjects and get to know them better than they could themselves verbalize. For the 2016 elections in the US, all adult Americans were categorized according to 32 personality types, adjusting the language of communication to specific people, and hinting at the political sympathies of the poll subjects to the polltakers, in order to be more persuasive on specific issues. In the USA it is so much easier, as the two main political parties have been developing voter databases for years, trying to pinpoint non-obvious common denominators of political beliefs for small groups of people. This way, parties may adjust their message to undecided supporters of the other party who can be convinced to stay at home—either by offering negative suggestions or by convincing them they need to go on vacation on the day of the elections. Similar practices are definitely controversial, because they are based on interference in the democratic process. Additionally, closely targeted advertising is only weakly regulated: public broadcasts, such as a television spot, can be grounds for legal action on infringement of personal rights or defamation, while when emitting a microtargeted advertisement, the defamed person may not even be aware of the fact. In 2019, Facebook introduced a public Ad Library in response to similar concerns. Revealing the actions of Cambridge Analytica in 2018 created a backlash against Facebook—which had done little to protect the privacy of its users. Nevertheless, all kinds of consumer-related data is collected by thousands of companies in every possible technical way, and Cambridge Analytica is not an isolated case. Facebook introduced strict limits to data gathering it is difficult to mine the information, also for scientific purposes. Abstracting from these practical considerations, this application of Big Data has huge scientific potential.

The analysis of Big Data reveals some interesting data distributions, often diverging from the bell curve. Normal distribution assumes that outliers are rare: following the three-sigma rule as much as 99.7 percent of the area under the normal distribution curve lies within three standard deviations from the center. It is typical for demographic phenomena, like age in a defined population or intelligence in standard assessment models. Many journals in the social sciences rely on this Gaussian distribution (Andriani & McKelvey, 2009). This may make it difficult to notice phenomena of different characteristics.

Natural events, such as avalanches, fires, and epidemics, often show an exponential distribution. This is a distribution of $y=kx^a$ regularity, where y and x are variables, a is an exponent, and k is a negligible constant. Exponential distributions show that small-scale events are very popular, but there are also a few major cases. One of the first observed examples of exponential distribution is Zipf's law, often synonymous with exponential distribution. Zipf was a Harvard linguist who concluded that a language's most frequently used word occurs twice as often as the second in row, three times as often as the third in row (Reed, 2001). Similarly, income follows the Pareto law: 20 percent of individuals receive 80 percent of the income. Similar interesting correlations may be observed in many social phenomena: let's mention here the size of enterprises measured by number of employees and market value (Gabaix, Gopikrishnan, Plerou, & Stanley, 2003), or the salaries paid to CEOs (Edmans & Gabaix, 2011). In classical sociological research, the analysis of social clashes in Chicago from 1881 to 1886 showed similar characteristics; the research took into account the number of employees and companies (Biggs, 2005).

Research on the Internet community confirms that online groups show an exponential character of researched features (Johnson, Faraj, & Kudaravalli, 2014). It is frequently the consequence of systemic complexity: in complex sets of codependent individuals, normal distribution fails to be the norm in favor of exponential distribution (Andriani & McKelvey, 2009). The number of website visits (L. A. Adamic & Huberman,

2000) or the number of referring links (Albert, Jeong, & Barabási, 1999) can be mentioned here. An important element of sales strategy of Amazon.com, which made the company so successful, was to accommodate "the long tail"—satisfying the needs of the niche customers, placed at the end of the demand distribution (Spencer & Woods, 2010). In open collaboration communities, exponential distribution may be applied to social actors. For instance, this is what the popularity of Web users looks like (Johnson et al., 2014). Similarly, rules of involvement in most Internet communities are so similar that we may invoke a 1 percent rule, where 1 percent of the population of the community generates 99 percent of the content (Hargittai & Walejko, 2008). The number of Wikipedia articles per user follows this regularity (Zhang, Li, Gao, Fan, & Di, 2014), and the top promile of editors provides as much as 44 percent of content (Priedhorsky et al., 2007). Still, when the number of active participants rises, the proportions may change dynamically (Van Dijck & Nieborg, 2009). Such interesting observations provide previously inaccessible knowledge about human behaviors in large communities.

Big Data research, however, uses large datasets. Fortunately for researchers, many large databases can be legally examined for free. Wikimedia project data may be openly downloaded with the use of the API[1] in many popular formats, including JSON, XML, PHP, and even HTML. This is important when confronted with the fact that commercial services often impose limitations on accessing their data—Twitter does make their API accessible[2] but with strict limits on queries and time scope. No big wonder—paid access to such data, through the company Gnip.com, is one of the more profitable products of the enterprise. What is worse, social media site licenses do not allow for making the source database available for review purposes, which means little research conducted on this data is verifiable. This is also true of research propagated by the social media sites themselves—in 2014, Facebook's Data Science team published an interesting analysis on the evolution of memes on the site. It was based on an enormous dataset, so it had a very strong background, one of the reasons being that it used data of over a

---

[1] Cf. https://www.mediawiki.org/wiki/API:Main_page and https://en.wikipedia.org/wiki/Special:Export
[2] https://dev.twitter.com/streaming/public

million statuses from half a million user accounts (E. A. L. Adamic, Lento, & Ng, 2014). However, because the research team did not make source data available, the academic community cannot verify results, nor can it use the database for other supplementary analyses. Corporations often limit access to Big Data, which makes it more difficult for the academic community to validate research results; it also creates circles of research elites that are privileged to access the data (McCarthy, 2016) This is grounds for the conflict of interest if the interpretation of the data is unfavorable for the corporations that gave access to the information and to the rest of the academic world (boyd & Crawford, 2012). In this sense, Facebook and similar corporations are undermining the development of social sciences, although they have more structured and complete data than most governments and statistical offices (Farrell, 2017).

For these reasons, large databases, access to which is neither paid nor limited, such as Wikimedia project databases, are invaluable. I include them in my research projects. Nevertheless, not all research conducted on large databases can be called Big Data analysis. For instance, with Maciej Wilamowski of the University of Warsaw we conducted data analysis from eight Wikipedia language versions. We researched 41,000 of the best articles across the projects, using the criteria of the individual project communities for assessing quality. We supported our research with a bot developed in PHP by my co-author. We ask a simple but important question: are standards for the best articles consistent or different among language editions of Wikipedia? If they are similar, we could assume that people have certain universal beliefs about the presentation of encyclopedic knowledge. In light of cultural globalization, similar organization of societies, identical technology and presentation, and cooperation across projects, this would not be surprising, especially given the visible, strong paraprofessional culture of Wikipedians. However, if they were inconsistent, we could conclude that standards for presenting knowledge are strongly influenced by local cultures and cannot be universalized. We showed significant differences in the number of words and characters for the best articles in the sample, with exponential distribution. We also noted a large discrepancy in the average number of images used to illustrate articles, the average number of bibliographical references, as well as numbers of external and internal links.

Above all, we found major differences among language versions. This led to the conclusion that there are divergences in social preferences, most likely conditioned by the culture of a language—because individual Wikipedias are defined by language, not by country (Jemielniak & Wilamowski, 2017). For instance, countries where East Romanic languages are spoken have a preference for more images, while the French show a strong inclination towards large bibliographies (from the viewpoint of the average absolute number of references within articles, although not so much from the perspective of saturation in comparison to numbers of words). It is interesting, because it suggests that the conviction about neutral objectivism of knowledge and ways to present it is largely a myth. This forms part of the wider stream of research in the sociology of knowledge.

Wikidata is a free-licensed database with massive potential for social science. It is yet another of Wikimedia projects but it contains very ordered data, easily exported in several formats. Unlike Wikipedia data, this project's data does not need time-consuming parsing, sanitation, and clean-up. Wikidata, in perspective, may contain most of the Wikipedia-relevant data which can be recorded in an unambiguous way, without referring to any specific language, such as dates of birth and death. The database is still developing but yields some interesting observations. For instance, with Natalia Banasik-Jemielniak and Wojciech Pędzich, we collected the lifespan data, in days, for more than 800 bishops from six countries who had died in the past 30 years, and compared it with analogous data for priests and male academics. We wanted to check if a group of people who receive millions of prayers live longer than those who do not. The source of inspiration was an observation that each Roman Catholic bishop receives a few millions of prayers yearly, on average, because the Mass is regulated by the Roman Missal, in which a fixed element of the congregation recites such a prayer. On a large dataset we did not observe a significant difference in lifespan between bishops and priests, although we found out they outlived regular priests—which, however, we explained in terms of pre-selection (only priests who are over 35 may become bishops) and material status. Naturally, the results do not prove the efficiency of prayers as such—as we could not account for the commitment of the praying, the intentionality, emotional attitude towards the prayer or simple physical proximity to the person to which the prayer was directed. Nevertheless, in a rather humorous project we managed to learn something that we were simply curious about but which was only possible with the use of Wikidata.

Without going into details, it is worth noting that Wikimedia project data (Wikipedia, Wikidata, Wiktionary, Wikivoyage, Commons) may be a phenomenal source of research material that is limited only by the researcher's imagination, the need to ask the right questions and to seek solutions to interesting problems. Even the structure of the data can be the subject of social analysis, because the way in which large groups of people organize and categorize information is also the source of social preferences, stereotypes, and beliefs (J. Adams & Brückner, 2015). However, even though the project did research large amounts of data, a question remains if it was a Big Data project, because such a project is the research of massive datasets, usually streamed, whose analysis needs to be supported with something more than classical statistical tools and which results in the emergence of either predictive conclusions or behavioral models. George et al. (2014) suggest that the size of a dataset should not be considered as important as the "smartness" of the acquired information and granularity of data about an individual.

Quite recently, Google has set up the datacommons.org that combines integrated, ordered, and cleaned-up data from Wikipedia, American Census Bureau, FBI, weather agencies, and American election commissions. This tool is worth keeping in mind with geography research.

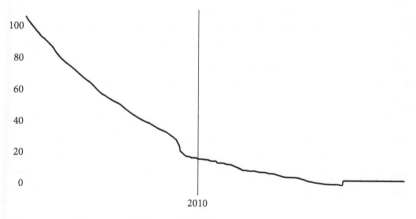

Figure 3.1 GOOGLE CORRELATE example 1

Stanford University's Large Network Dataset Collection datasets and those of Harvard University's Dataverse are also of great use.

An increasing number of interesting free tools supports the analysis of Big Data. GOOGLE CORRELATE[3] trend analysis allows the use of Google search queries whose popularity dynamics follows a defined trend. This may be plotted on a graph (Figure 3.1).

In the US, Google search queries that matched the plotted series between early 2004 and March 2017 were:

1. free web ($r = 0.9953$)
2. download ($r = 0.9933$)
3. free ftp ($r = 0.9932$)
4. Microsoft FrontPage ($r = 0.9932$)
5. amplifiers ($r = 0.9931$)
6. web page ($r = 0.9929$)
7. Japanese language ($r = 0.9929$)
8. comparisons ($r = 0.9927$)
9. pdr ($r = 0.9922$)
10. real media ($r = 0.9922$)

Each of the results may be visualized on a graph. Result 1 correlates with the plotted curve in Figure 3.2 as follows:

There is also a possibility of seeing a scatter plot; "free ftp" looks like this (Figure 3.3):

The interest in "free web," "download," "free ftp," and "Microsoft FrontPage" has plummeted. I am surprised that the interest in free web has dropped very similarly to the Microsoft WYSIWYG HTML editor, but this is understandable. The drop in searches for download and free FTP (a file exchange technology) also corresponds well with the transition to streaming content.

GOOGLE CORRELATE's feature that allows the input of time trends in a CSV format is much more interesting. Based on the available data on sales of a defined product, sickness rate, we can see which queries are correlated with the phenomenon. We may even check what queries are correlated with other queries—"losing weight" is strongly correlated

---

[3] https://www.google.com/trends/correlate/

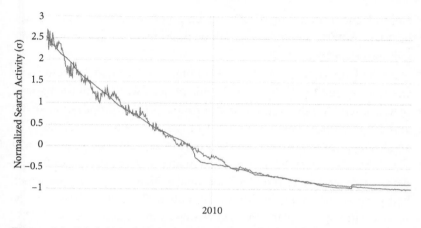

Figure 3.2 GOOGLE CORRELATE example 2 (plotted curve)
Source: https://www.google.com/trends/correlate/search?e=id:Ou5W8zluSUP&t=weekly&p=us

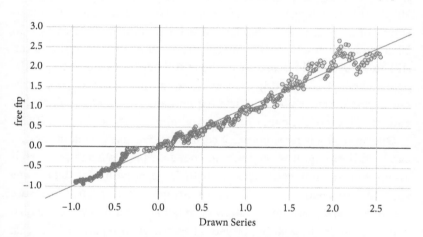

Figure 3.3 GOOGLE CORRELATE example 3 (scattered plot)

in US search results with phrases like "physical exercises," "losing kilograms," "whey," "increase of muscle mass," and "burning fat." The use of GOOGLE CORRELATE as even the only tool allows exploration of some quite serious research projects, or at least complements them.

Simple Google location and query data can serve practical social goals. In 2018, FINDER, an epidemiology project, based on mobile phone location data and Google searches for food poisoning, with the use of machine learning algorithms, allowed the Center for Disease

Control and Prevention (CDC), to pinpoint restaurants that needed health inspection with more than three times the accuracy of traditional methods (Sadilek et al., 2018).

At the same time, the tool had its limitations. De facto, the same data was used to run the Google Flu Trends project, which—on the basis of search query trends—estimated the probability of propagation of flu and denga viruses. The service was launched in 2008 and seemed to be an ideal application of Big Data (Ginsberg et al., 2009): a combination of search trends with CDC data resulted in an accurate estimate of flu epidemics two weeks ahead of the traditional epidemiologic models, which had great social value and life-saving potential. In 2013, however, the service had a spectacular failure, deviating from the actual results by 140 percent in the peak season for flu infections. Google Flu Trends had lost some of its predictive capabilities (Lazer, Kennedy, King, & Vespignani, 2014). This was largely a consequence of trusting in spurious correlations, of no bearing on infections, which contaminated the dataset. In 2015 the service was closed to public access, although historical data can still be viewed, and research teams may still apply to Google to put the data into better use. Putting exclusive trust in Internet-based data, without relying on any real-world data requires a precision of the algorithm and cleanliness of the data which are not fully accessible (Rogers, 2017).

One must simply remember that correlation data itself, without context, can be misleading. It is very easy to choke on Big Data and see correlations that do not exist because with large amounts of data come spurious correlations—which is catastrophic for science, because researchers are motivated to show correlations, and many commercial computer tools allow sifting of data in search of correlations. The scale of the problem is so large that some researchers simply conclude that "most of the published research is wrong" (Ioannidis, 2005).

Tyler Vigen brings a lighthearted perspective to the problem of "too much data" in *Spurious Correlations* (Vigen, 2015) and tylervigen.com. The correlation between US spending on science, space exploration, and development of technology on one side and suicides by hangings and suffocation on the other is worth a look (Figure 3.4):

In Big Data analysis the important irremovable constraints of the algorithms must be kept in mind. For example, even though online dating systems operate on tens of millions of user data and they develop matching algorithms that rely on preferences and psychological profiles,

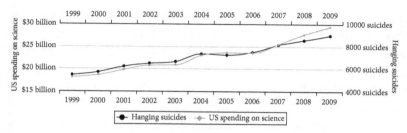

Figure 3.4 Correlation between US spending on science, space exploration, and technology versus number of deaths by hanging and suffocation
Source: tylervigen.com, used with permission.

research shows that they will not meet expectations (Finkel, Eastwick, Karney, Reis, & Sprecher, 2012). Moreover, one of the largest online dating services driven by algorithmic matching, OkCupid, provides a large amount of anonymized user data (Kirkegaard & Bjerrekær, 2016). This data can be used in research and exercises in using quantitative data (Kim & Escobedo-Land, 2015). Making it available, however, is an important ethical problem (Fiesler et al., 2015): there is a possibility to use seemingly unimportant data to create a profile and successfully behavior and features, or even maybe identify them, despite the obfuscation of identifying information. The issue is controversial and I consider the publication of such classified information risky, even if the publishing party considers the data to be correctly and fully anonymized (Fiesler, Wisniewski, Pater, & Andalibi, 2016).

It is worth making a distinction between Big Data analysis, machine learning, and Deep Learning, which can result in finding regularities in the data. Examples can include predicting poverty based on satellite photography (Jean et al., 2016), optimization of statistical analysis in questionnaires (Fu, Guo, & Land, 2018), prediction of prison violence (Baćak & Kennedy, 2018), classifying social media posts based on content analysis (Vergeer, 2015), or sentiment analysis in press articles (Joseph, Wei, Benigni, & Carley, 2016).

3.1.2 Social Network Analysis

Social network analysis (SNA) has quite a long history in social science (Carrington, Scott, & Wasserman, 2005; J. Scott, 1988). Its first famous application was related to weak ties (Granovetter, 1973)—a phenomenon that explains why, when looking for work, it is better to seek help from acquaintances instead of friends (Montgomery, 1992). The strength of weak ties resides in their length. They act as bridges, connecting indi-viduals socially far apart and exchanging information and resources across distances.

SNA is an excellent way to research online communities. It can also be applied offline, but it is in the virtual world that it has found popular application, because data on the relations and connections between ava-tars are easy to access online. It is also a new research field with much to be discovered. Some researchers claim that Internet social networks are based on weak ties (De Meo, Ferrara, Fiumara, & Provetti, 2014), or contacts acquaintances and strangers. This seems to explain the "Twitter revolutions" or social change movements in Tunisia, Egypt, Spain, or the international Occupy movement that relied on social media (Kidd & McIntosh, 2016). Other research shows that even people who know each other only online may form long-lasting and strong social ties (Ostertag & Ortiz, 2017), and the nature of social relations is an aggregate of online and offline acquaintance and contact (Chayko, 2014). Regardless, social network analysis will do a fine job, owing to easy access to data.

SNA is based on the research of ties within a network. It is usually a network of individuals or avatars, but the network can also be among devices and workstations. The two types of network connection are states (acquaintances, friends) and events (conversation, exchange, transaction) (Borgatti & Halgin, 2011). What else is measured? Within the connec-tions, one also may research the homophily, ways in which an avatar builds connections with similar others, and how they deal with those that are unlike themselves according to specified criteria such as polit-ical preferences, education, gender, or place of birth. Much data of this kind is available in the networks' public profiles. It is worth adding here that in network analysis it is hard to differentiate homophily from influence mechanisms—to observe whether a given reaction is the result of two people being similar and acting similarly, albeit independently, or whether this is the result of one person inspiring the other (Shalizi & Thomas, 2011).

In social network analysis, the focus is on the reciprocity/equivalence of connections, their transitivity (is the friend of our friend also our friend?), and density, strength of connections or centrality. Selection of these indicators makes sense only after establishing which of them is a good measure of what feature. Determining the number of contacts (e.g., phone calls) needed to confirm the presence of a bond is a valid methodological issue (Borgatti & Halgin, 2011).

There are many applications of SNA. Financial specialists serving on supervisory boards can be one subject of research (Mizruchi & Stearns, 1988). SNA is ideal for exploratory research—although it can form a tool of its own for a complete research project. It is also a good introduction to ethnographic research (Bellotti & Mora, 2016).

The purpose of social network analysis is to research the structure of connections and patterns of connections. Instead of categorizing individuals by features, the analysis is based on relations. The focus, as with the systemic approach, is set on the whole structure, the goal is to observe patterns, relations that allow to distinguish a subnet, observe cliques, or draw conclusions about the acting and organizing of individual units (nodes or objects) of the network (Wellman & Berkowitz, 1988). The nodes may be people, but also projects or teams, organizations, events, and even ideas. Defining a relation and confirming its occurrence are, naturally, conventional and dependent on the research perspective—a relation is presumably a result of close proximity, but comes with trust, membership in a group, and conflict. Noticing patterns of interaction improves understanding of the social mechanism, which adds valuable context to research of individuals. It is important in focusing on boundary spanning. It is a social phenomenon based on the observation that spreading information and new knowledge in organizations often depends on people who are well-networked and communicated, both inside and outside of the organization (Meyer & Rowan, 1977; Tushman & Scanlan, 1981). In some cases, we observe boundary spanning in sister organizations. It is especially visible in open software projects, where an important role is to communicate between the community of creators and users; people undertaking such roles often do this for different, unconnected projects and voice similar opinions in each case (Barcellini, Détienne, & Burkhardt, 2008). Discovering similar social relations networks is one of sociology's interesting contemporary challenges, also leading to theoretical developments (Erikson & Occhiuto, 2017; D. Wang, Piazza, & Soule, 2018).

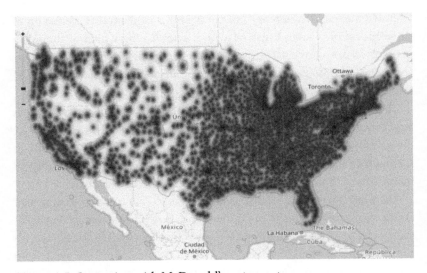

Figure 3.5 Saturation with McDonald's restaurants
Source: http://www.openheatmap.com/view.html?map=NonspeculativeCalcariferousOchidore

Many tools are capable of performing social network analysis, because there are many things to research. Some research can be completed exclusively with online tools. An interesting project is myheatmap.com (a free version of the tool was openheatmap.com)—allowing to input data from a CSV sheet or a Google Doc and visualizing it on a map (Figure 3.5). This way, by feeding the system with addresses of McDonald's restaurants, we may see their density:

Pete Warden developed the web crawler that collected Facebook profile information. The script was operational for six months and collected data from 210 million user profiles—saving given names, family names, locations, friends, and interests. Warden had intended to publish the dataset in 2010 after having it anonymized; however, upon learning of the intention Facebook's legal department threatened a lawsuit for breaching the service's terms of use by not obtaining written permission.[4]

---

[4] Warden's case is interesting in that Facebook's robots.txt file did not prohibit site indexing, and this is the traditional method websites use to signal whether their information can be processed. It is difficult to envision Google, for instance, requesting written permission to index each website's contents. Nonetheless, this is an important lesson to anyone using crawlers in social research.

As a result, Warden needed to delete the entire dataset (Giles, 2010). This was a shame, because many of the observations from the anonymized dataset might have been interesting. For instance, Warden remarked that groups of American cities, when analyzed in terms of Facebook friendships, form clusters, with strong connections within them and weak connections outside.[5] These clusters can sometimes but not always be explained geographically: it is hard, for example, to envision why Missouri, Arkansas, and Louisiana have stronger ties to Texas than to Georgia. The data was also used for other sociological observations. In the South, "God" ranked high on the list of top 10 liked pages, while sports and beer dominated in the North. The names Ahmed and Mohamed were especially popular in Alexandria, Louisiana. Such trivia, naturally, has little cognitive value on its own, but it could be a good start for quantitative research that could contextualize these observations and lead to actual discoveries.

As part of our research of unequal involvement in open-source projects, coauthored by Peter Gloor and Tadeusz Chełkowski and based on the ideas and data of the latter, we were able to indicate, based on the analysis of almost all Apache Foundation projects, that even though open source projects are frequently described as "open collaboration," in practice the element of collaboration is illusory (Chełkowski, Gloor, & Jemielniak, 2016). Our quantitative analysis—the first analysis of such an extensive dataset on open software—proved that the vast majority of open source programmers work independently. We also observed that the input of the individual project participants shows an exponential distribution.

We used network analysis to show the connections of all 4661 developers with their 263 projects (Figure 3.6). Apache Taglibs had the highest betweenness centrality, the degree to which it acts as an intermediary between other projects; this was a good indicator of the importance of a project. It was developed by 527 programmers over 15 years. It uses the popular Java Server Pages technology and is modular—which helps to explain its popularity. We correlated the betweenness in the network with the number of code lines, number of participants, and number

---

[5] https://petewarden.com/2010/02/06/how-to-split-up-the-us/

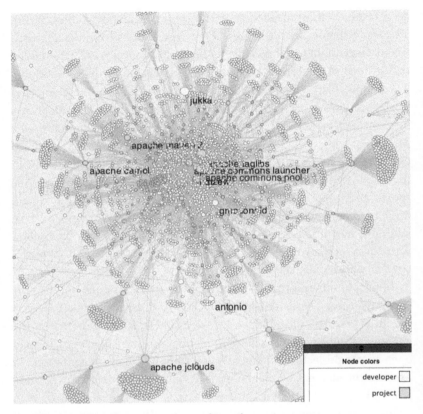

Figure 3.6 Social network analysis of Apache programmers
Source: Chełkowski et al., 2016.

of commits.[6] We observed a strong correlation between the number of contributors and the betweenness of a project ($r = 0.907$, $p < 0.001$, $N = 263$). When analyzing the programmer network, the user "jukka" with 6345 tasks had the highest betweenness level. This user participated in 20 projects; the correlation between the number of tasks and betweenness was $r = 0.222$ ($p < 0.001$, $N = 4660$)—it is meaningful but not strong, as other users had more tasks and less betweenness.

Thanks to the social network analysis, we were able to show that in open collaboration projects, the most involved users, in terms of

[6] More precisely, committal—the transferring of one's piece of code into the common repository.

number of tasks, do not need to play a central role. There are developers in the center of the social network who do have a moderate number of tasks, but who are of key importance to the network.

This observation was confirmed in other quantitative research on different open collaboration projects, such as Wikipedia—for instance, users with the highest edit count are not necessarily elected as organizational functionaries (Burke & Kraut, 2008).

As part of Internet process research, social network analysis is used in political marketing. For the last few years, active bot armies have been found on Twitter, Facebook, and other social media sites (Ferrara, Varol, Davis, Menczer, & Flammini, 2016). There is strong evidence that some states, especially Russia, use bots and armies of professional trolls and commentators to reach political goals (Aro, 2016). It is a fascinating subject for new research projects from the borderlands of sociology of politics and sociology of Internet, where different qualitative and quantitative research techniques need to be combined. When SNA and text analysis are combined with deep learning, it is possible to identify distinctive "virtual tribes," groups of people sharing word usage and behavioral patterns, often closely correlated with similar lifestyles, political choices, and worldviews (Gloor, Fronzetti Colladon, de Oliveira, & Rovelli, 2019).

How do we conduct social network analysis with the use of modern technology, but applied to offline research? For instance, the Human Speechome Project became the source of recognition for a linguist who installed cameras and microphones at his home and recorded the three first years of his child's language development (Roy et al., 2006; Tay, Jebb, & Woo, 2017). Geolocation and phone call data of users allowed to predict, with 95 percent accuracy, friendship relations (Eagle, Pentland, & Lazer, 2009), although because of the sudden decline of the phones' popularity as contact medium, the situation may alter significantly in the future. Analysis of phone calls of 65 million subscribers showed the relation between social network structure and diversity and access to socioeconomic opportunities (Eagle, Macy, & Claxton, 2010). Studying Twitter usage during a tsunami showed Twitter's usefulness for crowdsourced disaster management, but has to include opinion leaders and influencers, not just official governmental accounts (Carley, Malik, Landwehr, Pfeffer, & Kowalchuck, 2016).

Social network analysis of an archived corpus of Enron's employee emails led to some interesting conclusions on the dynamics of organizational crisis and informal communication (Diesner, Frantz, & Carley, 2005); in times of organizational crisis, inter-employee communication is intensified across organizational hierarchies. Email pattern analysis combined with machine learning allows the identification of top performers at work (Wen, Gloor, Fronzetti Colladon, Tickoo, & Joshi, 2019). In a wider perspective, all interactions within virtual teams beg for quantitative analyses. Collaborative Innovation Networks (COINs), based on distributed creative, IT-communication-savvy teams are the most efficient source of innovation, constituting a new research subject (Gloor, 2005).

MIT researchers (Olguín et al., 2009) conducted a project with the use of specially designed devices for research subjects to carry. Using the data, the researchers measured the length and number of interactions, proximity to other team members, and physical activity. This allowed them to reach conclusions on patterns of behavior in teamwork, and to quantify social reactions.

A similar project could be based on phone apps. Developing an Android/iOS app is expensive, but worth including in the total costs of a research grant if it will generate useful data. In any case, it will cost less than constructing a dedicated device, and will allow us to specify what kind of data we want to collect. At present, it is more difficult to come up with a research question than to access the data—the data is either already available or it is possible to obtain at a reasonably low cost. In any case, doing social network research is useful as a small component of a larger, Thick Big Data study and as a standalone project. There are many excellent textbooks on the topic (Hennig, Brandes, Pfeffer, & Mergel, 2012; McCarty, Lubbers, Vacca, & Molina, 2019; Robins, 2015).

3.1.3 Online Polls

Online behavior research based on existing data has the advantage of being non-invasive. When conducting such a study, researchers avoid the Hawthorne effect—the influence of the research on the results— although they will never avoid the influence of the need of self-presentation of the research subjects towards their reference groups. Thanks to this type of data we may observe racial preferences in matchmaking—the analysis of Yahoo's match-making portal user profiles showed that white heterosexual male Americans who express a preference usually indicate a lack of interest in black people, while female Americans excluded people of Asian descent (Robnett & Feliciano, 2011). It would be difficult to expect similarly strong declarations, potentially showing racial prejudice in a regular poll, although such questions are asked there frequently. Computational research based on large datasets has exposed a lack of accuracy of many traditional research methods—another example can be the discrepancy between declarations of people being in a specific place at a specific time when shown their mobile phone GPS data (Burrows & Savage, 2014).

Nevertheless, online social research is often based on active participation, for instance through experiments (Hergueux & Jacquemet, 2015). Sometimes the scope of experimental manipulation can be minor: for example, during a project co-run with Facebook on a sample of 61 million people, through differentiating access to information of whether a person's online friends have already voted in the US Congressional elections, research was done on the social influence on the political activity mobilization (Bond et al., 2012). This was research that raised serious ethical considerations, as it de facto interfered with the elections (Ralph Schroeder, 2014). These issues will be discussed later.

The poll is the easiest form of quantitative online sociological research with the participation of the research subjects. Emailed questionnaires used to be popular, but currently there are often no reasons not to use online questionnaires (Van Selm & Jankowski, 2006), or polls collected in face-to-face meetings. The advantage of online polls over traditional, paper-based ones is obvious: data is collected directly in the form of a database, usually allowing nearly instantaneous creation of simple analyses and charts. This has transformed the structure of the collected data, even during census studies (Aragona & Zindato, 2016). For this reason, the use of online tools to collect data is practically a standard, although we cannot assume that everyone uses the Internet and with distance, issues of controlling the sample or acquiring a sufficient number of responses will arise. Additionally, the Internet is used to contact the interviewees.

It makes no sense to abandon polls for some research questions, for instance when representativeness is important. For example, even though some research indicates that Facebook interaction analysis may provide more accurate predictions than polls (Chmielewska-Szlajfer, 2018), and that there is a visible correlation between Twitter mentions and political success (DiGrazia, McKelvey, Bollen, & Rojas, 2013), closer analysis shows that to reach political success, responsiveness and the ability to direct the narrative is of higher importance (Kreiss, 2016). Although Twitter mentions alone may be indicative of interest in politics, not the readiness to voice political support in elections (Jungherr, Schoen, Posegga, & Jürgens, 2017), it is problematic to replace political preference polls with Twitter analysis. In addition, news outlets and corporate accounts use Twitter in a more one-directional way than people do, with different hashtags and behaviors (Malik & Pfeffer, 2016), so their influence in the general poll may skew the results, if not sorted out.

This means that Big Data analysis can be used to create prognostic models but they should supplement polls, not replace them. It seems, however, that there is no escape from the increased use of the new methods of quantitative research, both those that are based on primary data, because the inclination to participate in traditional phone or paper-based polls is on the decline. It is additionally difficult to receive funding for such research, and technological changes are causing many households to get rid of their landlines. At the same time, people are eager not to answer phone calls that originate from unknown numbers. A system of unique IP addresses combined with browser data may identify people with the same precision levels as from phone polls. Nevertheless, the leading use of online polls directed towards the population are specialized research panels, which partially solves the representation problem.

Online polls are becoming increasingly popular as a research method, even though fewer people have Internet access than phone access (Couper, 2017). The disparities in technology exacerbate other kinds of inequality (Dutton & Reisdorf, 2017). In contrast to phone-based polls, online polls do not allow for a simple representative sampling (Schonlau & Couper, 2017). There are no good ways of unambiguously defining an individual's identity (one person may have several email addresses, each of which is difficult to link to a physical location or demographic characteristics). There is no census or list of individuals that subjects can be drafted from, although with social networks such as Facebook, authorization with social network credentials might eventually be useful.

For these reasons, non-random sampling is dominant, even in academic research, as its advantage is its affordability, even though there are sensible responses to the issue of sampling (Fricker Jr, 2016). "Opt-in" polls are used, where anyone declaring to meet the criteria can sign up (M. Callegaro et al., 2014). Recruitment is conducted through banners, social networks, distribution lists, or mailing lists. Unfortunately, voices have been raised about the problem of careless or simply deceptive participants, overrepresentation of certain social groups, and difficulties in reducing that overrepresentation (Bethlehem, 2010). These problems are especially visible in polls that offer remuneration to the participants.

Yet another problem of online polls is an error resulting from a large number of people deciding to answer only some of the questions (Couper, 2000). In classical polls we are nearly positive about the number of people who received invitations and when they were invited, but if online polls encourage participation by banners, we will receive inaccurate information about the number of views because of ad-blocking software even though marketing research and the analysis of traces left by web surfers have made measurements more precise. With emailed invitations or forum posts, the situation is even worse— often we will not know how many people withdrew from participation and why. At the same time, we need to remember that online polls, even though they are quite convenient from the viewpoint of data collection, may be problematic in reference to participants' privacy; they might also interfere with regular conversation in online communities (Cho & Larose, 1999).

To conduct online polls, both for large groups of participants who are strangers to us and for our own face-to-face polls, we can use many free tools. Google Forms (google.com/forms) does a good job for yes/no, multiple-choice and open-answer questionnaires (see Figure 3.7). It has an ergonomic and clear interface, the possibility of limiting access to specified Google accounts, conditions imposed on the sequence of questions, and the possibility of asking random questions within the section; there are no limitations on its free version, combined with an

Do you have any friends who download TV shows from the Internet?

60 responses

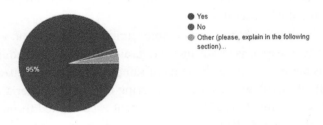

● Yes
● No
◉ Other (please, explain in the following
   section)...

95%

If you checked other in the previous question, please explain:

5 responses

I don't know

many of my friends like to download shows

Unsure, I know most stream content.

Lots of my friends download TV series from the internet. Even I do it. Often.

Downloads usually by torrents or other kinds of technology

Figure 3.7 Default presentation of a Google Forms questionnaire results

esthetic way of presenting or downloading the results as CSV files. I
have often used Google Forms in my quantitative research of Harvard
students—when I was trying to get their perception of the fairness of
sharing media files (Hergueux & Jemielniak, 2019). I studied 50 people
from one year group of the LL.M. and 60 from the next one—although
I used the traditional method of sitting in one room with my interviewees. I relied on computer-assistant personal interviewing (CAPI)
(Mario Callegaro, Manfreda, & Vehovar, 2015). My rationale was to
make absolutely sure all participants would be from my target group.
Additionally, it was my intention that the interviewees did not multitask
while filling the questionnaire—doing many things at once is a serious
risk in online research and may skew the results. Finally, because a single
cohort of LL.M. students has around 200 people, I wanted to present

the questionnaire to a few dozen students from each year. An emailed questionnaire has a low return rate (Cleary, Kearney, Solan-Schuppers, & Watson, 2014), and the disadvantage of online polls as such is the lack of or incomplete answers (LaRose & Tsai, 2014).

Among other tools, esurveycreator.com is free for researchers, and esurv.org, kwiksurvey.com and opinahq.com are free for everyone. They all contain many useful options, as does limesurvey.com. Among the paid tools, surveymonkey.com is popular, with some limitations in its free version.

When using polls, the researcher must exercise caution, as unintentional mistakes are easy to make (C. S. Fischer, 2009)—these result from the sequence or wording of questions. As this is true of all questionnaires, I will not explore these issues; however, in online polls on large samples, mistake leverage is particularly easy. When the study is conducted on a large group of anonymous people who are compensated or their participation (as with Amazon Turk), one needs to remember that the value of the data may be low—the respondents will be motivated to finish the poll as quickly as possible, and controlling their conditions during poll-taking, as well as the general demographics, may be impossible.

Online research also makes it unfortunately easy to introduce manipulations. For example, in a poll on risky sexual behaviors among Latinos, the precise analysis of answers led to the elimination of 11 percent of completed questionnaires because of suspected bad faith, and because it seemed that a single person had filled out as many as 6 percent of the questionnaires (Konstan, Simon Rosser, Ross, Stanton, & Edwards, 2005) who wanted to game the system.

3.1.4 Culturomics

The notion of culturomics was proposed by ten authors of an article in *Science* which was very important from the viewpoint of methods of online social research (Michel et al., 2010). Their painstaking work required the support of Google but with a striking outcome: they used a corpus of millions of digitized books, accounting for about 4 percent of all books that have been published in English.

With this database, they were able to come up with an original form of computational lexicography, for use in the research of linguistic, cultural, and sociological trends. One of their observations was that the English lexicon had 597,000 words in 1950, and 1.022 million in 2000; an annual increase of 8.5,000 over a 50-year period. Culturomics allowed the indexing of more words than any dictionary could. Similarly, it became possible to research trends in grammar, such as the tendency to creating regular past forms of previously irregular verbs. There was also an interesting result of a simple research of changes in the frequency of the use of specific terms—1939 visibly, and for good reasons, marked a sharp decline in the use of the term "the Great War" in favor of "First World War" and "Second World War."

The analysis of the most notable people born between 1800 and 1950 in samples of 50 people per year, with biographies acquired from Wikipedia, showed a visible trajectory of fame—the peak of the mentions for each individual was noted about 75 years after their birth. With time, fame came to notable people earlier and grew faster, although its timespan is shorter than what it had been, which is a good reason to research the phenomenon of celebrity not only in show business but also in academia.

Quite surprisingly for the knowledge of the contemporary world and sociology of politics, with time the publications increasingly often focused on current issues. References to 1880 had fallen by half by 1912. The same decline took only ten years after 1973. This could indicate that fewer books on history are being written and that people are more eager to forget it. The article contains other fascinating observations, but brings an interesting approach to digital sociology.

The co-authors of the *Science* article were Jean-Baptiste Michel and Erez Lieberman Aiden of Harvard University. They had also participated in the creation of the Google Ngram Viewer which allows research into cultural trends and frequency of word occurrence over time, based on the titles of Google Books. By 2015 the collection numbered 25 million volumes, about a fifth of the estimated 129 million of volumes published from the invention of the printing press until 2010 (Taycher, 2010). The Ngram Viewer plots very useful charts, similarly to GOOGLE CORRELATE, but based on the corpus of books within the repository, not on search terms. Unfortunately, it is limited to eight languages, and probably will not add more. Figures can be generated only for books published between 1800 and 2008. Out of curiosity, I counted the number of mentions and references to leading sociologists from 1920:

Figure 3.8 shows that Michel Foucault's ideas were as popular as those of Max Weber, while from 1996 the frequency of mentions of both sociologists similarly decreases. Zygmunt Baumans's plotted curve seems stable for years and resembles that of Erving Goffman. The creators of culturomics offer a tool on their website with which one can access data for the Ngram in a given set of queries.[7]

Other culturomics research from 2012 showed the dynamics of popularity of individual words in English, Hebrew, and Spanish, on the database of 10^7 words. With time, the number of words falling out of circulation increases, while the tempo of inflow of neologisms drops, although scanning errors have contaminated the data. At the same time, the 20–30 years before 2008 showed a rapid increase in the use of neologisms, most likely associated with technical vocabulary. Neologisms and evolution of language were noticeably affected by wars and other major historical events. The peak in the increase of word use was noted around forty years after their introduction into the language.

It is easy to notice changes in terminology when they are associated with wider social changes. This type of qualitative observations simply begs to be supplemented with deep qualitative research. For instance, the English word "gay" originally meant a joyous or eccentric person. In the 1960s, the homosexual community claimed the term (Oxford English Dictionary, 2018), as opposed to other terms of pejorative character. After twenty years, it replaced a neutral medical word: "homosexual" (see Figure 3.9).

This type of research can also be done on corpuses of magazines and popular press. The results can be fascinating. For instance, an analysis of thirty years' worth of world media reports on important events, combined with geographical analysis, was able to forecast, although retrospectively, revolutions in Tunisia, Egypt, and Libya, and the stability of Saudi Arabia (Leetaru, 2011).

Culturomics is useful not only in social research but also in the digital humanities, where a small revolution in favor of quantitative research is

---

[7] Accessible from: http://www.culturomics.org/Resources/get-ngrams

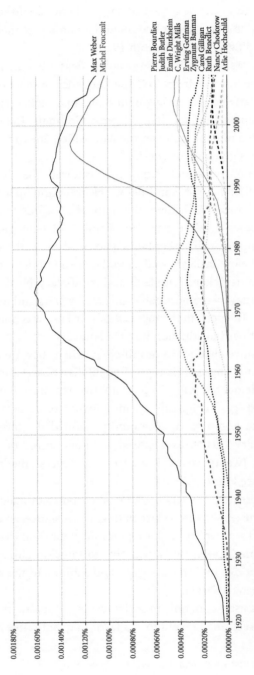

Figure 3.8 Reference Ngram for prominent sociologists

Source: https://goo.gl/bEwtS8

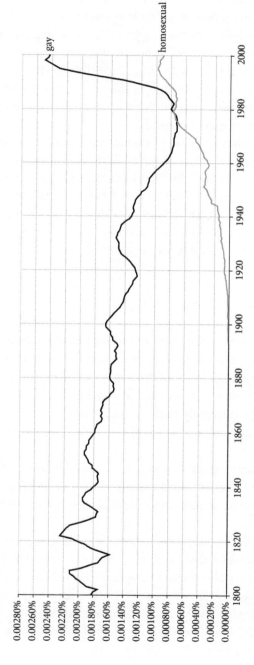

Figure 3.9 The Ngram of the use of the words "gay" and "homosexual"

Source: https://goo.gl/vGVMzd

taking (Nicholson, 2012). The use of Google Books corpus has some important limitations, based on a clear bias toward academic books and literary fiction, which distorts the image of the use of language and conclusions on culture and society, although the subset of novels seems robust (Pechenick, Danforth, & Dodds, 2015). This is why it is useful to approach the results obtained with the sole use of this method with a grain of salt. Nevertheless, culturomics is an incredibly valuable supplement to other kinds of digital research.

In the social sciences, the supplemental use of this method is still gaining its final shape, but in some areas, such as in changes of perception of professions (Mattson, 2015), it has a major cognitive sense. It is very useful in the research in sociology of fame and systems of social stratification (Van de Rijt, Shor, Ward, & Skiena, 2013). Other ways of computational text analysis for the purposes of sociological studies are also being shaped (Evans & Aceves, 2016).

3.1.5 Scraping

In online social research, it is often necessary to collect simple, repetitive data available on a website but not always accessible through an API. We can imagine, for instance, that we would need the prices of all children's books from Amazon's website—such a manual collection of this data would be extremely problematic, if feasible at all. However, even pure price data may be a source of serious socioeconomic analyses (Cavallo, 2018).

What is necessary is the "scraping" of data. Programming-savvy people write their own scripts for such purposes, or adapt existing code. Luckily, there are some easy-to-use tools at our disposal that I will describe later.

Data scraping in itself may impose some notional categories through the structure of scraped data, and, as a construct which is foreign to social sciences, it may also impose perspectives which are not typical to the social sciences, such as obsession with the data being up-to-date (Marres & Weltevrede, 2013). However, there is no escaping "investigative social sciences" based on the collection of detailed data from the Internet (McFarland, Lewis, & Goldberg, 2016).

Example 1: Donald Trump's tweets on climate

Let's assume I want to scrape all historical tweets by Donald Trump containing the phrases "climate" or "global warming." They are accessible from Twitter's advanced search page, but copying and pasting them would be time-consuming, and I may also want to analyze the number of retweets, reactions or replies. For such a simple project I can use a Chrome plugin, Web Scraper, developed by ScrapeHero team. It allows very easy data acquisition without any programming. A step-by-step guide is available here: https://www.scrapehero.com/how-to-scrape-historical-search-data-from-twitter/—the tool allows me to scrape the tweets into a CSV database, which I can work on in Excel. I only need to run both of the advanced searches, and after a couple of clicks I have my database. I immediately see that the numbers of retweets, comments, or favorites are in a text format. Unfortunately, thousands are rendered as "k," so instead of 6000 I see 6k. For just 125 tweets a manual correction is acceptable, for larger sets it would make a sense to run a conversion. I see that by far the most popular tweet about climate or global warming from Donald Trump is:

"Patrick Moore, co-founder of Greenpeace: 'The whole climate crisis is not only Fake News, it's Fake Science. There is no climate crisis, there's weather and climate all around the world, and in fact carbon dioxide is the main building block of all life.' @foxandfriends WOW!"
Donald Trump (@realDonaldTrump). March 12, 2019. Tweet.

The tweet makes the false claim that Patrick Moore, a climate change denier and an industry lobbyist had been a co-founder of Greenpeace, a claim that Greenpeace USA immediately disputed.[8]

For bigger projects I can use OctoParse—a handy installable tool that even in its free version scrapes data from different sources, allowing the use of simple templates for popular harvesting websites such as Twitter, Amazon, Booking, Instagram, YouTube, Google, and Yelp. This kind of data can be used for sentiment analysis. There are good corpuses of

---

[8] Patrick Moore was a president of Greenpeace Canada though. Since leaving the organization he has rejected the consensus of the scientific community on climate change, and insisting that there is no proof for human-caused increase in carbon dioxide. See more: https://en.wikipedia.org/wiki/Patrick_Moore_(environmentalist)

positive and negative words available. One can imagine e.g. studying the sentiment in certain phrases of official stock exchange companies' messaging. One useful tutorial on combining OctoParse scraping with sentiment analysis in Python can be found at: https://hackernoon.com/twitter-scraping-text-mining-and-sentiment-analysis-using-python-b95e792a4d64.

Additionally, some very useful tools not requiring coding include Google Sheets add-ons, such as Twitter Archiver, allowing free Twitter scraping, as well as Meaning Cloud, allowing a pretty solid sentiment analysis, and Wikidata Tools, which helps with querying Wikidata directly into Google Sheets.

Example 2: Quora

For this monograph, I will explain how to scrape data from Quora, arguably the most popular service used to ask questions, visited by 300 million active users. On Quora, people post rather longish answers to questions asked by others. For this demonstration, I assume that I wish to check if people who give most answers on Quora also ask the most questions.

Scraping can be performed with many tools and without skills in Python or R programming (which allows for more flexibility) although some knowledge of website construction might come in handy. For instance, understanding that the syntax of websites that use Asynchronous JavaScript And XML (AJAX) is much more complex than that of sites that use simple HTML with the added CSS requires so that the researcher knows that scraping these two types of websites can differ significantly. Here, I will use ParseHub (parsehub.com) but the reader may use any other service.

Quora's structure was one reason for its success over Yahoo!Answers, a service established in 2005 that met a similar need. Quora allows fluid interaction among its users, including asking and answering questions, commenting on, upvoting and downvoting answers, marking the answers with thematic categories, browsing the topics, with the pages that contain statistics of each (including the most frequently read providers of answers), and tracing whether within the questions, topics, or answers of selected users there is any new material.

Profiles of Quora users may be public or private, and the most popular authors are in the "top writer" program. The functions have remained practically unchanged for years. Quora does not make it easier to browse the answers in a homogenous structure, for instance on a comprehensive map of subpages or within a category tree, which makes it hard to assess the size of the database of questions and answers. The service is a gold mine of information for practitioners of online sociology, but it is difficult to perform quantitative analyses without data scraping.

The advantage of scraping as a method for collecting data is the automation of downloading bits of data, thanks to which we may benefit from the scale effect of a multitude of identically designed pages. Scraping tools, if set up properly, can extract data from the defined areas of the subpages. One needs to start with proper identification of the pages which have a repetitive layout. Taking into account that Quora is in the top 100 of the Web's most popular sites, it is no wonder its structure is schematic and repetitive: each answer to each question is served by the same content management system, optimized for search engines.

In order to display large sets of ordered data, websites use the division into connected subpages, i.e. allow the navigation through the use of internal links. Scraping tools may be adjusted to a pattern of navigation and the collection of specific data. For this example, I will focus on the subpages within Quora's/topic/"thread-name"/writers range. The scraping algorithm will acquire the title of the thread and move to the profile of the author. The author data is anonymized. The sequence is presented on Figure 3.10:

Profiles of individual authors are available under addresses with the syntax/profile/"user_name," where user data can be acquired, if the profile is set as public. Within the example, I will acquire only data about questions asked and answered. A user profile may look like this (Figure 3.11):

We provide these values at ParseHub and we indicate that they are to be scraped. The algorithm collects the data from the "top writers" profiles and automatically visits the next topic—if there was a map of subpages on Quora, it could be used to assist ParseHub in navigation; as it is absent, we move from one topic to another (Figure 3.12):

The algorithm will run until halted. Taking into account Quora's size, it is hard to assess how many topics need to be visited so that sufficient amounts of data for analysis can be acquired. The problem could be solved by supplementing the scraping with the "crawlers" or "spiders" which would first collect all the topic subpages.

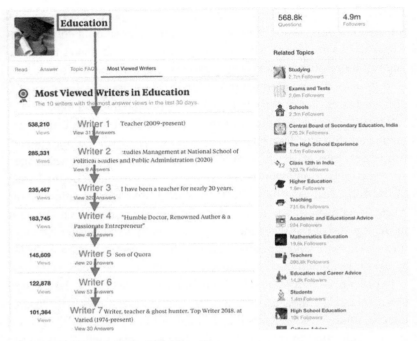

Figure 3.10 Scraping algorithm sequence

For those interested, the query algorithm is as follows:

The simple algorithm in Figure 3.13 acquired data of over 8000 users within 893 topics overnight. After a quick SPSS analysis of averages, it was apparent that the most-read authors are less eager to ask questions. On average, a member of the "top writers" category answered 244.99 questions, while asking 28.52. It may therefore be concluded that answering questions is a different social activity from asking them, and these two social roles—people sharing knowledge and people seeking knowledge—do not necessarily combine in one person, at least for the most popular providers of answers, which is counter-intuitive.

Naturally, data scraping in itself is only one side of the story. The other is, how much the data can be analyzed with the use of the basic statistical tools. Sometimes the use of more complex tools is required—these may be text mining, qualitative data analysis (QDA), or tedious Python/R processing. This example is a fundamental one—for the purpose of text mining, or linguistic analysis of the collected data there are many ready-made tools that do not require the user to have specialist

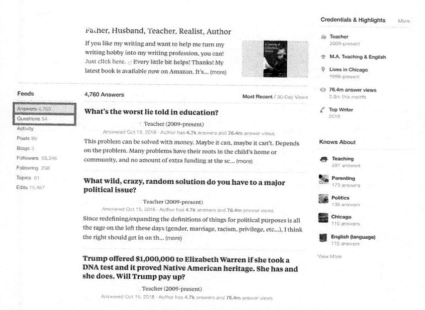

Figure 3.11 An example of an author's profile on Quora

Figure 3.12 Choosing related topics on Quora

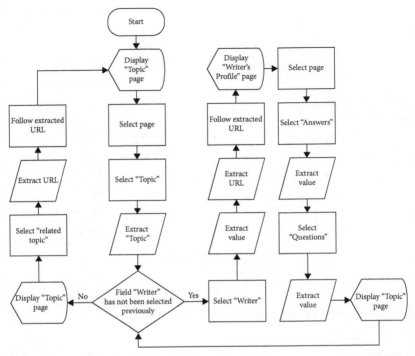

Figure 3.13 The scraping algorithm on ParseHub

preparation: IBM Watson Analytics, RapidMiner, Leximancer, and libraries such as Linguistic Inquiry or Word Count (LIWC), although these are mainly usable for research in English. Quantitative analysis may also be supported by the CAQDAS software to offer the researcher partial automation with coding or transcription. Sites such as Search Engine Scrapper or Lippmannian Device allow the user to research the frequency of specific word use on defined websites.

While scraping, we need to keep in mind that we are putting workload on the infrastructure of the services where we direct our queries. Therefore, if the websites offer making queries through their Application Programming Interface (API), this is definitely preferable to pure scraping; however, no such possibility exists for Quora. We also need to abide by the Terms of Service (TOS) and the rules included in the robots.txt file. Above all, what the researcher needs is common sense—and to limit the frequency of queries so as not to overload the servers.

In reference to the API, an example is Reddit.com, or the aggregator of comments and news items, which provides a very complex and detailed description of the availability of their data under reddit.com/dev/api. One may use the API also with no programming skills. For example, collecting the posts in the r/science thread can be done with the following syntax: reddit.com/r/science/top/.json?t=all&limit=100, where "top" indicates that we are interested in the most popular threads, "t" asks the API to sort the items by date, and "limit" imposes the limit of threads to be shown—100 is the maximum value. However, the results need further processing, unlike with data obtained through scraping. Also, the limitations of results to 100 is a serious limitation.

Working with APIs of different websites is facilitated with dedicated tools. Many data processing packages allows API access to data—as with tools like The Digital Methods Initiative Twitter Capture and Analysis Toolset (DMI-TCAT), RapidMiner, Tableau, Condor, or Gephi.

3.1.6 Other Useful Tools

It is beyond the scope of this monograph to cover all topics in detail. Its goal is not to present a complete and deep description of the tools of digital sociological analysis. Every method would deserve its own detailed description. However, people who have not used data mining software before will find it more rewarding to get a sense of its fundamentals, what limitations it imposes, and how to get started with their own data collection.

In this section, I offer concise descriptions of a few more tools, with some examples of their use. I am focusing on programs that do not require programming skills—assuming that readers who are proficient at programming will benefit more from the sections on qualitative studies, culture studies, and research ethics.

3.1.6.1 ScrapingHub

ScrapingHub.com was developed by people working on Scrapy.org. The latter is an excellent open source program to set up one's data crawlers, but it requires programming skills. ScrapingHub contains tools that can produce the same results with a visual editor, Portia. In Portia, we may choose the website that concerns us and, through an intuitive interface, mark the data we want. Portia works well with websites that do not allow for easy data export. It is a sensible alternative to ParseHub.

3.1.6.2 OctoParse

OctoParse.com is another service for easy automated collection of text- and image-based data, similarly to ParseHub. It works well with several webpage formats, including AJAX, dynamically created, or Javascript-based. The service is cloud-based, with the use of hundreds of servers, thanks to which the risk of the process being blocked by the website is minimized. Data can be scraped or accessed through the API. The free version comes with many limitations but it still allows research to be conducted on simple datasets. OctoParse can be installed on a desktop computer and comes with many pre-loaded templates for popular web-site scraping, including Twitter, Yelp, or Amazon.

3.1.6.3 COSMOS

COSMOS is a Java application for Windows, part of the socialdatalab. net service. It is available for free and may be useful in analyzing Twitter data based on country and demographic information. It allows the construction of custom enquiries, drawing the diagrams of retweets, frequency of occurrence of specific phrases, charts, maps, and word clouds based on frequency data. It is worth visiting the Social Data Science Lab service to read useful guides on hate speech online.

3.1.6.4 DiscoverText

DiscoverText.com is run by Texifter. It is a complex cloud-based tool combining machine learning, coding by human teams, and a variety of computer text analysis tools—coming from simply non-structural corpus, as well as from poll results and Twitter. Unfortunately, as of September 2018, the use of Twitter data requires the consent of the company behind it, but if such permission is granted, DiscoverText allows for many useful analyses.

3.1.6.5 Labs.polsys.net

This address hosts a family of simple, yet useful tools, with the added benefit of exporting the data to Gephi. I will describe a few that readers can experiment with.

Figure 3.14 Example network of interconnected music artists using Spotify Artist Network and Gephi

Spotify Artist Network, based on Spotify data, allows analysis of the network of interconnected music artists. It allows exporting of the network to Gephi for further analysis. It can show, for instance, that people listening to Johnny Cash are also interested in country music generally (see Figure 3.14). The structure of the network is homogeneous, but in a more general view there is a separate cluster of Southern US rock (with a high popularity of Lynyrd Skynyrd), and American folk.

NetVizz is a Facebook app allowing to scrape the data of the service's public pages and groups for academic research (Rieder, 2013). It originally enabled the scraping of non-public groups but this feature has been removed. Following the Facebook data leak scandals, revealed in 2018, the future of the application is uncertain. It also did not pass the Facebook's audit, as it was considered to not provide an added value for Facebook users[9]—but as of this writing (summer 2019), it still works. Thanks to NetVizz, we may analyze friendship networks, and demographic and relation data. It also allows analysis of the relations of likes among Facebook pages which enables the discovery of clusters of propaganda groups. It will be unfortunate to lose it.

The other tools are a YouTube data extractor and others that require a server-side installation and programming skills.

3.1.6.6 Chorus

Chorus (chorusanalytics.co.uk) is a free tool to scrape and visualize Twitter data (Brooker, Barnett, & Cribbin, 2016). Twitter is a

[9] See: https://perma.cc/PK4T-RM2E

tremendous source of data, as the access is completely public, although one needs to pay for the restricted use of historic data. We may therefore study interactions, communication networks, and connection clusters, with no fear of the deeper structure of interactions being hidden from us because of restricted permissions. Naturally, independent of technical availability, we need to control the issues of legality of access and use of the data.

3.1.6.7   Webometric Analyst

Webometric Analyst (Thelwall, 2009) is a free Windows tool that enables different kinds of analyses, such as the frequency of phrase occurrence or mentions of websites. It can be downloaded from lexiurl.wlv.ac.uk/index.html. It also allows visualization of the relations between sites or tweets. It uses the API of sites such as Mendeley, Microsoft Academic, or Google Books and allows the study of citations. Finally, it allows the creation and analysis of diagrams of relations based on social networks such as YouTube, Twitter, Tumblr, or Flickr.

3.1.6.8   Netlytic

Netlytic.org is a tool for text and social network analysis. It uses the APIs of Twitter, Instagram, YouTube, and Facebook's public groups but it also allows the researcher to study databases and RSS imports. With Netlytic we may identify popular topics and make impressive visualizations, including the geolocation of some data.

3.1.6.9   DigitalMethods.Net

DigitalNethods.net contains links to miscellaneous small tools, such as a Disqus discussion scraper (Disqus is one of the most popular commercial web forum systems), a tool enabling Amazon book analysis, a script collecting search suggestions on Google, and the scraping of GitHub project-related data.

3.1.6.10   WikiChron

WikiChron.Science enables convenient comparison of dozens of Wikimedia sites and projects with different criteria (Serrano, Arroyo, & Hassan, 2018) and chronologically, which gives it an advantage over other tools used in similar analyses, available from the repository at tools.wmflabs.org. It also allows visualization of query results, making work much easier.

3.1.6.11 Big Data Tools

Independent work with Big Data requires complex tools. Fortunately, many of these tools are free/open source but still require expertise in IT. Apache Hadoop (hadoop.apache.org) is one of the most popular tools and is capable of quickly processing large structured and unstructured data sets. It has many extra modules, including a scalable machine-learning project (Mahout). An alternative to Hadoop is Lumify (altamiracorp.com/index.php/lumify), which boasts easy 2D and 3D visualizations, dynamic histograms, or interactive geospatially organized dataviews. HPCC (hpccsystems.com) may be used in a similar way; this tool has been praised for its scalability and a well-developed Integrated Development Environment (IDE). All the tools are advanced and will make no sense to users who are not experienced coders, and the experienced coders are aware of them already.

Finally, RapidMiner (rapidminer.com) is an interesting alternative; its platform is easier to use and does not require coding skills—it is also available as free/open source but also offered as a paid web service. It is available for free to academics who cannot cover the cost from a grant.

3.1.6.12 Social Network Analysis—Other Tools

Social network analysis does not always require independent data collection but it does always require the data to be processed. Desktop software works well in this respect. The simplest solutions even encompass an MS Excel plugin—such as Node XL (nodexl.codeplex. com), which makes it easy to generate basic graphs. One of the more advanced tools is the Social Network Visualizer (socnetv.org). Like Gephi, this is a free/open source solution, also offered for free and allowing complex analyses, extending beyond standard measures. It also offers crawlers that analyze the reference networks based on a single URL, and an intuitive interface allowing an exploratory approach to data.

It is also worth looking at the possibilities offered by Intelligent Collaborative Knowledge Networks (ickn.org). For academic purposes, the developers allow the download of Condor, a convenient program allowing the use of data from emails, calendar, Skype, Facebook, Twitter, Wikipedia, and other sources, including user data.

3.1.6.13   MediaCloud

Media Cloud (mediacloud.org) is a simple, yet powerful open source platform developed by the MIT Center for Civic Media and the Berkman-Klein Center for Internet and Society at Harvard University allowing studying media ecosystems and tracking how stories and ideas are shared through online media, by analyzing millions of publications.

3.2 Qualitative Research

Qualitative social science research has often been the victim of its own success: it consists of a plethora of approaches, methods, tools, which despite bearing the same name offer diverging, or even conflicting, concepts.

In qualitative research of information systems (Sarker, Xiao, & Beaulieu, 2013), like social research, within one single typology, there are five streams of research (Ciesielska & Jemielniak, 2018; Creswell & Poth, 2017):

- hermeneutics,
- case study,
- grounded theory,
- ethnography,
- narrative research.

Despite some similarities, they have considerable differences in the practice of field research and in the collection of material. For instance, the goal of research based on grounded theory is to construct a theory that derives from qualitative data (Charmaz, 2014). For this reason, grounded theory research will be conducted differently from ethno-graphic research, even when the topic is the same (Prus, 1996). This will be true even if the analytical tools are similar or identical, as the philosophical assumptions as to the relation of the field to the researcher will differ (Konecki, 2008b). This is because ethnography is not designed to generate theories (Hammersley, 1990) and generalizations (Payne & Williams, 2005), but rather bases its external validation on thick description. Such discrepancies between offline and online research are consistently similar, both when employing grounded theory and ethnography. The former, in addition, makes a good choice for the use of online data.

In this monograph, I do not consider the nuances of qualitative research. Unlike with computational social sciences, founded on Big Data, whose canon is still in the making, the qualitative social sciences come with excellently described and developed methodologies. The goals of this book are only to present the set of new methods that fit online social research well, and to outline the differences between online and more traditional research methodologies. Those interested in the diversity of qualitative research or the use of grounded theory (Charmaz, Komorowska, & Konecki, 2013) will benefit from the existing literature (Ciesielska & Jemielniak, 2018; Flick, 2014; Hammersley & Atkinson, 1995).

For these reasons, this book will devoted only to the qualitative approaches that I have used. I will describe my experience with the digital ethnography I used in researching Wikipedia. I will also draw the readers' attention to specific differences related to case study, narrative analysis (Jemielniak, 2008a, 2008b), and interviews, assuming that these remarks will be sufficient to mark the most important differences between online and traditional social research. I will also describe the issues related to social studies of Internet-based culture.

3.2.1 Digital Ethnography

The subject literature contains many similar terms pertaining to online anthropological research (Jemielniak, 2013). Some are interchangeable and others are not. Each approach has its own way of referencing ethnographic tradition (Domínguez Figaredo et al., 2007). First, there is a skillful wordplay, referring to "netnographic" studies (Kozinets, 2002, 2010). Even though this name fits Internet ethnography well, it has been usurped by a marketing research tool with very weak link to ethnography, as it is not based on immersion in a culture.

The opposite pole is occupied by connective ethnography (Leander & McKim, 2003). It is based on researching a community by combining online and offline analyses, in long-term field studies, and with the use of social network analysis (Dirksen, Huizing, & Smit, 2010). In a similar context, cyberethnography is referenced (Rybas & Gajjala, 2007) as underlining the fact that behind the online messages actual people also take part in offline life, as opposed to virtual ethnography which may focus on online communities at the cost of a vital social context. As Miller and Slater observe: "ethnography means a long-term involvement amongst people, through a variety of methods, such that any one aspect of their life can be properly contextualized in others" (D. Miller & Slater, 2001, pp. 21–2)—which would suggest that purely virtual study cannot make valid claims. Even though this approach has some proper angles, we need to remember that ethnographic research of only online communities is also both possible and reasonable. Moreover, even the conviction that through physical proximity we are able to grasp each aspect of life seems pure fiction.

Above all, it is far from clear that the term "virtual ethnography" excludes conducting real-life research or complementing online research with interviews (Hancock, Crain-Dorough, Parton, & Oescher, 2010; Hine, 2000). In light of the multitude of terms, including "Internet ethnography" (Sade-Beck, 2008), "virtual space ethnography" (Guitton, 2012), or "online ethnography" (Markham, 2008), it seems worthwhile to stick to those that are most familiar. In mid-2019, "virtual ethnography" returned over 9000 hits in English in Google Scholar, "digital ethnography" almost 5000, while "networked ethnography" a mere 65. "Internet ethnography" barely crossed 1000 hits, and "cyberethnography" returned a little more than 600. Taking into account the popularity of digital humanities programs, I think that "digital ethnography" (Murthy, 2008; Underberg & Zorn, 2013) is a safe term for online ethnographic studies that encompass also the offline context (interviews, meetings, field research offline); "virtual ethnography" ought to be reserved for just online research.

Similar categorizations can be applied to digital and virtual sociology. We need to remember that the method of using the analyses is also important: we can fathom research which is conducted with both the traditional methods and online analysis but which will bear

Table 3.2 Online research terms

Term	Description
Internet sociology	A notion related to both the researching of online communities and to the study of Internet users, as well as products of online culture or human-bot interactions (see Introduction)
Networked sociology	A notion describing online and offline community research, with the possible additional use of quantitative tools
Digital sociology	A notion describing online community research, with the possible additional use of traditional research methods (such as interviews, observations)
Cybersociology	An older notion, replaced by "digital sociology" (Lupton, 2012; Rybas & Gajjala, 2007), also suggesting online research supplemented with offline analysis
Virtual sociology	A notion defining the research of online communities only in their online context (i.e. research of avatars, including bots)
Netnography	A marketing research method based on virtual simplified qualitative analysis, not connected with ethnographic research.

no traits of digital social sciences simply because the starting point and the goal of the research will be the understanding of real-life communities whose online presence will be merely additional. A list of the most common online research terms and their definitions is provided in Table 3.2.

In reference to both digital and virtual ethnography, the goal is to tell a good story that explains social reality, involving the readers in the everyday world and understanding the research subjects, based on long-term field studies as with traditional ethnography (Whyte, 1943/2012).

Some researchers claim that it is pointless to seek similarities between digital and classical ethnography (E. A. Buchanan, 2004). This claim does not hold water though. Online communities are not less complex in their interactions than their "real" counterparts—in addition, it would be hard to define a prototypical, real community (Paccagnella, 1997). A belief that we are facing something methodologically and subjectively new, is nothing more than placing older research methods in a privileged position, which can result from researchers having more experience with immersion in different brick-and-mortar cultures. Such immersion is typical of digital ethnography, where researchers immerse themselves in the culture they study; as with classical ethnography, it requires long-term participation in and deep engagement with the field. Similar criticisms were raised in the 1950s against organizational ethnography research in industrialized countries as not alien enough, not sufficiently exotic, or unfit for typical anthropological work (Gaggiotti, Kostera, & Krzyworzeka, 2016; Warner & Low, 1947). Ethnographies of the virtual worlds are simply ethnographies (Randall, Harper, & Rouncefield, 2007). There is no sense in arbitrarily separating the digital from the non-digital forms of human activity and labeling them "radically different" (Ruhleder, 2000). As Hine remarks (Hine, 2000, p. 65):

All forms of interaction are ethnographically valid, not just the face to face. The shaping of the ethnographic object as it is made possible by the available technologies is the ethnography. This is ethnography, in, of, and through the virtual.

Naturally, this does not mean digital ethnography does not require some modification of research tools (Nocera, 2002) but we may assume that it uses the prevailing theoretical and methodological frameworks to cater to a specific new research field. "Qualitative researchers who have thought carefully about internet ethnography accept that it should be employed and understood as part of a commitment to existing theoretical traditions" (Travers, 2009, p. 172). For this book, I will focus on the main discrepancies between traditional and online research. Therefore, I make general remarks on the issues related to ethnographic research while encouraging the readers to seek better and deeper descriptions (Atkinson, Coffey, Delamont, Lofland, & Lofland, 2001; Clifford & Marcus, 1986; Hammersley & Atkinson, 1995).

One of the best-known ethnographers, Geertz, wrote about ethnography (Geertz, 1973/2000, p. 6):

In anthropology, or anyway social anthropology, what the practitioners do is ethnography. And it is in understanding what ethnography is, or more exactly what doing ethnography is, that a start can be made toward grasping what anthropological analysis amounts to as a form of knowledge. From one point of view, that of the textbook, doing ethnography is establishing rapport, selecting informants, transcribing texts, taking genealogies, mapping fields, keeping a diary, and so on. But it is not these things, techniques and received procedures that define the enterprise. What defines it is the kind of intellectual effort it is: an elaborate venture in, to borrow a notion from Gilbert Ryle, "thick description."

The nature of ethnography is, therefore, not a set of tools but an "anthropological frame of mind" (Czarniawska-Joerges, 1992), thanks to which we can use our own reflexivity. It is being "a professional stranger" (Agar, 1980) to create a description that will enable an understanding of the local perspective. We offer a description of the researched culture in a way that gives the readers a feeling of co-participation in the discovery and comprehension of that culture, inviting the readers into the process of interpretation and creating an impression of independent immersion in the described reality (Clifford, 1983). The goal of ethnography is not an objective description of the reality but rather one interpretation, rooted in a reliable reflection of what the researcher considers important in the reality's hierarchies of domination, power relations, interests, or prejudices (Lichterman, 2017).

Anthropology used to be dominated by an approach typical of the natural sciences: the goal was to be completely impartial and dispassionate, as this was supposed to lead to objective reflections. It was thought possible to see the social world without constantly assigning meanings (Clifford & Marcus, 1986; Weick, 1969/1979).

This functional perception is anachronistic, it is clear that the researcher is an "interpretive lens": through whose experience knowledge, history, sensitivity, tastes, prejudices, and preferences, they filter and interpret the observed social reality, constantly negotiating and making sense of it (C. I. Gerstl-Pepin & Gunzenhauser, 2002). They reach under the cover of the social construction of reality (P. L. Berger & Luckman, 1967) without taking part in it. The belief in being able to get a neutral vision is an illusion. It may be a trick, but it interferes with reliable research (Golden-Biddle & Locke, 1997). The goal of ethnography is rather to present a subjective interpretation that will improve and expand our understanding of the world. We tell a credible, authentic academically rigorous story. The interpretation that is created in the process, naturally, needs to make sense to the researcher, but instead of striving for objectivity, which is impossible, it is fair to present and advance the researcher's starting position, privileges, and perspectives

(Haraway, 1988). This does not result in complete relativism but rather in awareness of intersubjectivity (Feinberg, 2007; Madden, 2017) and relying on this awareness as an ethnographic assumption (A. Gillespie & Cornish, 2010).

Ethnographers become academic tools—after absorbing the understanding of the local culture, with the exercise of proper care and diligence in reliable reporting of the perspective of the research subjects, they create interpretations whose main value is the better understanding of the cultures under examination (C. Gerstl-Pepin & Patrizio, 2009). The same researcher may interpret their studies in different ways—Wolf offers three takes on the same observation, and presents three genres of anthropological inquiry, separate in concept and in time from one another; the result is a fourth narrative on the role of an ethnographer (M. Wolf, 1992). For these reasons, attempts at playing a completely detached person and conducting a transparent narrative which excludes the author are de facto detrimental to the final result (Charmaz & Mitchell, 1996), by impoverishing it and stripping it of the key advantages of ethnography. The researcher is a fixture of ethnographic practice; attempts at ignoring and masking their influence on the process destroy the outcomes.

In some streams of anthropology, it is said that researchers should not, even in their own narrative, assume a privileged position, and that doing ethnography benefits when the differences in power and access to voicing one's opinions are reduced (Lassiter, 2001). Such beliefs are especially strong in the areas of anthropology that are associated with action research (Greenwood, González Santos, & Cantón, 1991; Jemielniak, 2006), where belief of science serving to describe the reality in an impartial and uninvolved way is rejected (Strumińska-Kutra, 2016). It is also characteristic of collaborative ethnography (Pietrowiak, 2014).

Because in ethnography it is vital to minimize the influence of one's assumptions and stereotypes, it is best started with as few preconceptualizations as possible. The culture is often treated performatively—the researcher assumes that it may not be possible to fit the culture into a standard theoretical model but rather that the unique model of the culture will reveal itself in the course of the research (Latour, 1986). Therefore, the characteristic element of ethnography is not to begin with hypotheses but with questions. During the study, the researchers accept what they see, although they wonder at everything and strive to understand even the simplest of things (Fetterman, 2009). This is the "anthropological frame of mind."

Actual research tools in ethnographic studies are secondary in character. There is a canon but nothing can stop researchers from doing ethnography with the use of less standard methods—or even, on occasion, with elements of quantitative studies, for instance to conduct a pilot study for a later list of research questions. The hallmark of ethnographic studies is the process of longitudinal immersion, attempting to understand the local logic. The most frequently used research tools and methods are observations (participative and non-participative), field notes, interviews, narrative and discourse analysis (Denzin & Lincoln, 1994) and analysis of photos, videos, or cultural artifacts.

The vast majority of ethnographic studies are based on participative observation (Ingold, 2014). Observations may be used to do case analyses, or to understand the event, or simply for wider analysis of how the researched community actually works. Observations are accompanied by a research log, or field notes—it is an essential element of ethnographic work, since it allows for more reflexivity, returning to previous interpretations, externalization of one's doubts (Emerson, Fretz, & Shaw, 2011; Sanjek, 1990), and a better understanding of one's own limitations and starting assumptions, including the status of power or private prejudices (Alvesson & Sköldberg, 2017). Without field notes, a researcher claiming to do ethnography may soon appear to be little more than a tourist, telling vacation anecdotes.

Ethnographic research also often uses qualitative interviews to complement observation data, allowing an interpretation voiced by participants in the local culture. Yet another useful supplementary method is narrative analysis. This chapter will be devoted to ethnography, and I will add some remarks on case analysis, narrative analysis, and interviews in the context of online community research.

I will describe the main differences between digital and traditional ethnography. The most important is that, in the virtual world, the subject of research is avatars, not people (R. Schroeder & Axelsson, 2006). Granted, most Internet traffic has migrated to Facebook, Instagram, or

LinkedIn—on those platforms users often are found under their real names, but other online services such as Twitter, Wikipedia, or internet forums allow to users to create "personae," avatars acting under a pseudonym and having their own style. By researching the behavior of avatars, we must keep in mind that one person may have several avatars, or several people may manage the same one. Moreover, a growing number of avatars are bots—accounts managed by algorithms, often without human supervision (Lokot & Diakopoulos, 2016). We therefore know both very little and a great deal about the people behind the avatars (Golder & Macy, 2014). We know a great deal because we may research their utterances, preferences, and interests. We know very little because we often lack the most basic demographic and geographical data. It is not rare to use different genders online and offline (Pearce & Artemesia, 2009). We may infer the geographical location of users just from the analysis of their network of friends (Compton, Jurgens, & Allen, 2014), however, the apparently simple task of differentiating utterances of actual people from those of bots is actually complicated (Clark et al., 2016), and acquiring potentially identifying data may be ethically problematic.

What practical problems does such differentiation present? In my Wikipedia research, I often encountered the problem of "sock puppetry,"[10] where a person establishes several user accounts to give the illusion that an idea is more widespread than it actually is. People who want an entry to appear on Wikipedia or want an editing principle to be changed will resort to sock puppetry. As a result, we may observe a "discussion" among several avatars who are really controlled by the same person. The problem is so common that there is a special group of high-trust functionaries, "checkusers," who have the tools to detect this kind of fraud and may access individual users' private data, like IP addresses or browser versions. Wikipedia administrators strictly control this access and do not use it arbitrarily. As a former checkuser, I know that sock puppetry is quite widespread, even though I encountered it only when other users reported suspected sock puppets. Therefore, it is only logical to assume that, many more careful perpetrators have gone unnoticed. The practical conclusion for digital ethnographers is that we need to

---

[10] https://en.wikipedia.org/wiki/Wikipedia:Sock_puppetry

differentiate the research of avatars from that of real people. At the same time, in many virtual communities people have an emotional bond with their avatars (Wolfendale, 2007). It is a good practice first to analyze purely virtual data and then contact selected user accounts with a request for a video conversation. Only then we can be sure that our research reaches actual people.

Digital ethnography is also different when it comes to "going native." In digital social sciences, we may get deeply involved as equals in the researched community. Classical anthropological research rather suggests the role of "marginal natives" (Lobo, 1990; Walsh, 2004) and "professional strangers" (Agar, 1980) and distancing of the researcher from their own culture (Leach, 1982; Narayan, 1993). It is not an absolute rule (Sperschneider & Bagger, 2003; Van Maanen, 1988/2011) and researchers are warned against identifying with the research subjects to a degree that would result in the loss of research perspective (Robson, 2002), but for purely practical reasons, researchers find it problematic to go native, as their outsider status is immediately visible. Still, even though the dream of being "the chameleon field-worker, perfectly self-tuned to his exotic surroundings" (Geertz, 1974, p. 27) in traditional anthropological studies is illusory, in case of online research it becomes really quite viable. Digital natives are not born, each member joined it as a stranger. What is most valuable in digital ethnography is the experience of going native and slowly coming to understand a community from within (Gatson & Zweerink, 2004). Naturally, this experience usually leads to adopting the logic of the researched community, but it is a fair price for reaching otherwise hermetic knowledge. As a result, unlike traditional ethnographic studies, digital ethnographies much more often have an autoethnographic character (Denzin, 2006; Kamińska, 2014; Rheingold, 1994). Observational research of this type may lead to the temptation of not informing the studied community of our role and goal of participating in the group. It is also a typical problem of offline research (Konecki, 1990) which has a direct impact on the possibility of giving informed consent to participating in the study. I will address this point in the chapter on research ethics. In specific circumstances, research conducted in concealment may be justifiable, however, experience has taught me that the best policy was to declare I am an academic on my profile and not conceal my willingness to conduct ethnographic research. Moreover, the division that Prensky (2001) makes between "digital natives" and "digital immigrants" has been criticized as inadequate and replaced with the notions of "visitors" and "residents" (White & Le Cornu, 2011).

With a theoretical easiness of going native comes the illusion of being able to permeate every community. This is illusory in a sense because one does not need to be born in a given place, from a given race, using a given language. In addition, the flexibility of self-presentation is related to those who conduct research and who have the freedom to manage and present their identity (P. Miller, 2012). Still, fluency in the local cultural code is a prerequisite. The situation is similar to attempts of permeating fandom. Someone who would like to present as a Bronie (Literat, 2017),[11] an adult fan of the cartoon *My Little Pony*, or as a Trekker, a fan of the *Star Trek* franchise, would need to know the series really well, should they want to have any credibility within the community. It is similarly hard to gain entry into a motorcycle gang, although it provides excellent chances for fantastic qualitative research (D. R. Wolf, 1991). In fact, the understanding of any organization's culture requires immersion into that organization.

It is no different with online communities which are similarly characterized by "deep diversity" of culture and context (English-Lueck, 2011). As Hine notes, "although the Internet feels like familiar territory for many of the people we study, it can seem quite strange and dangerous territory for a qualitative researcher" (Hine, 2013, p. 2). For Wikipedia users to consider me an true Wikipedian, I needed to perform tens of thousands of edits, discover where the important discussions were held, learn the jargon to understand seemingly simple lines like "fails to meet WP:NOTE, but no SD needed, submit to RfD rather" (an article subject is not notable enough but needs to be discussed because it does not fit the criteria for immediate deletion). Granted, because in many communities the records of all the discussions are easily accessible, we may consider enculturation a waste of time. It is definitely the opposite—it is enculturation that gives sense to the analysis of events. Only "insiderness [can be considered] as the key to delving into the hidden crevices of the organization"

---

[11] https://en.wikipedia.org/wiki/Bronies:_The_Extremely_Unexpected_Adult_Fans_of_My_Little_Pony

(Labaree, 2002, p. 98). One can imagine a para-ethnographic research based on available data, without learning the social dynamics of a community through participation. However, in the radical overflow of information, people with no deep understanding of the community, or at least a trusted guide, will be incapable of understanding what they see and where to look. For instance, external researchers of Wikipedia and new users of the project sometimes have a perception that the community is deeply conflicted. They may have this impression because Wikipedian culture radically rejects hierarchy and lacks the fear of superiors, typical of mainstream organizations, thus encouraging the expression of objections and doubts whenever one holds a different point of view (Jemielniak, 2016b). This leads, naturally, to situations where many people within Wikipedia or other Wikimedia projects are willing to express their opinions, radical points of view, or ask questions publicly, expecting answers, regardless of what role within the Wikimedia Foundation or a social movement is played by their debaters, simply because of the a-hierarchical ideology (Jemielniak, 2015). The awareness of this fact may become a serious impediment to the interpretation of the research.

A problem that is akin to going native is the lack of barrier between the field and home. In traditional ethnographic research, this border is defined by "going into the field," which is separated from home in space and time. In online research, the differentiation of time and place of research proves difficult. It is hard to separate taking field notes and deliberating on the material from using the Internet for personal or other professional purposes. The problem is similar to those classical ethnographies where the boundaries of work and life are blurred (McLean, 2007). It has serious consequences because it complicates a core component of the ethnographic method: researcher reflexivity (C. A. Davies, 2008). This reflexivity is largely ritualized, because within ethnographic research the way of speaking about one's doubts, failures, or shyness is rather conventional (Jemielniak & Kostera, 2010; S. Scott, Hinton-Smith, Härmä, & Broome, 2012). There are no good solutions to this problem, although, one may imagine symbolic measures like designating separate computers, one for research and one for personal use. In any case, what matters is knowing one's role.

It cannot go unnoticed that in digital ethnography, we observe a significantly different issue of being in the field (Rutter & Smith, 2005).

"Being on site" is a typical differentiating factor of classical ethnographic field research. Anthropology, in addition, is based on experiencing the researched cultures with all the senses (Bendix, 2005). The physical removal from home, travel, long-term relocation into a new environment and all-day round participation are undoubtedly factors that influence the researcher's state of mind. As already stated, it is a key element of the ethnographic interpretation machine, so such an important change needs to be taken into account. If we cannot be on site during our digital ethnographic research, as with traditional or organizational ethnography, we need to replace fixed physical co-presence with long hours of virtual participation, development of competences related to transmitting and receiving text-based and visual messages (Garcia, Standlee, Bechkoff, & Cui, 2009). Similarly to modern organization ethnographies, it seems clear that conducting field research without maintaining physical co-presence and spatial common experiencing is possible—especially as the participants of the researched communities act similarly within those communities (Burrell, 2009).

Digital ethnography is also different in the character of its interactions. In virtual communities, these are very often asynchronous; not everyone participated in the same discussion at the same time. Depending on the community and the topic, avatars may exchange comments almost synchronically. This is typical of heated discussions on forums, Facebook groups, Twitter, but also on Wikipedia, if the sides of the discussion are deeply involved. In some Internet forums or Wikipedia discussions, however, it is not uncommon for questions or comments to receive an answer after weeks, months, or even years. One needs to be aware of that issue because it shapes the dynamics of discussion. Although messages may resemble exchanges in a regular conversation, they are very different from this mode of communication (Ong, 2002). This mode is the result of interlocutors' awareness that they do not actually talk to one another; apart from the conversation, they participate in a collective process of establishing a public dialogic narrative or building a knowledge base. In this sense, we may speak of a new form of interpersonal interaction: a "monodialogue." A monodialogue is a conversation in which the recipient is primarily not the person that we are responding to; the recipient of our reply may never even learn that that there is a response.

Monodialogism directly influences different methods of observations (Garcia et al., 2009). We observe avatars instead of people (R. Schroeder & Axelsson, 2006; Williams, 2007). And because in many communities we have access to huge archives of older discussions, we may mistakenly assume that there is no difference in observing real-time interactions versus historical research. This is definitely not true. If we observe interactions in real time, we gain insights into the dynamics of the exchange. This awareness is not as easily obtained by a mere analysis of the recorded time of each utterance, although our ability to timestamp each utterance is indeed convenient. With historical analysis, we also lose the context of the current reactions of the community. We must remember that the more important discussions, controversies, and conflicts usually echo in other community-typical communication channels. For instance, typical Wikipedia discussions result in comments on Wikipedia groups on Facebook, mailing lists, IRC channels, and within private messages on different communicators. This makes it virtually impossible to recreate all of these comments after the fact. Moreover, wiki technology allows for the insertion of new messages without maintaining a linear flow of the text; one can insert a later message higher on the page to address a specific earlier fragment of communication. Because of this non-linearity, the recreation of the dynamics of a discussion is more time-consuming, even though timestamps and easy access to all versions of a page theoretically enable the reader to follow the chronology, unlike with some other platforms. Finally, having all interactions written down is a great benefit. This does not mean, however, that the researcher is absolved of the need to keep a research diary. Making notes and writing down reflections will launch the interpretive apparatus in the researcher's mind. Relying purely on archival quotes strips the ethnographic research of one of its greatest advantages—of iterative returning to the same observations and events, and assigning meanings to them (Weick, 1969/1979). A research journal also allows for more honesty—if ethnography, as a final text, is a narrative, written from a perspective (M. Wolf, 1992), the diary creates a safety valve, where doubts can be aired, where thoughts that we will not necessarily share in the final text will be sketched.

Furthermore, an important difference in the process of conducting online observation stems from the fact that, in some communities, one may perform it without having a user account; that is, in a way hidden from the participants. In other cases, one must enter the virtual world on its own terms and accept the forms of presentation of self in the community through a standardized avatar (Pearce & Artemesia, 2009). In turn, unlike with traditional ethnography, during virtual observations it is much more difficult to trace communication between the observed individuals—it is commonplace in virtual communities to use different communication channels and conducting discussions in the main thread simultaneously with "social life" discussions (Ducheneaut et al., 2010).

Digital ethnography, to a greater degree than its traditional counterpart, relies on being multi-sited (Marcus, 1995). In this context, it means concurrent research of more than one online community or a combination of online and offline research. It is a consequence of online communities: they often intermingle and overlap with other online and offline gatherings.

An important difference is that the digital ethnographer is in a less privileged position than the traditional ethnographer. The power of narration and control over communication is an issue that anthropologists have since long recognized as important (Fine, 1993). In traditional ethnography, however, we normally are alone in the field or in a team that will later publish observations that are collectively agreed upon—which, on a side note, is a strategy that is best chosen in an informed way, taking into account the pros and cons of ethnographic teamwork (Clerke & Hopwood, 2014). In digital ethnography, however, we never know whether we are crossing paths with other researchers who are analyzing the same events and utterances at the same time, or maybe even treat us as their research subject. In an extreme and purely hypothetical situation, we may envision a community of researchers studying one another, all with the mistaken impression that they are immersed in the local culture. Moreover, it is much simpler for others to verify our observations and thoughts. Unlike in traditional ethnography, where we may assume that the researcher creates the image of the community at a given moment which is inaccessible to others, and has full power over the narration, it is possible to confront the same data in digital ethnography even years later. Also, many online communities, perhaps because they work constantly with the written word, create their own meta-analyses of their culture, mythologies, histories—and are very protective of their monopoly on such artifacts. Inclusion of such native ethnographies into the academic circulation, in some form or another, remains an open issue.

Another characteristic of digital ethnography is the high interculturality of participants and the low homogeneity of the researched group, in contrast to more traditional communities. Usually, the hub of the community is a single common element, such as interests, common projects, or skills in using the same tool. Because of this element, the processes of enculturation and standardization of social norms are less formative and have less influence in the participants.

In digital ethnography, we also observe different social stigmas. Many of the traditional ways of stigmatizing in offline communities are based on race, age, or physical disabilities; but these are easier to mask online. Markedly, gender remains an important category of avatar classification, although hard to identify with certainty. Men dominate many online communities, this discriminates against women or discourages their equal participation. Still, in many other ways the Internet is egalitarian. As the popular 1993 *New Yorker* cartoon declares, "On the Internet, nobody knows you're a dog." On the one hand, everyone with Internet access may present more casually than face to face and in agreement with their tastes, at least in theory, with no demographic or material limitations. On the other hand, online communities are susceptible to other types of social stratification and identity construction (Ward, 2017). During a meeting in a loud disco, appearances, clothes, and body language play major roles; in online communities language competence plays first violin. Vocabulary range, using the lingo of the community, frequency and adequacy of the use of emoticons, and even typing speed may lead to strong assessments of an avatar.

Finally, although this trait is not typical of just online communities, it may be more difficult to address in the online context: ways of building one's status within the community may differ from our expectations. In traditional business organizations, there are fixed and relatively similar ways of playing out value and dedication, taking into account hierarchy, in addition to access to resource, money, and time,[12] but in

---

[12] As an example, in my research on software engineers, I noticed that managers view the amount of time that their employees spend at work, not the quality of the work done, as

virtual communities their unambiguous identification without being immersed in the field may become problematic. It is similar to traditional anthropological studies, but with online research, we are faced with the feeling that differences from our habits are negligible, which makes it more difficult to comprehend the situation. For example, in the Wikipedia community, in narratives of who is and is not valuable, the merit of writing well-developed encyclopedic articles arises more frequently that merely participating in discussions on the procedures and the whole bureaucracy of the project. However, an analysis of users who are elected the project's functionaries shows that they are almost always involved with the administration of the project, not only in content creation. Para-organizational structures are often bureaucratic and solidify the status quo (Konieczny, 2009; Shaw & Hill, 2014). Additionally, the actual quality of the articles is often of less importance than the mere number of edits—users becoming administrators on Polish Wikipedia usually have more than 2000 edits, and on English Wikipedia the count runs as high as 10,000—*editcountitis*, the obsession with the number of edits one has, is a serious problem within the community (Jemielniak, 2014). Inside Wikipedia, "one's edit count is a sort of coin of the realm" (Reagle, 2010, p. 157).

3.2.2 Case Study

The case study is a standard method of qualitative research, typical in studies of organizational change, when we may focus not only on a specific community but on the flow of an event. The case study is often used in ethnographic studies and for this reason, remarks and reservations from Chapter 2 also apply here. However, the goal of ethnography is to understand the cultural context and the local logic of a community as such, while case studies focus on the description and explanation of a specific event. This may be one reason why case study is perceived as easier than ethnography, as it does not require long-term environmental acculturation. It may be misunderstood as an "easy" way to do

---

indicative of the value of the employee; in other words, time was symbolic in showing loyalty and the devotion to the organization (Jemielniak, 2009).

qualitative and pseudo-qualitative studies—without using the full potential of thick qualitative interpretation and at the same time not having the advantages of clearly defined quantitative requirements.

The method is widespread both among researchers from post-positivist tradition, for whom it will allows the drawing of generalizations, and among academics associated with the interpretive tradition who are attempting to understand the logic of the situation in the local understanding (Hassard & Kelemen, 2010). Because the latter approach is closer to my practice, I will draw the readers' attention to the specifics of this kind of case study, based on online data, in the scope which supplements the remarks from the section on digital ethnography and assuming that case study also requires a deep understanding of the researched culture.

The idea of case analysis is therefore to comprehensively understand the specific social situation (Stake, 2005), which leads to knowledge situated in local context (Flyvbjerg, 2006). It is an issue of tracing the starting situation, reasons, course, and results of an event or a transformation. It may be an organizational or cultural change, social trend, or an event that visualizes important aspects of the phenomenon of our research interest. Extreme cases work quite well with case studies, as they more accurately visualize processes within the researched community (Eisenhardt, 1989). Therefore, some suggest focusing on extreme situations, and pay particular attention to critical incidents and social dramas (Pettigrew, 1990). In case analysis, we may use all tools at our disposal, such as questionnaires, SNA, interviews, sentiment analysis, observations, or all kinds of secondary data analysis. The differentiating factor of the method is the goal: the explanation of a peculiar or characteristic event or transformation.

During my Wikipedia research, I engaged in many debates. One of my observations was that the social structure of Wikipedia channeled interpersonal conflicts towards cooperation, through the set of rules. Thanks to the combination of this mechanism with the escalation of involvement and low entry barrier to content creation, Wikipedia uses motivation of those who want to prove they are right to create the world's largest encyclopedia.

In my book (Jemielniak, 2014) I used the analysis of a few cases to exemplify Wikipedia-characteristic processes which had been instrumental in the development of the communities, and in which I was not directly involved. It was a historical analysis. Unlike with case studies, which are done offline, on Wikipedia all interactions are archived. Naturally, all my remarks related to observations from chapter 2 also apply here and for someone who was not familiar with the community even the selection of cases which could be considered especially important or symbolic would be difficult, we need to remember that community discussions are millions of pages and tens of thousands of words long. Nevertheless, the possibility of tracing, step-by-step, the flow of a discussion which I considered momentous made the study easier.

One of the cases I analyzed was the "Battle of Danzig": an argument on English Wikipedia over whether the article describing the city ought to be titled with the Polish "Gdańsk" or the German "Danzig." The case was very old, as the conflict had run from 2001 to 2005, a decade before I took up my research. It could seem that, especially in light of rapid changes on the Internet, such old stories from a community have no value today. However, this conflict, which even the community considers one of the lamest edit wars ever,[13] shaped later community regulations and revealed distinct processes that are still observable. The edit war, which did have a substantial background but grew way out of proportion, is still a living thing among Wikipedia veterans, and similar debates still arise, such as whether the Ganges River should be rendered as "Ganga" (the English name of the river among native English speakers from India) or whether Mexico has an official language. It was possible for me to better describe and analyze these two cases via reaching for a historic event without which I would not have been able to contextualize the dynamics of discussion, references, developed rules of reaching consensus. As I was not personally involved in the discussion, I was able to distance myself from it and thus describe the increase of involvement, emotions, and even paranoia on both sides of the barricade.

Yet another possible approach to case studies is to draw purposefully from personal experience. For of one of my articles, I describes a debate in which I was personally and emotionally involved (Jemielniak, 2016a). I did a case study of controversial edits in the Wikipedia article "Glass ceiling," where I reacted as a participant, trying to remove a section of

---

[13] See https://en.wikipedia.org/wiki/Wikipedia:Lamest_edit_wars

the article which I considered sexist but which still cited a verifiable source and as such did not fall under the rules of expedited removal. My goal was not complete objectivity. Just the opposite, personal experience and going back to thoughts and feelings that accompanied me in the debate, and which were definitely purely subjective, brought the added value of being able to look into the perception and reactions of an expert Wikipedian. I showed how quickly subject conflicts can arise and how difficult it is, especially for people not accustomed to the rules of Wikipedia, to abstain from a move that would result in their accounts being blocked, regardless of merit.

A short autoethnographic case analysis showed that the extensive bureaucratic ruleset of Wikipedia, as well as lack of skills in reacting to pseudo-academic reasoning, not to mention personal attacks, could easily deter women from editing Wikipedia. Making references to own emotions and reactions made it easier for me to show how difficult, regardless of one's experience, it is to keep composed and react calmly in online discussions with people who are well-versed in the community regulations. In this case, personal experience and emotional involvement were therefore used as part of the method. In order, however, to make the best use of the elements of autoethnographic look, reflexivity and a large dose of caution are advised (T. E. Adams & Ellis, 2016)—as drawing from one's own experience needs even more academic consideration, to keep the researcher from falling into the trap of describing their experience in a disorderly fashion, under the pretense of scientific method (Atkinson & Delamont, 2006). The researcher also needs to bear in mind that personal experience is also socially constructed and interpreted post-factum (J. W. Scott, 1991).

Trust is the bedrock of social relations, however, it is visible in different organizational forms in different ways (Latusek & Cook, 2012; Sztompka, 1999). For many online communities, trust in people, including close project associates (Latusek & Jemielniak, 2007, 2008), has been replaced by trust in procedures. When users know each other only in the virtual world, this is mainly the result of the users bearing in mind they hold discussions with avatars, and the identity of the debaters is fluid. Case analysis, as a method, causes the research of community procedures and rules to become valuable here, as well as the discussion surrounding the establishment of the procedures and rules. Even in communities which seemingly do not construct complex rules, major regulatory rule is often played by the online platform (which makes specific forms of interaction and social signals possible) and the practice of their use. One example is the use of the period in texting and chat messaging in a way that signals reluctance to continue the interaction or that the message is less honest (Gunraj, Drumm-Hewitt, Dashow, Upadhyay, & Klin, 2016; Houghton, Upadhyay, & Klin, 2018). Similarly, detailed meaning can be assigned to the use of emoticons in specific contexts (Monica A Riordan, 2017). For these reasons, to make sense of the studied cases, or even to be able to define the start and end of the cases, we need to be well-versed in the rules of the community or to use the services of experienced guides. In other words, if, regardless of our age, we are "digital immigrants" or "guests," at least within the researched community, we need the support of the "natives," *vel* "inhabitants" so that we may be able to tell which case is interesting, how to read through it, and what communication nuances are important (Monica A. Riordan, Kreuz, & Blair, 2018).

3.2.3 Online Interviews

The use of interviews to research online communities is, naturally, possible and useful (Salmons, 2012, 2014). They may be conducted in one of a few different formulas, with each having its advantages and disadvantages (Kazmer & Xie, 2008): text-based chat, email or forum interviews, voice messenger interviews, videoconferences, ad face-to-face interviews with the representatives of online communities.

Having conducted several interviews with the use of a text chat client, I cannot recommend this method. It appears very attractive because it avoids the tedious transcription of the interview. However, the answers I got were superficial, shorter, and the interviewees could not be convinced to provide longer narratives. It also took longer to establish trust, something that other researchers have confirmed (Shapka, Domene, Khan, & Yang, 2016). This was most likely the consequence of a few factors. The main reason is that most people speak more freely and more easily than they write. In addition, most people write more slowly than they speak. Moreover, the specifics of a text chat interaction (be it IRC, Slack, Messenger) inspire shorter messages because especially in synchronous interactions, writing longer chunks of text forces the other person to wait for the message to be sent across, so the communication cannot be received on the fly. Even if in some conversation messages are split into single sentences, or even fragments, it can be hard to tell when the message has ended. Finally, chat-based interviews invite the interlocutors to multi-task. The temptation is simply too big; although the interview can be very important for the researcher, for the interviewee it may become simply one of several open tabs or windows, not necessarily a high-priority one. If interviewees are doing other things while giving their answers, it is hard for us to expect that their involvement in the study is high.

From this perspective, it might be safer to conduct the interviews via email (Meho, 2006); but this method comes with its own disadvantages, the main being the need to stick to the list of questions and the inability of ad hoc follow-up, which, of course, is not so much a problem with structured interviews (Al-Saggaf & Williamson, 2004; Gruber, Szmigin, Reppel, & Voss, 2008). The situation is similar with web forum interviews and para-focus forms (Ping & Chee, 2009). It is still worth remembering text-based chat interviews in especially sensitive cases, where visual contact may be an impediment to completing the study (Aupers, Schaap, & de Wildt, 2018; M. Davis, Bolding, Hart, Sherr, & Elford, 2004; Neville, Adams, & Cook, 2016). It is similar to researching people engaged in illegal activities (Barrattt & Maddox, 2016). In such situations, the researcher needs to pay special attention to building trust and research relations, and to enlisting the involvement of the interviewee so as to negate the losses of the narrative's saturation and richness (Hewson, 2016).

The problem of the casual character of messages, resulting from multi-tasking, is also characteristic of voice-based interviews with the use of voice messengers, but this approach does not require a separate description, as it is not much different from a phone interview. It is worth mentioning the benefits of using software that encrypts the communication, such as Signal, or technology that does not impose the need to install anything on our interviewee's computer; Jitsi comes to mind as worth recommending. It is a communication platform, based on free/open source software which enables convenient voice- and videoconferences in the browser. Similar functions are also offered by Google Hangouts, AppearIn, Zoom or Bluejeans, but these are commercial projects.

These tools can are easy to use in video interviews (Deakin & Wakefield, 2014). Among all the remote connectivity ways, this is the one that provides the best contact. It largely solves the problem of multitasking and enriches the interview with the possibility of reading facial expressions. Here, broadband connection is a must. Nothing will replace a live, face-to-face contact, though, as an important part of communication relies on body language and the direct reading thereof. We simply rely on the use of all the senses, and additionally, the building of trust and research relation is also based on co-experiencing the same reality—reacting to the same changes in the environment. Video interviews have an advantage which needs to be addressed here though—they allow to reach people whose location, when revealed, would put them in a risky position. From my experience in contacting interviewees who were in hiding because of their involvement with the free information movement, it may be the only way of accessing them. In such situations a video software interview could have immense advantages. It may also be the tool of choice for people working a lot and accustomed to corporate videoconferences. In video interviews, recording is also usually easier than with live ones—we have direct access to sound from two microphones, and environmental noise is usually lower than when meeting our interviewees in a public space. An obvious advantage is also the low time and financial costs involved in reaching the interviewee who may as well reside on the other side of the world (Lo Iacono, Symonds, & Brown, 2016).

The classical face-to-face interview is well suited to the research of communities that communicate mainly online. Participation in such communities usually allows determination of what conditions are the most beneficial for an interview—it is worth mentioning here that many online communities organize conferences, retreats, fandom meetings, or hackathons, which are interesting events, allowing to observe various rituals performed by the participants (Zukin & Papadantonakis, 2017). Additionally, such events allow interviews with people who may not be directly involved in the community but provide its infrastructure, organization of local structures, or perform community-oriented commercial activities. It is also helpful that during one visit, we may conduct multiple interviews. Some of the most interesting interviews in my research of Wikimedia communities were conducted during the

Wikimania conferences, annual events organized for community members in different parts of the world. The disadvantage that one needs to keep in mind is the preselection of people; the profile of online community members, who are both willing and active enough within the community to want to visit an international event, is very specific. Also, many online communities pay some attention to the anonymity of their participants (McDonald, 2015). During Wikimanias, for instance, people who do not wish to appear on any visual materials from the conference wear ID badges with different color lanyards. Many also appear under online nicknames instead of their real names.

Regardless of the method used to conduct interviews, it is definitely advisable for the process to undergo reflection, and that the reflection is included in the final version of the paper (Sutton, 2011).

3.2.4 Narrative Analysis

Classical narrative analysis or inquiry is used in traditional research, mainly in references to texts, although recorded speech is on occasion treated as narrative, for instance during narrative interviews (Hollway & Jefferson, 2000). These, especially the way of playing the narrative interviews out in a conversation, is directly linked to storytelling (Boje, 2001, 2008, 2014). Social scientists have become interested in the topic as a result of the narrative turn (R. J. Berger & Quinney, 2005). This turn is based on an observation that people make sense of their understanding of the world through their stories, with a defined structure, heroes, turns of events, and they negotiate the stories in an intersubjective way (Gabriel, 2004). Making a narrative is the typical form of social life (MacIntyre, 1981), and a personalized story is more suggestive than statistics (De Wit, Das, & Vet, 2008), which is associated with the perceived crisis of hierarchy of knowledge, described in more detail earlier in this book.

The narrative approach also draws from literary research (Bakhtin, 1984; Barthes, 1977), shifting the focus more to the text as such, and to a lesser extent on the possible intents of the author or the events surrounding the creation of the work (Czarniawska, 2004). The subject of the analysis is the narration in itself, and the source of the material can simply be the interviews. The intended purpose of the interviews is important: we search for recurring motives, ways of constructing the story of oneself and of others, and of creating order in the world (Walzer & Oleś, 2003). Persuasive strategies, the weight assigned to specific details, the order of events, the vocabulary, presentation of actors and their role, the construction of one's own image and identity—all combine to make the important elements that undergo narrative analysis and which are more important than seeking for material truths (Czarniawska-Joerges, 1994, 1998). The issue of the research lies in the focus on plot, based on a vision of the world, founded in a defined way within the presented chronology and with some assumptions as to the relations between events.

As Given (2006) remarks, the development of digital technologies has had a transformative impact on sociology, especially on narrative studies. The hallmark of many online communities is that most interactions are written and often archived. For these reasons, in online social research the use of methods associated with narrative inquiry, including literary aesthetics or hermeneutics comes almost naturally (Das & Pavlíčková, 2014). It does not require radical changes in the method. We need to take into account the issues raised in the previous two chapters, in addition to some more details.

Online conversations resemble persistent conversations (Erickson, 1999). Granted, they can be conducted dynamically, completely or partially synchronically, with the ongoing participation of the interlocutors, but they may also be archived. For this reason they can be analyzed after years with no loss of the message, as long as the context is understood. Naturally, we need to take into account the awareness which the participants have that whatever they say will be written down and that even a spontaneous exchange will have many asynchronous readers. Because of this, many Internet discussions may, or even should, be treated as forms of many-to-many public transmission, or the monodialogue, not private conversations, although this can be no excuse for ignoring ethical considerations on anonymity protection and privacy of the research participants.

Nevertheless, since some conversations are addressed to a mass audience, they can be treated as public discourse. Open discussions on Twitter on global warming (Fownes, Yu, & Margolin, 2018) may be treated not as a semi-private conversation but as a state of public debate. It would make sense to perform purely quantitative study of such a debate, as well as a social network analysis. Still, a qualitative inquiry fits great as well, either as a standalone method, or a complementary one. It is easy to imagine that one conducts a quantitative study, and then follows up with a narrative analysis of a selected subset of tweets or tweeters. The goal of such a study could be to focus on the way arguments are shaped, and recurring motives or typical conversation trajectories appear. In this sense, online research can benefit from Foucauldian concepts of discourse as systems of formulating and articulating ideas at a specific time, a great force shaping the world order (Foucault, 1980). Discourse serves to formulate meanings and consolidate social institutions; reaching these mechanisms is important from the viewpoint of social sciences. Inquiry in itself may be based on qualitative text analysis and on a quantitative approach (Elliott, 2005), though the use of sentiment analysis or the culturomics.

An important characteristic of online conversations is that they undergo the echo chambers effect: reinforcement of opinions when we stay in the company of other people but with similar views to ours (O'Hara & Stevens, 2015). In addition, digital propaganda makes spreads radical ideas online to convince people, to desensitize them to messages that would previously have been shocking, and to change the perception of what is normal and neutral (Lockie, 2017; Sparkes-Vian, 2018). For this reason, online narratives can be radicalized; para-anonymity makes it easy to use extreme arguments to shift the perceived medium ground. Additionally, because of the efficiency of trolling, discussions which are important from the viewpoint of information wars, are often waged by professional, hired disputants who are paid to pretend they are regular users, which is important for the political or business interests of their customers (Aro, 2016). The issues discussed do not always need to be related to politics and may reach into seemingly distant areas of vaccines, national pride, simply providing wider support for all kinds of anti-establishment and destabilizing tendencies (d'Ancona, 2017; Lewandowsky, Ecker, & Cook, 2017). In a sense, theoretically individual expression in social media, even if spontaneous, is also a specific form of political propaganda (Wojtala, 2018).

Online narratives, like offline culture texts, also have a literary character and may be analyzed as signs of cyber-folklore. A specific type, worth mentioning here, is the copypaste (Chess & Newsrom, 2015). These are once-popular texts, copied and pasted to be distributed for entertainment (Meder, 2008), chain letters and all kinds of spam. Their role has been taken over by social media posts which makes tracing them easier.

The differentiating factor of online narratives is that online messages and posts, more often than regular conversations, are a performance. The goal may be to play a narrative as such, in a form similar to artistic expression, or to participate in a ritual of enacting the feeling of community with others (Bar-Lev, 2008). Participation in online communities is often divorced from one's professional and social identity. It makes posting radical or absurd messages so much easier. A goal is not to convince others to adopt an idea but rather to evoke a reaction. From this, the phenomenon of completely voluntary and sadistic trolling arises, where asocial behaviors or messages aimed at upsetting the people on the other side of the screen (Buckels, Trapnell, & Paulhus, 2014; March, Grieve, Marrington, & Jonason, 2017). It is also interesting that concurrently with the development of trolling, we may observe the growth of pro-social behavior and attempts at ordering the dialogue and maintaining its level of culture, based on voluntary involvement of moderators; however, these attempts are rarely sufficient to create an aggression-free public discussion space (O'Connor & Mackeogh, 2007). On a side note, because of avatarization, we must constantly remember that the same person may troll from one account while providing support from another.

Trolling can often take the form of solidifying a normative; frequent areas of attack are feminist forums and digital places where feminist attitudes are voiced (S. Herring, Job-Sluder, Scheckler, & Barab, 2002). Internet forums are a frequent place for misogynists, online sexual harassment, gender-based derision, and other kinds of bullying (Moloney & Love, 2018). Online communities are not free from offline social divisions, biases, and stratifications (Rufas & Hine, 2018). Many online conversations lead to the radicalization and solidification of gender stereotypes (Banet-Weiser & Miltner, 2016), and are places of hateful messages aimed at silencing the opposite side (Jane, 2014). Such trolling is often met with defensive strategies (Stroud & Cox, 2018), some of which are controversial as they border on mob law (Kosseff, 2016). It is also important that the expressions of discrimination by men and women differ, which makes it difficult to create rules for gender neutrality (Dueñas, Pontón, Belzunegui, & Pastor, 2016).

There is no doubt that the awareness that even academic works, written from feminist viewpoints, are the subject of trolling may lead to self-censorship and withdrawal from discussions (Carter Olson & LaPoe, 2018). The reaction to trolling from the social environment, including professional media, is also an interesting research area. One of the more frequent pieces of advice is "do not feed the trolls" (Figure 3.15) and simply ignore them so that they are denied the pleasure of causing an emotional reaction. This advice taps well into the typical trolling strategy, which may be exemplified by the sentence "Trolling is an art," posted as a comment, and baiting unwitting disputants to point out the "mistake." Ignoring trolls, however, leads also to the ignoring of symbolic violence and shifting responsibility to the

Figure 3.15 "Do not feed the trolls"
Source: Pixabay

victim (Lumsden & Morgan, 2017). Naturally, this also may shift the perception of what is a common ground view, or a balanced position to the ideas expressed by the troll.

Trolling in itself can be of para-artistic character, meaning that it could to mask deep irony and provide entertainment (Dynel, 2016). Perhaps this is why some forms of trolling are accepted, and online conversations with the participation of trolls are often based on an unwritten social contract, according to which the response to trolling is more trolling and absurd escalation (Coles & West, 2016). It is the reason why trolling cannot be prevented, with the state of technology as it is now, based on automatic algorithmic filters and why human moderation is necessary (T. Gillespie, 2018). Narrative analysis of this kind of interactions ought to take their characteristics into account and remember that they form some kind of art or performative acting. Such art is also associated with other online culture products. I used trolling only as an example of specific narrative and activity and that other kinds of narratives may be examined, such as support groups, blogs, ways of self-creation, and self-narration in discussions, or conspiracy theories.

3.3 Research of Works of Culture

One of the major changes that we experienced as the result of the Internet revolution is the new way of spending free time, consuming and producing media (Livingstone & Das, 2013). Some even invoke the convergence of consumption and production in "prosumerism" (Bruns, 2008). Prosumerism is revealed in a large part of the population, passive consumers of films, television, music, and the like, presented by professional teams, which have become co-creators of that media. Naturally, the distribution of people actively involved in actual media production is lopsided: only a small minority is involved in this activity, and only a fraction can compete with professionally created art. Nevertheless, popular involvement in the production of culture has serious consequences for many branches, not only commercially, in the effect of falling prices of stock photos, but also socially. In many cases, competition is based on offering goods of comparable quality but at generously discounted prices, as "amateurs" who publish their works online are more concerned with fame than money (Shirky, 2009; Surowiecki, 2004). This transforms the system of perceived values and the spirit of capitalism (Yeritsian, 2017), but also creates new potential for exploitation, inequalities, and abuse (Dusi, 2017).

Some researchers are not happy with this change. Keen laments the "cult of the amateur" (Keen, 2007) and predicts plunging quality as the result of lack of professional standards for production and quality control; in consequence, he also forecasts the doom of culture. The argument is hyperbolic, although, according to the Gresham-Copernicus law, bad money drives out good money, and competition from people who are not subject to quality control standards and procedures or professional ethics may have devastating consequences for cultural production (Helberger, Leurdijk, & de Munck, 2010). We need to remember, however, that the conviction of the growth of the role of amateur work is partially a myth—cutting out the intermediaries in the distribution of works from professionals to final clients is more noticeable (Brabham, 2012). Perhaps the concentration on the dichotomy of professionally produced versus amateur-driven culture ought to be abandoned in favor of the circulation of culture (Jenkins, 2006).

Spontaneous and bottom-up culture is closely connected to open collaboration communities and the gift economy. The idea of the prosumer revolution relies less on the actual mass production of works of culture than on the possibilities offered, and the emergence of ahierarchical online communities focusing on spontaneous creation (Benkler & Nissenbaum, 2006).

Digital communing reshapes what we perceive as ownership (Kostakis, 2018), and leads to other serious cultural changes, within the perception of value, or intellectual property and authorship (Pouwelse, Garbacki, Epema, & Sips, 2008). These notions arose in a world where the entire system of circulation of works of culture was aimed at the separate roles of active creators and passive recipients, and law maintained the business model including major intermediaries (publishers) and enforced the resulting monetary transactions.

From the perspective of sociology, the notion of self-agency underwent its own transformation (Sztompka, 1991) of culture participants—it is both increased, as forecast by the enthusiasts of prosumerism (Knott,

2013), but limited, through the control of platforms and computer systems (Ritzer, 2015; Ritzer & Jurgenson, 2010; Van Dijck, 2009).

3.3.1   Remix Culture and Politics

Cultural production of online communities has only recently become available to social scientists for research. Professional online communities have been widely researched (Ciesielska, 2010; Coleman, 2013; Dahlander, Frederiksen, & Rullani, 2008; Lakhani & Wolf, 2003); however, movements based on amateur, spontaneous participation and creation of culture are just now becoming objects of interest of the representatives of social sciences (Boellstorff, 2008; Pragnell & Gatzidis, 2011; Steinmetz, 2012). It is surprising, as the movement of free culture and information was initially developed with involvement of social scientists, including those who used qualitative methods (Kelty, 2004).

The phenomenon of spontaneous culture co-creation has major consequences, as it is associated with changes in interpersonal hierarchy and relations. The metamorphosis of culture consumers to producers (Lessig, 2004), also through remix culture (Lessig, 2008) results in a cultural change within the legal (Benkler, 1999; Lessig, 2004), economic (Benkler, 2003, 2013) or social areas (Zittrain, 2008). Portals such as 9gag or Imgur, where people spontaneously share pictures and videos, which are often simply popular pictures of movie frames with added commentary, are more popular than professional services, created by full-time, paid crews. It is even more visible in the social networks geared for media production and sharing, such as TikTok, used by more than half a billion people, or Instagram, with over one billion users. It is also worth mentioning that in the face of the collapse of the job market for the young, the development of "do-it-yourself" careers of bloggers, vloggers, web musicians or even meme creators is useful for the development of professional competences and portfolio associated with the more traditional job market (Bennett, 2018).

Remix culture is based on the strong social acceptance of derivative works—in simple words, remakes of original works (Cheliotis, 2009). A remix is a delicate balance between the original work and skillful combination of popularly recognizable contexts and artistic traces

(B. M. Hill & Monroy-Hernández, 2013). Contrary to appearances, people participating in the remix culture or the associated fandom culture, despite their casual attitude to copyright law, have their own code of behavior (Hetcher, 2009). They allow, granted, to make extensive use of the existing works, mixing of movie and quotes or images, but with simultaneous adhesion to the idea of authorship— not so much as formal recognition of the original author in terms of remuneration, but rather in the acknowledgement of and homage to the creative input. As research proves, even children, when using software that enables the use of others' code, pay attention to whether others notice their work—while not paying attention to whether they will be automatically mentioned as original authors by the algorithm (Monroy-Hernandez, Hill, Gonzalez-Rivero, & boyd, 2011).

Naturally, this approach results in culture clashes with the norms of copyright law and with the expectations of the groups that rely on their creativity for a livelihood. Although online creators often invoke the right to quote, some corporations which are copyright owners do not acknowledge this interpretation (Freund, 2014). Usually the law is on the side of the latter group, although the social feeling of justice is increasingly more divergent from it (Chused, 2014; Hergueux & Jemielniak, 2019). Courtroom confrontations are very rare. Derivative works, thanks to their popularity, also increase the popularity of the originals. For example, remix culture contributed to a revival of interest in Lego products (Einwächter & Simon, 2017). The prosumer movement, even though its subcultures have praised rebellion and opposition to corporations on occasion, is also a source of free labor for these corporations. This is so not only in the area of promotion but also by providing content to distribution platforms (Sugihartati, 2017).

In open collaboration communities, this type of creation of content takes place in a networked participatory environment. Produsers (Bruns, 2008), people who use and create at the same time, usually while remaining anonymous, strengthen and grow the common output—Internet content—through continuous improvements to its material. The effects of their work are not products in the classical sense, as produsers are not purely producers. The works continue the activity of others, often very imitative and derivative. The wide availability of editing tools increases the number of people involved in produsage and presumption, i.e. the combination of creative and utilitarian/consumption activity, as well as the Read/Write culture (Lessig, 2004). Even Internet users who are not co-creating anything at the moment, may—at any time, with no preparation or the need to acquire competences—become co-producers. This leading role is less often played by those who create and remix the works, in favor of those who disseminate this culture, acting as transmitters (Frank, 2011)—because they also take pains to pore through the works, categorizing, describing, and commenting on them. The creation is very derivative, partly because cyberculture is based on the communal, not the individualistic, aspect of culture. Maybe this is the secret to the popularity of Creative Commons licenses which enable the users to reuse the works for non-commercial purposes, or even with no restrictions at all, as long as they credit the original author (Carroll, 2006).

Potentiality resulting from unlimited access to media—in this case to Internet social media—gives the produsers both nearly absolute freedom of expression and the power of shaping the contents accessible online and returning to the previous works, following the quote according to which "the Internet never forgets." One function of this radically democratized and pluralist medium is the possibility of expressing one's opinion and critique, including political protests, and as a result, social involvement (Castells, 2013a, 2013b; Milan, 2013), whose influence on the issues of interest to sociologists, such as political system, national culture, customs, or even demographics, cannot be overestimated.

The Internet grants entry to a new dimension of political involvement to but at the same time in ways which used to be reserved for political cartoon satire—press caricature or grassroots street art in public spaces. Partial or complete anonymity of such works of involved art is becoming an option for many Internet users (Mouffe, 2008). They live in a virtual space which, in its fluidity and temporariness, resembles Marc Derbyshire's (2008) idea of non-places (Augé, 1995). Permanent change of the cyberspace and the transience of its functioning allow unlimited social and culture-creation activity (Dahlberg, 2007). The Internet is therefore also an ideal discursive platform for grassroots social-political activity (Jordan & Taylor, 2004), which uses art to propagate ideas.

The agency of anonymous works of digital art results from their placement between the reality that they serve to comment on and potentiality (Agamben, 1999). It is based on how these works of digital art can influence the reality through their virtual existence (Leadbeater, 2008; Van Dijck, 2009). An important example of such subjectivity is the potential influence of the Internet and modern technologies on powerful grassroots social movements. For instance, an important area of research is the role of Facebook and Twitter during post-election riots in Iran in 2009, during the revolution in Egypt, and later during the 2011 Arab Spring (Bruns, Highfield, & Burgess, 2013; Christensen, 2011; Khondker, 2011; Lotan, Graeff, Ananny, Gaffney, & Pearce, 2011), or the Spanish Los Indignados movement (Castells, 2013b), or Ukrainian EuroMaidan (Bohdanova, 2014; Onuch, 2015) in 2013 and 2014, as well as the #MeToo phenomenon. Similarly, more technologically advanced groups get involved in the hacktivism, which is social activity through hacking (Coleman, 2014), in the form of website cracking, or simply Denial of Service (DoS) attacks—causing websites to stop working because of excessive traffic.

Even though "Twitter revolutions" and the role of online publications in shaping social change are criticized as a fancy of the media (Mejias, 2010; Morozov, 2009), the influence of technology in the increased agency of individuals is far from obvious (Christensen, 2011; Segerberg & Bennett, 2011), and activism becomes "slacktivism" (Kristofferson, White, & Peloza, 2014; Skoric, 2012)—involvement that requires just a few clicks and gives the feeling of having completed a duty and provided a distraction from actual activities—spontaneous, online community-created satire both social and political, as well as purely entertainment-oriented, are cultural phenomena that require the attention of the social sciences and that bear importance on the emerging social reality.

3.3.2 Research of Humor

Ethnographic researchers claim that the true understanding of culture is confirmed if the researchers start to understand the jokes of their inter-viewees, meaning that they possess similar cultural capital. It is similar to the native knowledge of a language—understanding irony is one of the most difficult competences of a language (Banasik & Podsiadło, 2016). In the words of Dougherty, a cartoon "requires that the viewer be familiar with current issues and debates, savvy about the cultural context, and capable of analytical judgments" (Dougherty, 2002, p. 258), and similarly, a joke requires complex understanding the cultural context. For researchers of culture, jokes are a source of knowledge about social sentiments, including political views (Virno, 2008), making them the point of interest of historical studies (Granger, 1960; Wood, 1994), sociology, anthropology, or political science (Klumbytė, 2012). We may even state that in many communities, research into jokes and their comic imaginarium—to coin a joke, focusing on "anecdotal evidence"—may be of higher cognitive value for cultural analysis than focusing on the research of pure facts (Jemielniak, Przegalińska, & Stasik, 2018). This is one reason why researching online humor, both in the sense of studying jokes of selected online communities and going deep into the research of the rules of communities focused on cultural production is worthy of deeper sociological analysis, even if it is underestimated.

Political memes, like graffiti, may be seen in categories of political involvement (Mouffe, 2008) or simply social critique of the activity of the state. Laughter and jokes are some of the most popular techniques of civic resistance—in their democratized form they are a way of negotiating social reality which is accessible to anyone (Friedman, 2012). An important catalyst for the textual and visual political satire is mass media—printed newspapers for political comic strips and caricatures (DeSousa, 1982; Gamson, 1992), and more recently, the online space for older and newer forms. Extreme cases of the increased reach of such works of culture are caricatures of the Prophet Muhammad (Sturges, 2015; Weaver, 2010a), which caused actual physical violence. These channels of communication allow jokes to question the symbolic order: they celebrate its critical function and control, watchdog spheres, allowing for wide circulation of contents.[14]

---

[14] The attitude of different communities to picture culture is interesting in itself. As part of my ethnographic study of the Wikipedia community I participated in a discussion about image filtering. Simply put, the Wikimedia movement community wanted to decide whether logged-in users should have an additional setting at their disposal. Upon loading an article that contains photos or pictures that can be considered controversial, the person would see a warning instead of the actual picture. The setting would not even have to be a default one, with an opt-in, so only people who wanted such an option enabled would need to find it and set it. The Wikimedia community, in the movement's largest vote, collecting 24,000 participants in 2011, supported this solution, and the Wikimedia Foundation's Board of Trustees published a resolution encouraging the development of technical means to enable Wikimedia users set what contents they would like to be concealed. Despite strong support, a group of active Wikimedians considered similar solutions as potentially leading to censorship. A few

"Humor appears when people resolve two conflicting images in ways that make sense within distorted systems of logic. The processes by which organization members set up such puzzles for others to solve—and the processes by which these are actually solved—say much about the ways organization members work and play together" (Kahn, 1989, p. 46). Analyses of ludic behaviors in organizations and communities (Hunter, Jemielniak, & Postuła, 2010) have been increasing in popularity in the social sciences.

Similarly, organizational humor is often presented as a weapon of symbolic violence between employees and their superiors (Fleming & Spicer, 2007; Jemielniak, 2007). Totalitarian organizations, including governments, also see humor as a threat (Oring, 2004). There are at least two reasons: irony deconstructs and disarms official organizational propaganda but also allows individuals to see their roles from a distance (Kunda, 1992). The larger the discrepancy of power between individuals and organizations, including the structures of the state, the more humor becomes a defensive weapon of the weakest: examples reach far beyond the obvious, in anti-totalitarian opposition (Benton, 1988) and encompass customer-producer relations, visible in popularity of jokes about Microsoft (Shifman & Blondheim, 2010), the movement of African American emancipation (Weaver, 2010b), and female emancipation (N. A. Walker, 1988). A daily dose of humor allows us to create and make sense of professional roles and builds opposition to managerial control (Lynch, 2009). In a way, organizational rhetoric, used to strengthen the expected behavior and reinforce the hierarchy, is undermined through deconstructive ambivalence of spontaneous employee resistance (Höpfl, 1995) expressed through humor—both within commercial organizations and social movements.

These processes have a carnivalizing character, according to Bakhtin (Bakhtin, 1984) who cited the example of medieval carnivals to show the crucial role of unofficial and spontaneous ludic behavior in maintaining the social contract. Temporary suspension of dominant norms and hierarchies allows people from lower social echelons a moment of

---

large projects conducted their own polls, leading to the conclusion they did not want image filtering to be enabled, with similarly massive support of the idea (79% on Spanish Wikipedia, 81% on French Wikipedia, 85% on German Wikipedia). As a result, the idea was abandoned as the risk of forking [what's this?] was too high.

freedom, while making them aware of the fixed order of things. Jokes and spontaneous humor in organizations and communities, like the carnival, are the realm of temporary freedom from the prevailing discourse and the fixed system of domination. In humorous tales—jokes, drawings—we find messages that escape the control of formal hierarchy, thanks to which they can be of use for socio-cultural analysis.

The goal of ethnography, according to Agar, is to reach the "notion-points," carriers of cultural topoi and archetypes, and making a specific translation of them, which allows the interpretation of the culture in its context (Agar, 2006). Even though Agar did not reference online research, cyberculture is especially rich in such points. Ironic messages are one of the more interesting areas for researching them.

Analysis of humor, including political satire, is especially useful when new, not yet solidified, cultural changes are studied. For this reason, it is useful to analyze online community phenomena and their cultural works. Online humor is a specific form of creativity in that it makes perfect use of the creative character of participating in culture (prosumerism) with an easy form of participation: all that is needed is paraphrase, deconstruction, or combining an image and a comment to arrive at a comic effect. This is how memes are born.

3.3.3 Online Memes

Apart from blogs, thematic forums, and social media, where discussions can be held and social movements started, the most valuable tool of social critique can be found in memes (Shifman, 2014b). Although it seems impossible to trace the genesis of individual memes, it is easy to pinpoint the creator. In "The Selfish Gene" (Dawkins, 1976), Dawkins presented the term "meme" to define extra-genetic behaviors and cultural phenomena that spread from one person to another—starting with language norms and ending with sports traditions. With the development of the Internet, the term "meme" started to be used in reference to the processed (remixed) cultural contents that are made available online (Brake, 2014; Knobel & Lankshear, 2007). Internet memes, in their essence, emerge from the world of the anonymous pan-individual network which does not belong to anyone (J. M. Adams,

2014); at the same time it forms the quintessence of democratized and pluralized digital culture, created by the widely understood prosumer crowd. The latest and most elegant academic definition of the phenomenon may be ascribed to Davison in "The Language of Internet Memes," where he writes: "an Internet meme is a product of culture, usually a joke, which increases its influence through online propagation" (Davison, 2012, p. 122).

Socio-cultural researchers have been focusing on individual cases to trace the shaping of Internet memes. They concentrated on meme creation and migration (Shifman, Levy, & Thelwall, 2014), memes' role in expressing prejudices (Woźniak, 2016), specific relations (Wiggins & Bowers, 2015), cultural logic (Shifman, 2014a), or the importance of memes for specific subcultures and individual identities (Nissenbaum & Shifman, 2017).

A meme, as an element of mass culture, has become a means of commenting on the prevalent socio-cultural reality. In this sense, Internet memes are the direct descendants of the culture of socio-political satire at its peak. The ridiculing online humoristic memes comment on events or messages using text elements with visual and audio-visual ones (Da Silva & Garcia, 2012). Memetic nonsense is based not only on notional deconstruction of intellectual art but also on playing with the social norm (Katz & Shifman, 2017).

Many comments are inappropriate or use very dark humor (Burroughs, 2013) and resemble trolling (Greene, 2019). "Memetic activism," also known as "snarktivism," is a defense tactic against the contested actions of politicians, international corporations and non-governmental campaigns that simplify social problems. The best example is the use of 4chan platform by the anti-capitalist Occupy Wall Street movement in 2011 (Coleman, 2011; Milner, 2013b). The Occupy movement was recognized as a meme by the Know Your Meme portal (Bratich, 2014). 4chan, in contrast, is said to have popularized memes in contemporary culture. At the same time, it is a radically anti-systemic community, building identity based on a contemptuous attitude to "normies," who are people following social norms (Nagle, 2017). One of its most infamous campaigns was convincing gullible users that upon drilling a hole in their iPhones they would be able to use mini-jack head-/earphones with their devices, or that heating a mobile phone in a microwave would charge its batteries. 4chan also popularized the "pedobear" (a pedophile-associated mascot) meme, spread rumors about Steve Jobs having a heart attack which caused a momentary plunge in Apple stock prices, or provided the possibility of coordinating large-scale social resistance actions, such as Distributed Denial of Service (DDoS) attacks work-places by sending massive amounts of queries to a server so that the server's website is inaccessible. The Anonymous movement was also established on 4chan (Coleman, 2014). 4chan is also the cradle of Internet memes.

The satirical character of online memes comes from locality—in their form, they are definitely represent contemporary Americanized global culture (Shifman & Boxman Shabtai, 2014), however, their content is often of high social-political importance only on a local scale (K. V. Anderson & Sheeler, 2014). The meme's message is understand-able only in a specific socio-cultural context, even though it is composed of signs that are understandable for supranational communities of the Internet (Shifman & Boxman Shabtai, 2014). Creative use of Internet memes as social involvement and the critique of local political stage is apparent in the audiovisual "Harlem Shake" meme. A joke meant as a dance happening (a group of people listens to a piece of music without moving a muscle just to start a frantic dance at one point; the happening is recorded and edited to expose the contrast between the two states), gained a political dimension when young people in some Middle Eastern countries performed dance moves inspired by African American culture while wearing in traditional Muslim clothes. In Egypt, the ruling Muslim Brotherhood arrested the people responsible for the local version of the international fad (Werbner & Modood, 2015). Something similar happened in Russia. Such clashes and transfers of cultural contents are a hallmark of political potential carried by the culture of virtual communities (Tsing, 2011). This use of memes simply begs for social network analysis supple-mented by interviews with the participants in and distributors of the memes, and finalized with a socio-political analysis of the context and the reasons for the power of the memes.

As we can see, the role of political satire, including humorous provocation, which is reflected in slacktivism, snarktivism and trolling cannot be overestimated (Milan, 2013). Carefully tracing memes can both help us understand contemporary civic society and understand the way social media spreads information—including politically loaded pop-cultural contents—which prosumer online communities consider socially important. Internet audience of the contemporary socio-political stage participate in the remixing, processing, and popularization of contents. At the same time, it creates new, efficient channels of distribution whose research is also the domain of contemporary sociology.

Internet memes can be divided into "image (or visual) macros" which are remixes of familiar pictures with a comment (see Figure 3.16), and "reaction Photoshop," the use of a familiar picture or a symbol in a new context (Shifman, 2014b). An image macro can be "This is bait":

It became popular on 4chan as a comment signaling that the message leans towards trolling and was, naturally, the starting point for numerous remixes. The picture is one of the most popular memes of all time, although the issue of propagation and popularity of memes is a complex one and therefore worthy of different research approaches (Zannettou et al., 2018). The problem of quantitative research is the lack of clear distinction when a derivative work becomes independent and ought not to be treated as a derivative anymore.

Figure 3.16 "This is bait". Example of an image macro
Source: https://knowyourmeme.com/memes/bait-this-is-bait

Figure 3.17 "Chubby Bubbles Girl"
Source: https://knowyourmeme.com/memes/chubby-bubbles-girl/

The examples of "react Photoshop" are a photo of a police officer pepper-spraying seated demonstrators from the Occupy movement, edited into medieval paintings[15] or variations of the "Chubby Bubbles Girl," (Figure 3.17) a girl running away from whatever the creators put in the background:

With memes, we can express an infinite number of ideas in a specific semiotic form which is also characterized by unlimited flexibility (Milner, 2013a). Memes use the structural properties of the given work of culture as a set of templates for free use and reuse in a new context (Massanari, 2015). In 2004, Glen Whitman, a blogger for Agoraphilia, coined the term "snowclone." It is related to sentences such as "grey is the new black," where the words *grey* and *black* can be replaced with any other nouns ("X is the new Y"). Satirists may therefore use the original photo or a ready-made picture from the resources of Internet portals such as Meme Generator or Rage Comic Builder, and afterwards adorn them with a humorous text in an original or altered form, to create a joke which may become popular. Such "image macros" are easy to produce and the most image repositories even provide trending backgrounds which are recommended when creating a meme. It would be an interesting research question to analyze which pictures are most often recommended and used by the meme generator websites.

Memes are an efficient transmitter of social moods, as they combine surprising forms and concepts (the variations on the British poster from World War II: "Keep Calm and Carry On", Figure 3.18) (Virno, 2008).

---

[15]   See https://knowyourmeme.com/memes/casually-pepper-spray-everything-cop

Figure 3.18 "Keep Calm and Carry On"
Source: http://knowyourmeme.com/memes/keep-calm-and-carry-on

One of the more interesting examples are the "advice memes"—a variation of image macros, bearing the picture of a person giving "bad advice," pasted on a colorful spinning background with a repetitive pattern of a duck or bear. At first, the advice came from funny animals, however, the form itself was also used for political critique—in the USA, during the discussion on national debt, the giver of bad advice was Barack Obama or the economist Paul Krugman (Vickery, 2014). Rintel summarizes this in a blog post: "Whatever we call it, internet comment culture is a reinvigoration of an active public voice. It's a combination of popular culture and folk culture, appropriating and mashing together objects and ideas from media industries and objects and ideas created from whole cloth" (Rintel, 2011).

"Advice memes" can evolve. For instance, a study of the "confession bear" meme shows that the initial use of the image only for humorous purposes on Reddit evolved after some time and caused the publication of a series of memes with serious content, also mentioning rape, molestation, and addiction, in a way that contested the dominant discourse of culture. This generated long community discussions, related to both the honesty of confessions and the suitability of memes as the carrier of such confessions, as well as the possible regulations within participatory culture of the portal (Vickery, 2014). Ways of using memes can also be of research interest, to show how communities with seemingly no norms aspire to self-regulation—often returning to those standards of behavior patterns that they themselves contest at the rhetoric level (Gal, Shifman, & Kampf, 2015). Analysis of memes may therefore be based not only on the analysis of images which we recognize from visual sociology but also on the research of readership, contexts of creation and distribution, and expression of meme-related social norms, as well as deeper auto-analyses of memes that are sometimes created by the communities.

Internet memes represent a phenomenal growth of digital culture of social commentary, becoming a new tool of political agency in public opinion (Davison, 2012). It is worthwhile to include meme analysis into research projects, drawing on the achievements and tools of cyber cultural studies (C. W. Anderson & Revers, 2018; Nissenbaum & Shifman, 2017).

According to Google Trends, in the English version of the search tool, in USA memes reached the same level of interest as Jesus in 2012. They are now are four times as popular (Figure 3.19):

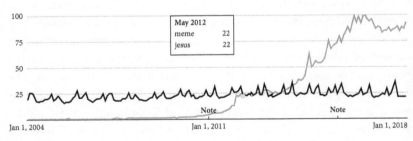

Figure 3.19 Google Trends results for "jesus" and "meme"
Source: https://goo.gl/tTLn5R

4

Research Ethics

Accepting ethic norms involves naturalization of beliefs, assuming them as unalterable truths (Law, 2004). Social sciences have been inscribed with certain standards for years. In the last twenty-five years, the practice of having research projects approved by ethics committees has become institutionalized, in some cases leading to extreme bureaucracy and changing the character of the issue, shifting the weight from the personal moral obligation of the researcher and an issue that requires high flexibility and individualism (Adler & Adler, 2012) towards a set of forms to be filled out, pseudo-warrants of the safety of the research subjects (Alderson & Morrow, 2006). However, Internet research has opened the eyes of the sociologists to new problems and caused reconsideration of some issues of research ethics.

In the early stages of online research, the classical approach to social studies was considered sufficient. After all, we learnt a lot from abuse from academia in medicine[1] as well as from the studies in social sciences, that would likely be controversial nowadays, such as in Zimbardo's prison experiment. Researchers felt comfortable, as they also relied on the premise that the information online is already public. It quickly turned out, however, that Internet research can be more dangerous than its traditional counterparts and presents many new associated risks and ethical issues for the research subjects.

For example, a Usenet study of pornographic materials conducted in the 1990s included a careless collection of personal data, statistics, and data on the files viewed by users. In the associated grant proposal, the author assumed that people who are just blocking access to their files

---

[1] In the infamous Tuskegee Study, African American men with syphilis went for years without treatment, despite the availability of antibiotics. Cf.: http://www.cdc.gov/tuskegee/timeline.htm

Thick Big Data: Doing Digital Social Sciences. Dariusz Jemielniak, Oxford University Press (2020).
© Dariusz Jemielniak.
DOI: 10.1093/oso/9780198839705.001.0001

may be pedophiles (J. Thomas, 1996). Even though this is an extreme case of irresponsible research, in less obvious cases we may cause trouble to the research subjects, even unwillingly. One typical safeguard in social sciences in many countries is the approval of research projects by an Institutional Review Board for human-subjects research, but these boards are not always populated by researchers aware of the risks that come with online research.

A simple assumption that online we are dealing with the same kind of research on people as with offline research also does not make sense; the scope of the possible identification online is visibly different, and conversations are also carried out by non-human actors—bots, be it openly declared or concealed.

The potential of Big Data sheds new light on possible threats. A group of several researchers has come with ten rules of Big Data research (Zook et al., 2017):

1. Acknowledge that data are people, represent them, and influence them, and that data can do harm.
2. See that privacy is not binary and that it may be scalable.
3. Take active steps against reidentification of the data, for instance through cross-referencing with other datasets.
4. Practice ethical data sharing with clear information for the research subjects how the data will be used, informed consent, and possibility of having research subjects withdraw their data.
5. Consider the limitations of your data; "Big Data" is not necessarily "better data," data that enhances knowledge, or that has sensible context.
6. Debate the tough ethical choices. Even if Big Data research does not need to be approved by an IRB, discussing your new and ongoing research from an ethical viewpoint is worthwhile, both in academic environments and in student groups.
7. Get involved in developing a code of conduct for your organization, research community, or industry.
8. Design your datasets and management systems for auditability.
9. Engage with the broader consequences of your research—leave the race for citations, reputation or resources and consider whether the research is conducted for the betterment of the general public.

10. Have enough intuition and common sense to know when to break these rules—for instance, in the face of an epidemic outbreak which could necessitate the breach of privacy.

In 2012, the Ethics Working Committee, as part of their activity within the Association of Internet Researchers, published guidelines for online researchers.[2]

- The greater the vulnerability of the community/author/participant, the greater the obligation of the researcher to protect the community/author/participant.

- Because "harm" is defined contextually, ethical principles are more likely to be understood inductively rather than applied universally. That is, rather than one-size-fits-all pronouncements, ethical decision-making is best approached through the application of practical judgment attentive to the specific context.

- Because all digital information at some point involves individual persons, consideration of principles related to research on human subjects may be necessary even if it is not immediately apparent how and where persons are involved in the research data.

- When making ethical decisions, researchers must balance the rights of subjects (as authors, as research participants, as people) with the social benefits of research and researchers' rights to conduct research.

- Ethical issues may arise and need to be addressed during all steps of the research process.

- Ethical decision-making is a deliberative process, and researchers should consult as many people and resources as possible in this process, research review boards, ethics guidelines.

The issue of ethical duties in online research is still evolving and the canon is being shaped (Fiesler et al., 2016). The development of research methods in Internet research has led to deep debates on previously obvious dogmas (Baym & Markham, 2009), especially in informed consent, perception of the research subjects' identity, their right to privacy, or

---

[2] https://perma.cc/7F7W-ENAY

borders between public and private messages. Acknowledging the merits of the guidelines, I will develop them further in this chapter, and present the ethical problems that must be carefully considered when conducting Internet sociology research.

4.1 Internet as the Source of Infamy

In discussing research ethics, I would like to begin with the story of Justine Sacco,[3] Director for Public Relations at Interactive Corp. On December 20, 2013, while boarding a plane to South Africa, she tweeted: "Going to Africa. Hope I don't get AIDS. Just kidding. I'm white!"

The tweet implied that Sacco believed that her white privilege made her immune to the HIV virus, and stigmatized non-whites (Nakayama, 2017).

At the time of boarding, she had only 170 followers—a rather small circle, sized for typical acquaintance conversations. Her tweet, however, went viral after it was seen and retweeted by Sam Biddle, journalist for Valleywag (a Gawker company) with 15,000 Twitter followers (Laidlaw, 2017). During the 11-hour flight when Sacco had no Internet access, her tweet was answered by tens of thousands of people, and the hashtag #HasJustineLandedYet added more heat. Sacco was fired, her family denounced her, and employees of the hotels where she had booked rooms threatened to go on strike if she tried to check in.

There is no doubt the tweet was racist in character, or at least boorish and insensitive. A stupid, embarrassing tweet—however, did Sacco deserve public infamy? She tweeted publicly, but can we assume that it could be read by others, apart from her friends and acquaintances? Or is it that she had the mistaken feeling of anonymity (Chaudhry, 2016)? This one tweet, albeit scandalous, destroyed her professional life (Ronson, 2015). Naturally, we can say she deserved all of it. Nevertheless, not providing an excuse for the contents of the contemptuous tweet, we cannot fail to see that hate speech is omnipresent on the Internet and noticeable in comments to practically every social-political article

---

[3] I am using Sacco's full name as the case is publicly known. She has also responded to the case under her own name.

(Erjavec & Kovačič, 2012); it is a frustrating but also inseparable element of online discourse—and normally does not bring such punishment.

Justine Sacco became a symbol—joining the hunt against her became an embodiment of opposition to racism. People passed judgment—regardless of whether her tweet was purely racist, whether it was a stupid joke with racist innuendo, or whether—as Sacco said later—it was a pastiche of information bubble that Americans closed themselves in and a parody of racism (Laidlaw, 2017). As a result, she became the object of mass condemnation and cyber-bullying (Chisholm, 2014). Such social shaming is a controversial issue—as with every mob law it is hard to notice nuances, hold deliberations, or allow the target person to provide an answer, but easy to deal out serious consequences (Norlock, 2017).

A similar fate befell the "dog poop girl," a Korean woman who was photographed not cleaning up after her dog when he pooped on a train. The photo became popular on social media, people were quick to identify her name and place of work—as a result she lost her job and needed to go into hiding (Solove, 2007). We function in a society of control, where mass communication metes out infamy by a group of anonymous online users on an unprecedented scale (Ronson, 2016).

Sacco returned to Interactive career after a few years, and even made peace with Biddle, who in the meantime had also became the target of cyber-bullying (Biddle, 2014). From this and many similar stories, a simple conclusion can be drawn: if even PR specialists are not able to carry out the communication within social networks, we must not assume that our research subjects will have enough sense to control the outcomes of their posts. It is worth remembering these cases when we consider what data to use.

The ethical standard of all research, including online (Dutton & Pipler, 2010), is fourfold: anonymity, privacy, informed consent, confidentiality. I will describe each.

4.2 Anonymity

Research subject anonymity means we will take all steps necessary to keep their identities from becoming known.

In traditional, especially qualitative research, study subjects are often consulted to check what details could identify them. In online social sciences, naturally, we cannot rely only on the opinion of the research subjects. It is responsibility of the researcher to see how some messages can be identifying.

In practice, we often quote fragments of online messages in our academic work. If in traditional social research the use of quotes from others' statements, especially without mentioning the names of the speakers, is permissible, in online research it sometimes becomes problematic.

Some academics claim that online pseudonyms and avatars ought to be protected as carefully as actual identities (Langer & Beckman, 2005). This is the consequence of nicknames unambiguously identifying their users in their environments, and which can be important elements of their identity (Wolfendale, 2007). Others claim we may treat online behaviors as public, and apply text analysis standards rather than those of interviews (Bassett & O'Riordan, 2002) and therefore treat the duties of personal data protection more loosely. The latter approach, however, evidently does not take into account the ethical issue in any research— the possible consequences. Regardless of the paradigmatic, methodical, or interpretative convention we adopt, we must not cause situations, where as a result of our activities, serious breaches of privacy occur. The assumption "[B]ut the data is already public" does not hold water. As an example the 2008 research of Facebook profiles, where student data was made public, shows that we need to exercise caution and assume that unforeseen consequences may arise (Zimmer, 2010). Granted, the researchers of the study attempted to anonymize the database, but it was insufficient—and taking into account the power of Big Data, with time providing anonymity will become more difficult. Web users are typically unaware that they leave a wealth of identifying traces—and to partly identify a person it may be sufficient to just combine the specific, unique version of a web browser and the user's IP address.

Moreover, even if users consciously make some data public, it does not mean those users will never want to remove it. A risk arises that the study will become an archive of information which the users will want to de-publicize and remove from the original source—the possibility of revoking the agreement for the publication of private data is an important element of the research participant's rights.

Special diligence is needed for sensitive subjects. For instance, in interviewing the users of the Silk Road, a system of illegal trade within the TOR network, Barratt and Maddox undertook special safety measures to secure access to the gathered material and not to collect any identifying data, or follow criminal motives in interviews, when such motives were mentioned by the interviewees (Barrattt & Maddox, 2016). If the police or the court requested data, Barratt and Maddox could truthfully say that they had no incriminating evidence.

The 2017 research of publications based on data used without the consent of the research participants showed that the vast majority of researchers disregard some possible threats, do not take protective measures, and often ignore the ethical aspect of such analysis (D. R. Thomas, Pastrana Portillo, Hutchings, Clayton, & Beresford, 2017). There is no golden rule that guarantees anonymity; everyone needs to weigh the risks, so careful reflection is required each time.

4.3 Privacy

The issue of privacy is primarily related to the influence of the research subjects on the scope of personal data which is collected in the research.

This area is associated with what is considered public data and what bears the characteristics of private data. Some people believe that privacy died with the dawn of social media and the Internet. It would be wise to say that such a strong judgment is exaggerated, and the question of separating the private from the public sphere, as well as the changing cultural meanings thereof, are of key importance to the related discussions (Marx, 2001).

Regardless of the virtualization of social life, a hard differentiation of public sphere and private sphere has already been discussed in the brick-and-mortar context (E. Goffman, 1963; Jemielniak & Jemielniak, 2002). The proliferation of new technologies also causes borders to become fluid and constantly redefined (Anthony, Campos-Castillo, & Horne, 2017).

Online, the division between public and private communication is even more blurred. Traditional division into "publishing" (public-type messages, such as newspapers, radio shows, TV shows) and "conversations" (private messages) loses its meaning. In reference to produsage, or the mixing of the roles of content producers and users, it is difficult to apply the conceptualizations transmitted straight from media theory or copyright law. In online social life, publications resembling newspaper political discourse can be found alongside conversations and behaviors that are actually extremely private, even intimate. Sometimes distinguishing the two becomes possible only by understanding the wider context—as some dialogs, although technically available to third parties, may in their intent and practice be designed as two-way interactions.

What is worse, even if we define the border between the public and the private, technological changes may move that border. As danah boyd observes (boyd, 2008), the introduction of the search function on Usenet or in discussion lists led to a rapid change: individual communities that used to function in quasi-closed groups suddenly became accessible to outsiders who could join conversations without being aware of the context. Moreover, people used to participate in discussions which they could safely consider local, with limited and defined circle of addressees, which changed radically post-factum. A similar situation can be observed with Facebook comments—where the audience and availability of the post are decided by the author who has the power of publicizing others' comments without their consent, even after the exchange has finished. How much technology has been invading into the redefinition of the prevailing social and legal borders can be illustrated by what happened in the USA regarding mugshots. It was a long-established legal rule in many states for people to be able to browse the photos of detainees with their personal data at a police station—as part of public access to information, as well as social control of local safety. With the onset of information technologies, mugshots are routinely scanned by commercial companies and made available, at a modest fee, to anyone. Standard customers include recruitment agencies who neither care whether the arrest was justified or not, nor tell the candidates why their applications were rejected.

The second source of income for such companies are people who wish their photos to be removed—each company is, naturally, paid separately. Not many people, even those who are absolutely innocent, can afford to defend their rights in court, and companies defend their position by insisting that they are merely reflecting public archives. It is of no importance to them, therefore, whether a given person has had the record expunged, or even if they were convicted at all—as they could have been arrested by mistake (Bode & Jones, 2018). This obviously causes a serious problem with privacy resulting from the application of new technologies which rendered previous regulations inadequate (Sarah Esther Lageson, 2016; Sarah E Lageson & Maruna, 2018; Slane, 2018).

It may be wise to abandon attempts at fixed classification and public–private division online, or at least to treat privacy as falling along a continuum (boyd, 2008). In the previous examples of Internet infamy we can clearly see that many Internet users have problems distinguishing whether they are taking part in public discourse or a private conversation. Sometimes blog developers write "publicly," in the sense that they want to reach new undefined audiences, but also wish to be "public" only within a defined scope (boyd, 2005). Many people do not realize that they are putting their privacy at risk and they often publish their private information unknowingly—with the obvious example being not logging out of public computer terminals (Wakeford, 2003).

Therefore, it is important to note the degree to which the transmitting person can control the circle of recipients, but also the intent with which they use the specific communication tools, as well as their perceived (not actual) privacy—the physical access barrier for third parties. In this sense, we may assume that the data has a public character when access is public and the participants also perceive their messages as public, without doubts (Rosenberg, 2010). The matter of their perception can therefore be important, even in reference to such public-oriented media as Twitter (Williams, Burnap, & Sloan, 2017). Sveningsson Elm suggests that the assessment of private and public character of online data can also be based on the criteria of contents (Sveningsson Elm, 2009), thus attempting to assess how private the collected data is.

The inevitable rush for data collection and enjoying the possibilities offered by modern technologies by social scientists ought to be accompanied by more diligence in the protection of privacy. Technology allows for more invasiveness of messages, and reaching towards intimate details. Even simple online polls, may lead to breaches of physical, psychological, or informative privacy. They can often cause breaches of conversation privacy in online communities (Cho & Larose, 1999).

As Whiteman remarks, we observe distinct evolution of thinking about data privacy online: from treating all messages which are technically publicly available as public, to higher problematization of matters and taking into account intents, perception, and contents of data (Whiteman, 2012). For this reason, when gathering data online, we need to reflect upon the collected information and make grounded decisions on whether and how the research participants ought to be able to influence the data pertaining to them. It is additionally easy to fall into negligence and lack of reflection on the possible breaches of privacy—for example, two Danish authors collected the data on approximately 70,000 users of the OKCupid dating service and published it in The Open Science Network, a platform serving the exchange of valuable datasets. They thought everything was in order as the database contained no names—however, it was quickly observed that the identity of the individual users could be deduced based on the database's demographic and geographic information or nicknames, and the answers within the database touched on very intimate preferences, orientations, and personal life (Zimmer, 2018).

At the same time we cannot fail to notice that technological revolution has created a situation in which many people purposefully and independently collect data on themselves, keeping a sort of research diary which is very valuable to sociology (Purdam, 2014), and make the diaries freely available. There will definitely be more of this data available, for instance following the growing popularity of the *Quantified Self* movement and its different versions (Lupton, 2016; Przegalińska, 2015b), that quantify and archive indicators, such as pulse, stress levels, breathing capacity, or number of steps taken. As a result of their popularity, we may even speak of a revolution in Big Data research in combination with biological and medical sciences (Swan, 2013), although they also have unexpected side effects, such as the increased neoliberal belief of the society that health is primarily a private issue (Maturo, Mori, & Moretti, 2016). The spread of remote measurement technologies and the archiving of health indicators also create serious threats to privacy: enough said that the Fitbit sportband, which published the wearer's data publicly, easily allowed detection of when the wearer was having sex

(Austen, 2015). Tracker users often also do not pay attention to the fact that the aggregated data, including theirs, is afterwards sold and used for commercial purposes, like preparing individual offers, which can be controversial in health insurances (Spiller et al., 2018).

4.4 Informed Consent

Informed consent means giving the research participants a chance, upon presenting them with reliable and legible assumptions of the project, to decide whether they want to participate. In ideal conditions, besides applying due diligence to the complete and clear explanation of what the research is about, it is important to present these assumptions to the research participant in advance and in writing.

Naturally, in the case of informed consent the issue lies in the division of things public and private—as we assume that publicly available information normally does not require additional consent. Online, unlike anywhere in the past, we observe the clash of two research traditions: interview-based research that requires informed consent every time a message is used, and observational research, where we assume the observed communities are unaware of the process of the study, especially if they are observed in public space (Sixsmith & Murray, 2001). However, unlike with public space understood in its physical sense, where the borders between public and private are signaled by architecture and are relatively fixed, online these orders can undergo unexpected changes, as a consequence of the introduction of new technologies and simply following the changes of data organization on websites (boyd, 2008). In researching online communities we therefore need to exercise caution and not treat observation studies as a buzzword that lets us avoid the "problem" of requiring informed consent of the participants. Unlike with classical observations, in online communities we can easily reach the observation subjects, even after many years from having observed them, which can actually be a good method for supplementary research.

Nevertheless, if we guarantee full anonymity, in online observation studies we can often assume that the requirement of informed consent depends on the research topic and especially in issues which are definitely uncontroversial and belonging to general sociology, informed consent of the observation subjects is not necessary, especially if we use aggregated data, where no information on the level of individuals can be concluded. Still, we should receive informed consent if it is feasible, if only because the right to remove one's data is a major privilege. We need to approach the issue with our eyes open. Some researchers even suggest that concealed observations in non-public chatrooms or forums are unethical by definition, and even potentially illegal (Sveningsson Elm, 2009)—however, this seems to be an excessively radical approach and one which leaves out the key aspect of the goal of research, the expected gains, and the possible risks for the research subjects, which is actually a well described problem in many books on research methodologies in the offline world. It is difficult to assume that we always need to apply stricter criteria for online research than for offline studies.

Research of illegal behaviors or study of data from illegal sources is a special case of using data without informed consent of the research subjects. In those cases, attempting to obtain informed consent would most likely result in distorted outcomes. Then, abandoning informed consent can make sense—as the British Society of Criminology remarks, at the same time restating that covert research needs to justify the use of such methods through the potential gains (British Society of Criminology, 2015). When I researched Harvard student attitudes towards piracy and perception of permissibility of sharing media files, I took the following precautions:

- I did not write down names of the study participants; instead, I used codes;

- At the beginning of interviews and questionnaires, I stated clearly I did not want the participants to divulge identifying data;

- in the questionnaires and interviews, I avoided potentially identifying questions, and I removed those fragments which could have the same effect;

- I deleted recordings after they were transcribed;

- I stored the transcripts on an encrypted partition;

- I collected only such data that could be distilled into categories encompassing many people. For example, I excluded information on the home country but not the continent of the participants, although this complicated my analysis and made it impossible to draw conclusions on, for instance, the relation of my study area with the home country GDP.

Besides these precautions, I described the goal of the research to my participants, gave them a description along with my contact details, and explained both the associated risks and the possibility of withdrawing from the study at any time, including after the questionnaire and interview.

Similarly, with research interviews conducted with some selected participants of a community, informed consent is so much more important. In my research practice, after interviewing hundreds of people, only one research participant decided to leave the study upon learning its purpose. I still claim the reaction of this person was exaggerated, and the risks they were trying to see non-existent. However, when they told me they would like to abandon the study, I did not try to dissuade them. I accepted the decision, only offering my apologies for wasting their time. It is definitely better and safer not to press people to take part in a study, although, naturally, the conditions may vary and be related to the study area, availability of the research subjects, or the importance of the research topic. As an analogy, although in a different context, "no" means "no." It is our duty to read the signals and give the interview participant genuine opportunity and conditions to express their true opinion about whether they want to participate in the study.

Similarly to traditional studies, it is clear that consent to take part in the study ought to be informed (be preceded with the necessary information), voluntary (with no pressure, actual and perceived alike), and competent (voiced by the person who is sufficiently stable and cognitively mature).

The last part presents a problem with online research. Granted, some portals introduce certain controls, requiring their users to be of legal age, of for Facebook to be at least thirteeen). However, these controls are based on self-declarations. It is the ethical duty of the researcher to exercise limited trust and assume that our participants can be younger than they declare to be. Even though young people may be less out of control in their digital communication as it is sometimes assumed (Hodkinson, 2017), we should still remember that many people, even adults, sign the research consent without knowing exactly what they are doing (Varnhagen et al., 2005). Additionally, even in traditional studies people often show far-reaching hospitality and friendliness, just because the researcher is interested in them, and it is advised to be especially cautious when doing online research.

4.5 Data Ownership

In previous chapters, I indicated that data from many social networks can be technically available but legally—not so. As Solove (Solove, 2004) remarks, we live in times of "digital dossiers" which are compiled about ourselves practically everywhere but rarely under our complete control. Granted, the EU and USA lawmakers are attempting to regulate this market, as seen in the European Union's GDPR of 2018—however, this is a complicated market and companies constantly devise new tricks to compile rich sources of interconnected customer data.

At the same time, they are jealously guarding the data, seeing it as the important source of competitive advantage. For these reasons, corporations, when writing their Terms of Use, often take a protective position and do not allow external researchers to gather data, even of no identifiable character. The matter is complicated by the fact that in international academic teams, different legal jurisdictions can be present and some activities may be legal to some, but illegal to others (Dutton & Pipler, 2010).

Yet something else is crucial here—even though from the legal perspective the data could be owned by the corporation, from the ethical viewpoint we also need to take into account the social aspect—and ponder whether some of the data can be perceived by users as belonging to them or whether there is some data that does actually belong to the users. The examples that come first to mind are pictures and drawings— even after receiving permission to use the data from the owner of the website, when reusing any creative works we ought to remember the moral rights of the authors. This creates a contradiction: we need to be diligent in guaranteeing the anonymity of our sources so that their privacy is respected but at the same time, they hold personal copyrights for what they publish, and have some common-sense right to attribution.

The case is complicated in that authors often publish their works with conviction that it is worthy of distributing further and deserving acclaim, and we can also be aware that quoting these works can expose the authors to ridicule.

In such situations we need to abide by the central rule—that of protecting the research participants from the risks that they themselves see, even if we consider them irrational, and the risks that we perceive and the participants cannot fathom or find impossible. If we see a pathetic poem on a public forum we need to really deeply consider if it is worth quoting, even if the author is eager to share it. It is quite possible that describing this work will draw the attention of a wider audience and the questionable poet will want to have their work forgotten in a few years.

The dichotomy between attribution and the need to protect the sources can often bring us to radical theoretical positions (S. C. Herring, 1996). In practice, the decision of what we consider a published work and what is a private message needs to be context-based and taken on a case-by-case basis.

4.6 Data Confidentiality

The rules of research ethics often extend beyond public information. Before the publication sees the light of day, large sets of data are created. They are often sensitive, such as audio/video recordings or transcripts of interviews with the names of people and avatars. When keeping conducting a research diary, we often make observations or reflections for our own use, without any intention of publishing them, but also in a way that allows identification of research participants. It is good practice to mask the identity of the research subjects at as early a stage as possible but even leaving a note that a few different quotes come from the same person may cause trouble (if the quotes can be easily found online), while removing this information could make future analyses problematic if not impossible. Similarly, although recordings are to be erased after they have been transcribed, transcription can be time-consuming and depend on a researcher's style of work but also on the availability of research grants.

Researchers in the digital social sciences are burdened with the need for higher awareness in digital security and guaranteeing data confidentiality. Because of this, they should master the tools for safe communication and data storage. Below is the abridged version of advice that I prepared for a workshop for the Nieman Foundation fellows, who as journalists—are often exposed to higher risks of digital attacks.

Secure voice and text message communication can be achieved with Signal, a free/open source application that enables encryption of connections and communication between people in the best possible way, and that has been recommended by Edward Snowden and Bruce Schneier. Signal's algorithm is increasingly often used by corporations, such as Facebook.

If we want to go online in a way that makes it more difficult to identify us, we need a Tor browser or a good Virtual Private Network (VPN) service. The latter is useful when using public wireless hotspots, and increases our safety and therefore that of our data. VPNs are something we recommend to our informants, especially if they reside in countries that actively monitor the online behavior of Web surfers, like China, or that block access to some popular services. (Turkey blocked access to Wikipedia in 2017 and in Russia, LinkedIn access is limited.) It is important not to use free VPN services offered by little-known companies because of the documented cases of abuse of privacy. At worst, free VPNs may, without warning, hand over the control of our computers to potentially criminal botnets (Razaghpanah et al., 2017).

We should also keep some things in mind when selecting research equipment. If we conduct research in places where hacking is a possibility, it is advisable to replace a traditional laptop with a Chromebook,[4] or at least use this equipment in fieldwork, if surveillance is a possible threat. As of 2019, many Chromebooks come with the possibility of installing both Linux and mobile Android applications, which improves their usefulness. Chromebooks usually store user data in the Google cloud, so breaking into them requires breaking through Google's safety

---

[4] Complete academic work on a Chromebook is difficult, as applications are rare. Nevertheless, the number of tools in reference management is growing (Paperpile in combination with Google Docs works even better than EndNote, Mendeley, or Zotero, but requires the full version of the Chrome browser).

systems, not local, equipment, safeguards which definitely raises the entry barrier for cyber burglars.

Speaking about clouds, some researchers are still averse to storing store data in the cloud, seeing a safety threat. This view is unjustified. Google or Dropbox cloud-stored data is protected from outside intervention, although it is imperative to use two-factor authentication, which is needed to authorize any new device that we log in from for the first time. (This feature should also be enabled on Facebook.) Yet data can be made even more secure with hardware tokens, available from sources like Google. Their daily use is somewhat problematic, so they are recommended only to those who face high risk of cyber burglary.

Cloud storage also makes the data available to other researchers we cooperate with in a safe way—also requiring a password and subject to personal control, unlike with email, whose hijacking is easier (and this is why data should not be emailed). Using the cloud is also very useful, providing backups in case of downtimes, fire or theft; in the latter two cases local backups may be insufficient. Nevertheless, cloud storage can be subject to different jurisdictions from our local one, so we may unwillingly break the law and be subject to responsibilities which are not present in our home location. Another potential element of risk is that data can be subject to inside interventions—breaches of confidentiality by the cloud server owner. Most companies that offer popular cloud storage declare they protect our data and do not have access to it themselves, but such declarations cannot guarantee freedom from intervention in the future. Therefore, for the most sensitive data we should use Vivo or Boxcryptor; both allow encryption of cloud-stored data. Whoever breaks into our cloud storage without a separate password-protected application will not be able to decipher the contents; such protection will also work for the cloud storage operator who will see only encoded data. As an alternative, we may consider SpiderOak—a cloud storage service specializing in data encryption and safety, where encryption is performed on the side of the local machine.

Data encryption is also required on the local computer. Since we have folders and files containing sensitive data, they need to be protected, and the password needed to log into the operating system is definitely insufficient. Windows users can launch the system's BitLocker encryption service; Mac users have FileVault at their disposal. Both solutions are good, although it is worth considering the more convenient, free, and free/open source VeraCrypt—an excellent disk and data encryption tool that works across many platforms. It makes life easier, since we can read a Windows-encrypted pendrive on a Mac and the other way round.

Apart from the use of advanced tools, we need to exercise common sense and safety hygiene. Research data must not be encrypted with the same passwords we use with any Web service. Yahoo, LinkedIn, or MySpace password leaks show that even the largest corporations do not always keep their promises of user safety.[5] It is advisable to use password managers, such as LastPass or 1Password for less important passwords. More critical ones, such as email, social networks, bank accounts, or research data, would benefit from not using password managers and the use of complex passwords backed up by mnemonics. For example, we can use the first letters from the refrain of our favorite song, replacing some letters with numbers ("When you stand up and feel the warmth/But the sunshine never comes" can result in "Wy5uaftwBt5n3") and adding special characters. An element of a password built this way can be enriched with part of the name of the service—therefore "guaWy5uaftwBt5n3!" could be an easy-to-remember password for The Guardian service.

---

[5] I recommend http://haveibeenpwned.com, where we can check whether our email addresses and associated passwords have been found in one of the major data leaks.

5

Final Remarks

In this monograph I presented the variety of approaches and tools to conduct social research of and through the online world. I explained why the Internet ought to be the subject of sociological studies, and why even traditional social sciences projects ought to include elements of online research. I identified three trends that are strictly connected with the development of communication technology and networks (online transformation of interpersonal relations, crisis of expert knowledge, and the sharing economy). I indicated their importance in many areas, and the need for deep and recurring social science analyses due to the high changeability of the phenomena.

I then described the main quantitative approaches, focusing on those that do not require long-term specialist training. I highlighted those qualitative methods that may be used to interpret quantitative research and be a starting point for qualitative analysis. I outlined the possibilities of doing online cultural studies—studying products of Internet culture as a valid method of doing social sciences. Finally, I outlined the ethical considerations that every author of a digital study ought to consider.

My goal was to write an introductory methodological monograph and a reference book, which therefore should also include a solid literature review that would broaden knowledge in the indicated areas and trace my own line of thought. I also tried to include the basic technical issues, to encourage readers to do their own research.

Thank you for reading this book. I hope that it has proved useful. I am parting with you with the use of a meme—the last page of the Internet.[1]

---

[1] See: https://knowyourmeme.com/memes/the-last-page-of-the-internet

Thick Big Data: Doing Digital Social Sciences. Dariusz Jemielniak, Oxford University Press (2020).
© Dariusz Jemielniak.
DOI: 10.1093/oso/9780198839705.001.0001

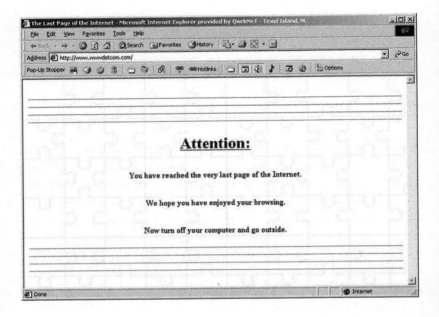

References

Adamic, E. A. L., Lento, T., & Ng, P. (2014). The evolution of memes on facebook. *Facebook Data Science*, https://www.facebook.com/notes/facebook-data-science/the-evolution-of-memes-on-facebook/10151988334203859.

Adamic, L. A., & Huberman, B. A. (2000). The nature of markets in the World Wide Web. *Quarterly Journal of Electronic Commerce, 1*(1), 5–12.

Adams, J., & Brückner, H. (2015). Wikipedia, sociology, and the promise and pitfalls of Big Data. *Big Data & Society, 2*(2). Retrieved from http://journals.sagepub.com/doi/abs/10.1177/2053951715614332.

Adams, J. M. (2014). *Occupy Time: Technoculture, Immediacy, and Resistance after Occupy Wall Street* (First edition). New York, NY: Palgrave Macmillan.

Adams, T. E., & Ellis, C. (2016). *Handbook of Autoethnography*. London—New York: Routledge.

Adler, P. A., & Adler, P. (2012). Keynote address tales from the field: Reflections on four decades of ethnography. *Qualitative Sociology Review, 8*(1), 10–32.

Agamben, G. (1999). *Potentialities: Collected Essays in Philosophy*. Stanford: Stanford University Press.

Agar, M. (1980). *The Professional Stranger: An Informal Introduction to Ethnography*. New York: Academic Press.

Agar, M. (2006). Culture: Can you take it anywhere? *International Journal of Qualitative Methods, 5*(2), 1–16.

Aigraine, P. (2012). *Sharing. Culture and the Economy in the Internet Age*. Amsterdam.

Al-Saggaf, Y., & Williamson, K. (2004). Online communities in Saudi Arabia: Evaluating the impact on culture through online semi-structured interviews. *Forum Qualitative Sozialforschung/Forum: Qualitative Social Research, 5*(3), DOI:10.17169/fqs-17165.17163.17564.

Albert, R., Jeong, H., & Barabási, A.-L. (1999). Internet: Diameter of the World-Wide Web. *Nature, 401*(6749), 130–1.

Alderson, P., & Morrow, V. (2006). Multidisciplinary research ethics review: Is it feasible? *International Journal of Social Research Methodology, 9*(5), 405–17.

Alles, M. (2014). Thick data: Adding context to big data to enhance auditability. *International Journal of Auditing Technology, 2*(2), 95–108.

Aloisi, A. (2015). Commoditized workers: Case study research on labor law issues arising from a set of on-demand/gig economy platforms. *Comparative Labor Law & Policy Journal, 37*, 653–90.

Alvesson, M., & Sköldberg, K. (2017). *Reflexive Methodology: New Vistas for Qualitative Research*. London—Thousand Oaks—New Delhi: Sage.

Anderson, C. W., & Revers, M. (2018). From counter-power to counter-Pepe: The vagaries of participatory epistemology in a digital age. *Media and Communication, 6*(4), 24–5.

Anderson, K. V., & Sheeler, K. H. (2014). Texts (and tweets) from Hillary: Meta–meming and postfeminist political culture. *Presidential Studies Quarterly, 44*(2), 224–43.

Andriani, P., & McKelvey, B. (2009). Perspective-from Gaussian to Paretian thinking: Causes and implications of power laws in organizations. *Organization Science, 20*(6), 1053–71.

Anthony, D., Campos-Castillo, C., & Horne, C. (2017). Toward a sociology of privacy. *Annual Review of Sociology, 43*(1), 249–69. Retrieved from https://www.annualreviews.org/doi/abs/10.1146/annurev-soc-060116-053643.

Aragona, B., & Zindato, D. (2016). Counting people in the data revolution era: Challenges and opportunities for population censuses. *International Review of Sociology, 26*(3), 367–85.

Aro, J. (2016). The cyberspace war: Propaganda and trolling as warfare tools. *European View, 15*(1), 121–32.

Arvidsson, A., & Colleoni, E. (2012). Value in informational capitalism and on the Internet. *The Information Society, 28*(3), 135–50.

Asongu, S. A. (2018). Conditional determinants of mobile phones penetration and mobile banking in Sub-Saharan Africa. *Journal of the Knowledge Economy, 9*(1), 81–135.

Atkinson, P. (2013). Ethnography and craft knowledge. *Qualitative Sociology Review, 9*(2), 56–63.

Atkinson, P., Coffey, A., Delamont, S., Lofland, J., & Lofland, L. (eds.). (2001). *Handbook of Ethnography*. Thousand Oaks: Sage.

Atkinson, P., & Delamont, S. (2006). Rescuing narrative from qualitative research. *Narrative Inquiry, 16*(1), 164–72. Retrieved from https://www.jbe-platform.com/content/journals/10.1075/ni.16.1.21atk.

Augé, M. (1995). *International Journal of Selection and Assessment*. London: Verso.

Aupers, S., Schaap, J., & de Wildt, L. (2018). Qualitative in-depth interviews: Studying religious meaning-making in MMOs. In V. Sisler, K. Radde-Antweiler, & X. Zeiler (eds.), *Methods for Studying Video Games and Religion*. New York—London: Routledge.

Austen, K. (2015). The trouble with wearables. *Nature, 525*(7567), 22–4.

Azzellini, D. (2018). Labour as a commons: The example of worker-recuperated companies. *Critical Sociology, 44*(4–5), 763–76. Retrieved from http://journals.sagepub.com/doi/abs/10.1177/0896920516661856.

Babones, S. (2016). Interpretive quantitative methods for the social sciences. *Sociology, 50*(3), 453–69. Retrieved from http://journals.sagepub.com/doi/abs/10.1177/0038038515583637.

Baćak, V., & Kennedy, E. H. (2019). Principled machine learning using the super learner: An application to predicting prison violence. *Sociological Methods & Research, 48*(3), 698–721.

Bainbridge, W. S. (1999). Cyberspace: Sociology's natural domain. *Contemporary Sociology, 28*(6), 664–7.

Baker, L. M. (2006). Observation: A complex research method. *Library Trends, 55*(1), 171–89.

Bakhtin, M. M. (1984). *Rabelais and His World* (Vol. 341). Bloomington: Indiana University Press.

Banasik, N., & Podsiadło, K. (2016). Comprehension of ironic utterances by bilingual children. *Psychology of Language and Communication, 20*(3), 316–35. Retrieved from https://content.sciendo.com/view/journals/plc/20/3/article-p316.xml.

Banasik-Jemielniak, N., Jemielniak, D., & Pędzich, W. (2018). Do millions of prayers increase one's longevity? A cohort study of the impact of intercessory prayers on the mortality of Roman Catholic bishops. *Journal of Medical Internet Research (preprints)*, DOI:10.2196/preprints.12150.

Band, J., & Gerafi, J. (2013). Wikipedia's Economic Value. *SSRN Working Paper*, DOI:10.2139/ssrn.2338563.

Banet-Weiser, S., & Miltner, K. M. (2016). #MasculinitySoFragile: Culture, structure, and networked misogyny. *Feminist Media Studies, 16*(1), 171–4. Retrieved from https://doi.org/10.1080/14680777.2016.1120490.

Bar-Lev, S. (2008). "We are here to give you emotional support": Performing emotions in an online HIV/AIDS support group. *Qualitative Health Research, 18*(4), 509–21. Retrieved from http://journals.sagepub.com/doi/abs/10.1177/1049732307311680.

Barabási, A. L., Jeong, H., Néda, Z., Ravasz, E., Schubert, A., & Vicsek, T. (2002). Evolution of the social network of scientific collaborations. *Physica A: Statistical Mechanics and Its Applications, 311*(3), 590–614.

Barcellini, F., Détienne, F., & Burkhardt, J.-M. (2008). User and developer mediation in an open source software community: Boundary spanning through cross participation in online discussions. *International Journal of Human-Computer Studies, 66*(7), 558–70. Retrieved from http://www.sciencedirect.com/science/article/pii/S1071581907001437.

Barrattt, M. J., & Maddox, A. (2016). Active engagement with stigmatised communities through digital ethnography. *Qualitative Research, 16*(6), 701–19.

Barthes, R. (1977). Introduction to the structural analysis of narratives. In *Image, Music, Text*. New York: Hill and Wang.

Bassett, E. H., & O'Riordan, K. (2002). Ethics of Internet research: Contesting the human subjects research model. *Ethics and Information Technology, 4*(3), 233–47.

Bauman, Z. (2003). *Liquid Love: On the Frailty of Human Bonds*. Cambridge: Polity Press.

Bauman, Z. (2007). *Consuming Life*. Cambridge, UK–Malden, MA: Polity.

Bauwens, M. (2006). The political economy of peer production. *Post-autistic Economics Review, 37*, 33–44.

Bauwens, M. (2009). Class and capital in peer production. *Capital & Class, 33*(1), 121–41.

Bauwens, M. (2012). Thesis on digital labor in an emerging P2P economy. In T. Scholz (ed.), *Digital Labor: The Internet as Playground and Factory*. London—New York: Routledge.

Bauwens, M., & Kostakis, V. (2014). From the communism of capital to capital for the commons: Towards an open co-operativism. *tripleC: Communication, Capitalism & Critique. Open Access Journal for a Global Sustainable Information Society, 12*(1), 356–61.

Bauwens, M., Kostakis, V., & Pazaitis, A. (2019). *Peer to Peer: The Commons Manifesto*. London: University of Westminster Press.

Baym, N., & Markham, A. (2009). *Internet Inquiry: Conversations about Method*. London-New Delhi-Thousand Oaks: Sage.

Beck, U. (2002). *Individualization: Institutionalized Individualism and Its Social and Political Consequences* (Vol. 13). London—New York: Sage.

Beigel, F. (2014a). Introduction: Current tensions and trends in the World Scientific System. *Current Sociology, 62*(5), 617–25. Retrieved from http://journals.sagepub.com/doi/abs/10.1177/0011392114548640.

Beigel, F. (2014b). Publishing from the periphery: Structural heterogeneity and segmented circuits. The evaluation of scientific publications for tenure in Argentina's CONICET. *Current Sociology, 62*(5), 743–65. Retrieved from http://journals.sagepub.com/doi/abs/10.1177/0011392114533977.

Bellotti, E., & Mora, E. (2016). Networks of practices in critical consumption. *Journal of Consumer Culture, 16*(3), 718–60.

Bendix, R. (2005). Introduction: Ear to ear, nose to nose, skin to skin: The senses in comparative ethnographic perspective. *Etnofoor, 18*(1), 3–14. Retrieved from http://www.jstor.org/stable/25758082.

Benkler, Y. (2002). Coase's penguin, or, Linux and the nature of the firm. *Yale Law Journal, 112*(3), 369–446.

Benkler, Y. (1999). Free as the air to common use: First Amendment constraints on enclosure of the public domain. *NYU Law Review, 74*, 354.

Benkler, Y. (2003). Freedom in the commons: Towards a political economy of information. *Duke Law Journal, 52*, 1245–76.

Benkler, Y. (2004). Sharing nicely: On shareable goods and the emergence of sharing as a modality of economic production. *Yale Law Journal, 3*(15), 273–358.

Benkler, Y. (2011). *The Penguin and the Leviathan: How Cooperation Triumphs over Self-interest*. New York: Crown Business.

Benkler, Y. (2013). Practical anarchism peer mutualism, market power, and the fallible state. *Politics & Society, 41*(2), 213–51.

Benkler, Y., & Nissenbaum, H. (2006). Commons-based peer production and virtue. *Journal of Political Philosophy, 14*(4), 394–419.

Bennett, A. (2018). Conceptualising the relationship between youth, music and DIY careers: A critical overview. *Cultural Sociology, 12*(2), 140–55. Retrieved from http://journals.sagepub.com/doi/abs/10.1177/1749975517750760.

Benton, G. (1988). The origin of the political joke. In C. Powell & C. Patton (eds.), *Humor in Society: Resistance and Control* (pp. 85–105). New York: St. Martin's Press.

Berg, M., & Seeber, B. (2016). *The Slow Professor: Challenging the Culture of Speed in the Academy*. Toronto: University of Toronto Press.

Berger, P. L., & Luckman, T. (1967). *The Social Construction of Reality: A Treatise in the Sociology of Knowledge*. Garden City, N.Y.: Doubleday.

Berger, R. J., & Quinney, R. (2005). *Storytelling Sociology: Narrative as Social Inquiry*. Boulder: Lynne Rienner Publishers.

Berghel, H. (2017). The new science wars. *Computer, 50*(11), 72–6.

Bergquist, M., & Ljungberg, J. (2001). The power of gifts: organizing social relationships in open source communities. *Information Systems Journal, 11*(4), 305–20.

Bethlehem, J. (2010). Selection bias in web surveys. *International Statistical Review, 78*(2), 161–88.

Beverungen, A., & Lange, A.-C. (2018). Cognition in high-frequency trading: The costs of consciousness and the limits of automation. *Theory, Culture & Society, 35*(6), 75–95. Retrieved from https://doi.org/10.1177/0263276418758906.

Biddle, S. (2014). Justine Sacco is good at her job, and how I came to peace with her. *Gawker,* http://gawker.com/justine-sacco-is-good-at-her-job-and-how-i-came-to-pea-1653022326.

Biggs, M. (2005). Strikes as forest fires: Chicago and Paris in the late nineteenth century. *American Journal of Sociology, 110*(6), 1684–1714. Retrieved from http://www.journals.uchicago.edu/doi/abs/10.1086/427675.

Bijker, W. E., Bal, R., & Hendriks, R. (2009). *The Paradox of Scientific Authority: The Role of Scientific Advice in Democracies.* Cambridge, MA: MIT Press.

Blok, A., Carlsen, H. B., Jørgensen, T. B., Madsen, M. M., Ralund, S., & Pedersen, M. A. (2017). Stitching together the heterogeneous party: A complementary social data science experiment. *Big Data & Society, 4*(2), 2053951717736337.

Blok, A., & Pedersen, M. A. (2014). Complementary social science? Quali-quantitative experiments in a Big Data world. *Big Data & Society, 1*(2), 1–15. DOI:10.1177/2053951714543908.

Bode, L., & Jones, M. L. (2018). Do Americans want a right to be forgotten? Estimating public support for digital erasure legislation. *Policy & Internet, 10*(3), 244–63. Retrieved from https://onlinelibrary.wiley.com/doi/abs/10.1002/poi3.174.

Boellstorff, T. (2008). *Coming of Age in Second Life: An Anthropologist Explores the Virtually Human.* Princeton: Princeton University Press.

Bohdanova, T. (2014). Unexpected revolution: the role of social media in Ukraine's Euromaidan uprising. *European View, 13*(1), 133–42.

Boje, D. M. (2001). *Narrative Methods for Organizational and Communication Research.* London—Thousand Oaks, Calif.: SAGE.

Boje, D. M. (2008). *Storytelling Organizations.* London—Thousand Oaks, CA—New Delhi: Sage.

Boje, D. M. (2014). *Storytelling Organizational Practices: Managing in the Quantum Age.* New York: Routledge.

Bok, D. C. (2009). *Beyond the Ivory Tower: Social Responsibilities of the Modern University.* Boston: Harvard University Press.

Bond, R. M., Fariss, C. J., Jones, J. J., Kramer, A. D., Marlow, C., Settle, J. E., & Fowler, J. H. (2012). A 61-million-person experiment in social influence and political mobilization. *Nature, 489*(7415), 295–8.

Borgatti, S. P., & Halgin, D. S. (2011). On network theory. *Organization Science, 22*(5), 1168–81.

Bornakke, T., & Due, B. L. (2018). Big–thick blending: A method for mixing analytical insights from big and thick data sources. *Big Data & Society*(1), DOI: 10.1177/2053951718765026.

Botsman, R., & Rogers, R. (2010). *What's Mine Is Yours: The Rise of Collaborative Consumption.* New York: HarperBusiness.

Bouwman, M. G., Teunissen, Q. G., Wijburg, F. A., & Linthorst, G. E. (2010). "Doctor Google" ending the diagnostic odyssey in lysosomal storage disorders: Parents using internet search engines as an efficient diagnostic strategy in rare diseases. *Archives of Disease in Childhood, 95*, 642–4.

Bowman, D. M., Woodbury, N., & Fisher, E. (2016). Decoupling knowledge and expertise in personalized medicine: Who will fill the gap? *Expert Review of Precision Medicine and Drug Development, 1*(4), 345–7. Retrieved from https://doi.org/10.1080/23808993.2016.1199949.

boyd, d. (2005). Blogging outloud: Shifts in public voice. *LITA conference,* http://www.danah.org/papers/LITA.html

boyd, d. (2008). Facebook's privacy trainwreck. *Convergence: The International Journal of Research into New Media Technologies, 14*(1), 13–20.

boyd, d., & Crawford, K. (2012). Critical questions for big data: Provocations for a cultural, technological, and scholarly phenomenon. *Information, Communication & Society, 15*(5), 662–79.

Brabham, D. C. (2012). The myth of amateur crowds. *Information, Communication & Society, 15*(3), 394–410. Retrieved from https://doi.org/10.1080/13691 18X.2011.641991.

Brake, D. R. (2014). Are we all online content creators now? Web 2.0 and digital divides. *Journal of Computer-Mediated Communication, 19*(3), 591–609.

Brannen, J. (2005). Mixing methods: The entry of qualitative and quantitative approaches into the research process. *International Journal of Social Research Methodology, 8*(3), 173–84.

Bratich, J. (2014). Occupy all the dispositifs: Memes, media ecologies, and emergent bodies politic. *Communication and Critical/Cultural Studies, 11*(1), 64–73.

Brickell, C. (2012). Sexuality, power and the sociology of the internet. *Current Sociology, 60*(1), 28–44.

Brickhouse, N. W., Dagher, Z. R., Letts IV, W. J., & Shipman, H. L. (2000). Diversity of students' views about evidence, theory, and the interface between science and religion in an astronomy course. *Journal of Research in Science Teaching, 37*(4), 340–62. Retrieved from https://onlinelibrary.wiley.com/doi/abs/10.1002/%28SICI%291098-2736%28200004%2937%3A4%3C340%3A%3AAID-TEA4%3E3.0.CO%3B2-D.

British Society of Criminology. (2015). Statement of Ethics. http://www.britsoccrim.org/ethics/.

Brooker, P., Barnett, J., & Cribbin, T. (2016). Doing social media analytics. *Big Data & Society, 3*(2), 2053951716658060.

Brosnan, C., & Kirby, E. (2016). Sociological perspectives on the politics of knowledge in health care: Introduction to themed issue. *Health Sociology Review, 25*(2), 139–41.

Bruns, A. (2008). *Blogs, Wikipedia, Second Life, and Beyond: From Production to Produsage.* New York, NY—Frankfurt, Germany: Peter Lang.

Bruns, A., Highfield, T., & Burgess, J. E. (2013). The Arab Spring and social media audiences: English and Arabic Twitter users and their networks. *American Behavioral Scientist, 57*(7), 971–898.

Bryman, A. (2007). Barriers to integrating quantitative and qualitative research. *Journal of Mixed Methods Research, 1*(1), 8–22. Retrieved from http://journals.sagepub.com/doi/abs/10.1177/2345678906290531.

Buchanan, D. R. (1992). An uneasy alliance: Combining qualitative and quantitative research methods. *Health Education Quarterly, 19*(1), 117–35. Retrieved from http://journals.sagepub.com/doi/abs/10.1177/109019819201900108.

Buchanan, E. A. (ed.) (2004). *Readings in Virtual Research Ethics: Issues and Controversies.* Hershey—London—Melbourne—Singapore: Information Science Publishing.

Buckels, E. E., Trapnell, P. D., & Paulhus, D. L. (2014). Trolls just want to have fun. *Personality and Individual Differences, 67,* 97–102. Retrieved from http://www.sciencedirect.com/science/article/pii/S0191886914000324.

Burke, M., & Kraut, R. (2008). Taking up the mop: identifying future Wikipedia administrators. Paper presented at the CHI, Florence.

Burrell, J. (2009). The field site as a network: A strategy for locating ethnographic research. *Field Methods, 21*(2), 181–99. Retrieved from http://journals.sagepub.com/doi/abs/10.1177/1525822X08329699.

Burroughs, B. (2013). FCJ-165 Obama trolling: Memes, salutes and an agonistic politics in the 2012 presidential election. *The Fibreculture Journal, 22,* 258–77.

Burrows, R., & Savage, M. (2014). After the crisis? Big Data and the methodological challenges of empirical sociology. *Big Data & Society, 1*(1), 2053951714540280. Retrieved from http://journals.sagepub.com/doi/abs/10.1177/2053951714540280.

Callegaro, M., Baker, R., Bethlehem, J., A., G., Krosnick, J. A., & Lavrakas, P. J. (eds.). (2014). *Online Panel Research: A Data Quality Perspective.* New York: Wiley.

Callegaro, M., Manfreda, K. L., & Vehovar, V. (2015). *Web Survey Methodology.* London—New Delhi—Thousand Oaks: Sage.

Camargo Jr, K., & Grant, R. (2015). Public health, science, and policy debate: Being right is not enough. *American Journal of Public Health, 105*(2), 232–5.

Campbell, J., Fletcher, G., & Greenhill, A. (2009). Conflict and identity shape shifting in an online financial community. *Information Systems Journal, 19*(5), 461–78.

Capodieci, A., Budner, P., Eirich, J., Gloor, P., & Mainetti, L. (2018). Dynamically adapting the environment for elderly people through smartwatch-based mood detection. In F. Grippa, J. Leitão, J. Gluesing, K. Riopelle, & P. Gloor (eds.), *Collaborative Innovation Networks. Studies on Entrepreneurship, Structural Change and Industrial Dynamics* (pp. 65–73). Cham: Springer.

Carley, K. M., Malik, M., Landwehr, P. M., Pfeffer, J., & Kowalchuck, M. (2016). Crowd sourcing disaster management: The complex nature of Twitter usage in Padang Indonesia. *Safety Science, 90,* 48–61. Retrieved from http://www.sciencedirect.com/science/article/pii/S0925753516300431.

Carrington, P. J., Scott, J., & Wasserman, S. (2005). *Models and Methods in Social Network Analysis* (Vol. 28). Cambridge: Cambridge University Press.

Carroll, M. W. (2006). Creative commons and the new intermediaries. *Michigan State Law Review, 45,* 45–66.

Carter Olson, C., & LaPoe, V. (2018). Combating the digital spiral of silence: Academic activists versus social media trolls. In J. R. Vickery & T. Everbach (eds.), *Mediating Misogyny: Gender, Technology, and Harassment* (pp. 271–91). Cham: Springer International Publishing.

Carvalho Nascimento, E. C., da Silva, E., & Siqueira-Batista, R. (2018). The "use" of sex robots: A bioethical issue. *Asian Bioethics Review,* https://doi.org/10.1007/s41649-41018-40061-41640.

Castells, M. (2000). Toward a sociology of the network society. *Contemporary Sociology, 29*(5), 693–9.

Castells, M. (2013a). *Communication Power*. Oxford: Oxford University Press.

Castells, M. (2013b). *Networks of Outrage and Hope: Social Movements in the Internet Age*. New York: John Wiley and Sons.

Cavallo, A. (2018). Scraped data and sticky prices. *The Review of Economics and Statistics, 100*(1), 105–19. Retrieved from https://www.mitpressjournals.org/doi/abs/10.1162/REST_a_00652.

Chambers, D. (2013). *Social Media and Personal Relationships: Online Intimacies and Networked Friendship*. London: Palgrave Macmillan.

Charmaz, K. (2014). *Constructing Grounded Theory*. London—Thousand Oaks—New Delhi: Sage.

Charmaz, K., Komorowska, B., & Konecki, K. (2013). *Teoria ugruntowana: Praktyczny przewodnik po analizie jakościowej*. Warszawa: Wydawnictwo Naukowe PWN.

Charmaz, K., & Mitchell, R. G. (1996). The myth of silent authorship: Self, substance, and style in ethnographic writing. *Symbolic Interaction, 19*(4), 285–302.

Chaudhry, I. (2016). "Not so black and white": Discussions of race on Twitter in the aftermath of #Ferguson and the shooting death of Mike Brown. *Cultural Studies? Critical Methodologies, 16*(3), 296–304.

Chayko, M. (2014). Techno-social life: The Internet, digital technology, and social connectedness. *Sociology Compass, 8*(7), 976–91.

Cheal, D. (2015). *The Gift Economy*. London-New York: Routledge.

Cheliotis, G. (2009). From open source to open content: Organization, licensing and decision processes in open cultural production. *Decision Support Systems, 47*(3), 229–44.

Chełkowski, T., Gloor, P., & Jemielniak, D. (2016). Inequalities in open source software development: Analysis of contributor's commits in Apache software foundation projects. *PLoS ONE, 11*(4), e0152976.

Cheok, A. D., Levy, D., & Karunanayaka, K. (2016). Lovotics: Love and sex with robots. In K. Karpouzis & G. N. Yannakakis (eds.), *Emotion in Games* (pp. 303–28). London—New York: Springer.

Chess, S., & Newsrom, E. (2015). *Folklore, Horror Stories, and the Slender Man: The Development of an Internet Mythology*. London-New York: Palgrave.

Cheung, C. C., Krahn, A. D., & Andrade, J. G. (2018). The emerging role of wearable technologies in arrhythmia detection. *Canadian Journal of Cardiology, 34*(8), 1083–7.

Chisholm, J. F. (2014). Review of the status of cyberbullying and cyberbullying prevention. *Journal of information systems education, 25*(1), 77–87.

Chmielewska-Szlajfer, H. (2018). Opinion dailies versus Facebook fan pages: The case of Poland's surprising 2015 presidential elections. *Media, Culture & Society, 40*(6), 938–50. Retrieved from http://journals.sagepub.com/doi/abs/10.1177/0163443718756065.

Chmielewska-Szlajfer, H. (2019). National Internet pro-voting campaigns and local watchdog websites: Practicing civil society online. In *Reshaping Poland's Community after Communism: Ordinary Celebrations* (pp. 125–79). Cham: Springer International Publishing.

Cho, H., & Larose, R. (1999). Privacy issues in Internet surveys. *Social Science Computer Review, 17*(4), 421–34. Retrieved from https://doi.org/10.1177/089443939901700402.

Christensen, C. (2011). Twitter revolutions? Addressing social media and dissent. *The Communication Review, 14*(3), 155–7.

Chused, R. H. (2014). The legal culture of appropriation art: The future of copyright in the remix age. *Tulane Journal of Technology and Intellectual Property, 17*, 163–216.

Ciambrone, D., Phua, V., & Avery, E. N. (2017). Gendered synthetic love: real dolls and the construction of intimacy. *International Review of Modern Sociology, 43*(1), 59–78.

Ciechanowski, L., Przegalinska, A., Magnuski, M., & Gloor, P. (2019). In the shades of the uncanny valley: An experimental study of human–chatbot interaction. *Future Generation Computer Systems, 92*, 539–48.

Ciesielska, M. (2010). *Hybrid Organisations. A Study of the Open Source—Business Setting.* Copenhagen: Copenhagen Business School.

Ciesielska, M., & Jemielniak, D. (eds.). (2018). *Qualitative Methodologies in Organization Studies: Theories and New Approaches.* London-New York: Palgrave.

Clark, E. M., Williams, J. R., Jones, C. A., Galbraith, R. A., Danforth, C. M., & Dodds, P. S. (2016). Sifting robotic from organic text: A natural language approach for detecting automation on Twitter. *Journal of Computational Science, 16*, 1–7.

Cleary, A., Kearney, B., Solan-Schuppers, N., & Watson, I. (2014). Research in a time of financial constraints: Carrying out representative postal surveys. *Irish Journal of Sociology, 22*(1), 102–6.

Clerke, T., & Hopwood, N. (2014). *Doing Ethnography in Teams: A Case Study of Asymmetries in Collaborative Research.* New York: Springer.

Clifford, J. (1983). On ethnographic authority. *Representations*(2), 118–46.

Clifford, J., & Marcus, G. E. (eds.). (1986). *Writing Culture: The Poetics and Politics of Ethnography.* Berkeley: University of California Press.

Cockayne, D., Leszczynski, A., & Zook, M. (2017). #HotForBots: Sex, the non-human and digitally mediated spaces of intimate encounter. *Environment and Planning D: Society and Space, 35*(6), 1115–33.

Coleman, E. G. (2011). Hacker politics and publics. *Public Culture, 23*(3), 511–16.

Coleman, E. G. (2013). *Coding Freedom.* Princeton—Oxford: Princeton University Press.

Coleman, E. G. (2014). *Hacker, Hoaxer, Whistleblower, Spy: The Many Faces of Anonymous.* New York: Verso Books.

Coles, B. A., & West, M. (2016). Trolling the trolls: Online forum users constructions of the nature and properties of trolling. *Computers in Human Behavior, 60*, 233–44. Retrieved from http://www.sciencedirect.com/science/article/pii/S0747563216301285.

Compton, R., Jurgens, D., & Allen, D. (2014). Geotagging one hundred million twitter accounts with total variation minimization. Paper presented at the IEEE International Conference on Big Data.

Cook, K. S. (2010). Trusting doctors: The decline of moral authority in American medicine–By Jonathon B. Imber. *The British Journal of Sociology, 61*(2), 391–2.

Couldry, N. (2012). *Media, Society, World: Social Theory and Digital Media Practice.* Cambridge: Polity.

Couldry, N. and Mejias, Ulises A. (2019). *The Costs of Connection: How Data Is Colonizing Human Life and Appropriating It for Capitalism.* Stanford, CA: Stanford University Press.

Couper, M. P. (2000). Web surveys: A review of issues and approaches. *Public Opinion Quarterly, 64,* 464–94.

Couper, M. P. (2017). New developments in survey data collection. *Annual Review of Sociology, 43,* 121–45.

Creswell, J. W., & Poth, C. N. (2017). *Qualitative Inquiry and Research Design: Choosing among Five Approaches.* London—New Delhi—Thousand Oaks, CA: Sage.

Curran, J. (2013). Big Data or "Big Ethnographic Data"? Positioning Big Data within the ethnographic space. Paper presented at the Ethnographic Praxis in Industry Conference Proceedings.

Czarniawska, B. (2004). *Narratives in Social Science Research.* London-Thousand Oaks-New Delhi: Sage.

Czarniawska-Joerges, B. (1992). *Exploring Complex Organizations: A Cultural Perspective.* Newbury Park, Calif.: Sage Publications.

Czarniawska-Joerges, B. (1994). Narratives of individual and organizational identities. In S. Deetz (ed.), *Communication Yearbook* (Vol. 17, pp. 193–221). London: Sage.

Czarniawska-Joerges, B. (1998). *Narrative Approach in Organization Studies.* Thousand Oaks, Calif.: Sage Publications.

d'Ancona, M. (2017). *Post-truth: The New War on Truth and How to Fight Back.* New York: Random House.

Da Silva, P. D., & Garcia, J. L. (2012). YouTubers as satirists: Humour and remix in online video. *JeDEM-eJournal of eDemocracy and Open Government, 4*(1), 89–114.

Dahlander, L., Frederiksen, L., & Rullani, F. (2008). Online communities and open innovation. *Industry and Innovation, 15*(2), 115–23.

Dahlberg, L. (2007). Rethinking the fragmentation of the Cyberpublic: From consensus to contestation. *New Media & Society, 9*(5), 827–47.

Dale, J., & Kyle, D. (2016). Smart humanitarianism: Re-imagining human rights in the age of enterprise. *Critical Sociology, 42*(6), 783–97. Retrieved from https://doi.org/10.1177/0896920516640041.

Das, R., & Hodkinson, P. (2019). Tapestries of intimacy: Networked intimacies and new fathers' emotional self-disclosure of mental health struggles. *Social Media + Society, 5*(2), 2056305119846488. Retrieved from https://journals.sagepub.com/doi/abs/10.1177/2056305119846488.

Das, R., & Pavlíčková, T. (2014). Is there an author behind this text? A literary aesthetic driven approach to interactive media. *New Media & Society, 16*(3), 381–97. Retrieved from https://journals.sagepub.com/doi/abs/10.1177/1461444813481296.

Davies, C. A. (2008). *Reflexive Ethnography: A Guide to Researching Selves and Others.* London—New York: Routledge.

Davies, H. (2015). Ted Cruz using firm that harvested data on millions of unwitting Facebook users. *The Guardian, 11,* https://www.theguardian.com/us-news/2015/dec/2011/senator-ted-cruz-president-campaign-facebook-user-data.

Davis, M., Bolding, G., Hart, G., Sherr, L., & Elford, J. (2004). Reflecting on the experience of interviewing online: Perspectives from the Internet and HIV study in London. *AIDS Care, 16*(8), 944–52. Retrieved from https://doi.org/10.1080/09540120412331292499.

Davis, T. (2010). Third spaces or heterotopias? Recreating and negotiating migrant identity using online spaces. *Sociology, 44*(4), 661–77. Retrieved from https://doi.org/10.1177/0038038510369356.

Davison, P. (2012). The language of internet memes. In M. Mandiberg (ed.), *The Social Media Reader* (pp. 120–34). New York—London: NYU Press.

Dawkins, R. (1976). *The Selfish Gene*. Oxford: Oxford University Press.

De Meo, P., Ferrara, E., Fiumara, G., & Provetti, A. (2014). On Facebook, most ties are weak. *Communications of the ACM, 57*(11), 78–84.

De Wit, J. B., Das, E., & Vet, R. (2008). What works best: Objective statistics or a personal testimonial? An assessment of the persuasive effects of different types of message evidence on risk perception. *Health Psychology, 27*(1), 110–15.

Deakin, H., & Wakefield, K. (2014). Skype interviewing: Reflections of two PhD researchers. *Qualitative Research, 14*(5), 603–16. Retrieved from http://journals.sagepub.com/doi/abs/10.1177/1468794113488126.

Delgado-López, P. D., & Corrales-García, E. M. (2018). Influence of Internet and social media in the promotion of alternative oncology, cancer quackery, and the predatory publishing phenomenon. *Cureus, 10*(5), e2617.

Denzin, N. K. (2006). Analytic autoethnography, or déjà vu all over again. *Journal of Contemporary Ethnography, 35*(4), 419.

Denzin, N. K., & Lincoln, Y. S. (eds.). (1994). *Handbook of Qualitative Research*. Thousand Oaks, Calif.: Sage Publications.

Derbyshire, S. (2008). The ethical dilemma of ethical committees. *Sociology Compass, 2*(5): 1506–22.

DeSousa, M. A. M., M. J. (1982). Political cartoons and American culture: Significant symbols of campaign 1980*. *Studies in Visual Communication, 8*(1), 84–98.

Dew, K., Chamberlain, K., Hodgetts, D., Norris, P., Radley, A., & Gabe, J. (2014). Home as a hybrid centre of medication practice. *Sociology of Health & Illness, 36*(1), 28–43.

Dickins, M., Browning, C., Feldman, S., & Thomas, S. (2016). Social inclusion and the Fatosphere: The role of an online weblogging community in fostering social inclusion. *Sociology of Health & Illness, 38*(5), 797–811. Retrieved from https://onlinelibrary.wiley.com/doi/abs/10.1111/1467-9566.12397.

Diesner, J., Frantz, T. L., & Carley, K. M. (2005). Communication networks from the Enron email corpus "It's always about the people. Enron is no different." *Computational & Mathematical Organization Theory, 11*(3), 201–28.

DiGrazia, J., McKelvey, K., Bollen, J., & Rojas, F. (2013). More tweets, more votes: Social media as a quantitative indicator of political behavior. *PLoS ONE, 8*(11), e79449.

Dirksen, V., Huizing, A., & Smit, B. (2010). "Piling on layers of understanding": the use of connective ethnography for the study of (online) work practices. *New Media & Society, 12*(7), 1045–63.

Domínguez Figaredo, D., Beaulieu, A., Estalella, A., Cruz, E. G., Schnettler, B., & Read, R. (2007). Virtual Ethnography. *Qualitative Social Research, 8*(3), http://www.qualitative-research.net/index.php/fqs/article/view/274/601.

Dougherty, B. K. (2002). Comic relief: Using political cartoons in the classroom. *International Studies Perspectives, 3*(3), 258–70.

Dourish, P., & Gómez Cruz, E. (2018). Datafication and data fiction: Narrating data and narrating with data. *Big Data & Society, 5*(2), 2053951718784083.

Ducheneaut, N., Yee, N., & Bellotti, V. (2010). The best of both (virtual) worlds: Using ethnography and computational tools to study online behavior. *Ethnographic Praxis in Industry Conference Proceedings, 1*, 136–48. Retrieved from https://anthrosource.onlinelibrary.wiley.com/doi/abs/10.1111/j.1559-8918.2010.00013.x.

Dueñas, D., Pontón, P., Belzunegui, Á., & Pastor, I. (2016). Discriminatory expressions, the young and social networks: The effect of gender (Expresiones discriminatorias, jóvenes y redes sociales: la influencia del género). *Comunicar: Revista Científica de Educomunicación*, 46(24), 67–76.

Duhigg, C. (2012). How companies learn your secrets. *The New York Times*, 16, http://www.nytimes.com/2012/2002/2019/magazine/shopping-habits.html.

Dusi, D. (2017). Investigating the exploitative and empowering potential of the prosumption phenomenon. *Sociology Compass*, 11(6), doi.org/10.1111/soc1114. 12488.

Dutton, W. H., & Pipler, T. (2010). The politics of privacy, confidentiality, and ethics: Opening research methods. In W. H. Dutton & P. W. Jeffreys (eds.), *World Wide Research: Reshaping the Sciences and Humanities*. Cambridge: MIT Press.

Dutton, W. H., & Reisdorf, B. C. (2017). Cultural divides and digital inequalities: Attitudes shaping Internet and social media divides. *Information, Communication & Society*, 22(1), 18–38.

Dynel, M. (2016). "Trolling is not stupid": Internet trolling as the art of deception serving entertainment. *Intercultural Pragmatics*, 13(3), 353–81.

Eagle, N., Macy, M., & Claxton, R. (2010). Network diversity and economic development. *Science*, 328(5981), 1029–31.

Eagle, N., Pentland, A. S., & Lazer, D. (2009). Inferring friendship network structure by using mobile phone data. *Proceedings of the National Academy of Sciences*, 106(36), 15214–8.

Eastwood, H. (2000). Why are Australian GPs using alternative medicine?: Postmodernisation, consumerism and the shift towards holistic health. *Journal of Sociology*, 36(2), 133–56. Retrieved from http://journals.sagepub.com/doi/abs/10.1177/144078330003600201.

Edmans, A., & Gabaix, X. (2011). The effect of risk on the CEO market. *Review of Financial Studies*, 24(8), 2822–63.

Einwächter, S. G., & Simon, F. M. (2017). How digital remix and fan culture helped the Lego comeback. *Transformative Works and Cultures*, 25, https://doi.org/10.3983/twc.2017.01047.

Eisenhardt, K. M. (1989). Building theories from case study research. *Academy of Management Review*, 14(4), 532–50.

Elliott, J. (2005). *Using Narrative in Social Research: Qualitative and Quantitative Approaches*. London-New Delhi-Thousand Oaks: Sage Publications.

Emerson, R. M., Fretz, R. I., & Shaw, L. L. (2011). *Writing Ethnographic Fieldnotes*. Chicago: University of Chicago Press.

Emke, I. (1992). Medical authority and its discontents: A case of organized non-compliance. *Critical Sociology*, 19(3), 57–80.

English-Lueck, J. (2011). Prototyping self in Silicon Valley: Deep diversity as a framework for anthropological inquiry. *Anthropological Theory*, 11(1), 89–106.

Erickson, T. (1999). Persistant conversation: An introduction. *Journal of Computer-Mediated Communication*, 4(4), 10.1111/j.1083-6101.1999.tb00105.x.

Erikson, E., & Occhiuto, N. (2017). Social networks and macrosocial change. *Annual Review of Sociology*, 43(1), 229–48. Retrieved from https://www.annualreviews.org/doi/abs/10.1146/annurev-soc-060116-053633.

Erjavec, K., & Kovačič, M. P. (2012). "You don't understand, this is a new war!" Analysis of hate speech in news web sites' comments. *Mass Communication and Society, 15*(6), 899–920.

Evans, J. A., & Aceves, P. (2016). Machine translation: mining text for social theory. *Annual Review of Sociology, 42*, 21–50.

Faasse, K., Chatman, C. J., & Martin, L. R. (2016). A comparison of language use in pro-and anti-vaccination comments in response to a high profile Facebook post. *Vaccine, 34*(47), 5808–14.

Farrell, H. (2017). How Facebook stymies social science. *The Chronicle of Higher Education*, https://www.chronicle.com/article/How-Facebook-Stymies-Social/242090.

Feinberg, R. (2007). Dialectics of culture: Relativism in popular and anthropological discourse. *Anthropological Quarterly, 80*(3), 777–90. Retrieved from http://www.jstor.org/stable/30052723.

Ferrara, E., Varol, O., Davis, C., Menczer, F., & Flammini, A. (2016). The rise of social bots. *Communications of the ACM, 59*(7), 96–104.

Fetterman, D. M. (2009). *Ethnography: Step-by-step* (Vol. 17). Thousand Oaks—London—New Delhi: Sage Publications.

Fiesler, C., Wisniewski, P., Pater, J., & Andalibi, N. (2016). Exploring ethics and obligations for studying digital communities. Paper presented at the Proceedings of the 19th International Conference on Supporting Group Work.

Fiesler, C., Young, A., Peyton, T., Bruckman, A. S., Gray, M., Hancock, J., & Lutters, W. (2015). Ethics for studying online sociotechnical systems in a big data world. Paper presented at the Proceedings of the 18th ACM Conference Companion on Computer Supported Cooperative Work & Social Computing.

Fine, G. A. (1993). Ten lies of ethnography: Moral dilemmas of field research. *Journal of Contemporary Ethnography, 22*(3), 267–94.

Finkel, E. J., Eastwick, P. W., Karney, B. R., Reis, H. T., & Sprecher, S. (2012). Online dating. *Psychological Science in the Public Interest, 13*(1), 3–66. Retrieved from http://journals.sagepub.com/doi/abs/10.1177/1529100612436522.

Fischer, C. S. (2009). The 2004 GSS finding of shrunken social networks: An artifact? *American Sociological Review, 74*(4), 657–69.

Fischer, F. (2009). *Democracy and Expertise: Reorienting Policy Inquiry*. Oxford: Oxford University Press.

Fleming, P., & Spicer, A. (2007). *Contesting the Corporation: Struggle, Power and Resistance in Organizations*. Cambridge, UK—New York: Cambridge University Press.

Flick, U. (2014). *An Introduction to Qualitative Research*. London—New Delhi—Thousand Oaks, CA: Sage.

Flyvbjerg, B. (2006). Five misunderstandings about case-study research. *Qualitative Inquiry, 12*(2), 219–45.

Fotaki, M. (2014). Can consumer choice replace trust in the National Health Service in England? Towards developing an affective psychosocial conception of trust in health care. *Sociology of Health & Illness, 36*(8), 1276–94.

Foucault, M. (1980). *Power/Knowledge: Selected Interviews and Other Writings, 1972–1977*. New York: Pantheon Books.

Fownes, J. R., Yu, C., & Margolin, D. B. (2018). Twitter and climate change. *Sociology Compass, 12*(6), e12587. Retrieved from https://onlinelibrary.wiley.com/doi/abs/10.1111/soc4.12587.

Frade, C. (2016). Social theory and the politics of big data and method. *Sociology, 50*(5), 863–77. Retrieved from http://journals.sagepub.com/doi/abs/10.1177/0038038515614186.

Frank, R. (2011). *Newslore: Contemporary Folklore on the Internet.* Jackson: University of Missisipi Press.

Frenken, K., & Schor, J. (2017). Putting the sharing economy into perspective. *Environmental Innovation and Societal Transitions, 23*, 3–10.

Freund, K. (2016). "Fair use is legal use": Copyright negotiations and strategies in the fan-vidding community. *New Media & Society, 8*(7), 1347–63.

Fricker Jr, R. D. (2016). Sampling methods for online surveys. In N. G. Fielding, R. M. Lee, & G. Blank (eds.), *The SAGE Handbook of Online Research Methods* (pp. 184–202). London—Thousand Oaks—New Delhi: Sage.

Friedman, L. (2012). Wit as a political weapon: Satirists and censors. *Social Research, 79*(1), 87–112.

Fu, Q., Guo, X., & Land, K. C. (2018). Optimizing count responses in surveys: A machine-learning approach. *Sociological Methods & Research.* Retrieved from http://journals.sagepub.com/doi/abs/10.1177/0049124117747302.

Fuchs, C. (2010). Labor in informational capitalism and on the Internet. *The Information Society, 26*(3), 179–96. Retrieved from https://doi.org/10.1080/01972241003712215.

Gabaix, X., Gopikrishnan, P., Plerou, V., & Stanley, H. E. (2003). A theory of power-law distributions in financial market fluctuations. *Nature, 423*(6937), 267–70.

Gabriel, Y. (2004). *Myths, Stories, and Organizations: Premodern Narratives for our Times.* Oxford—New York: Oxford University Press.

Gaggiotti, H., Kostera, M., & Krzyworzeka, P. (2016). More than a method? Organisational ethnography as a way of imagining the social. *Culture and Organization, 23*(5), 325–40.

Gal, N., Shifman, L., & Kampf, Z. (2015). "It gets better": Internet memes and the construction of collective identity. *New Media & Society, 18*(8), 1698–714. Retrieved from https://doi.org/10.1177/1461444814568784.

Gamson, W. A. S., D. (1992). Media discourse as a symbolic contest: The bomb in political cartoons. *Sociological Forum, 7*(1), 55–86.

Garcia, A. C., Standlee, A. I., Bechkoff, J., & Cui, Y. (2009). Ethnographic approaches to the internet and computer-mediated communication. *Journal of Contemporary Ethnography, 38*(1), 52–84.

Gatson, S. N., & Zweerink, A. (2004). Ethnography online":natives" practising and inscribing community. *Qualitative Research, 4*(2), 179–200.

Geertz, C. (1973/2000). *The Interpretation of Cultures.* New York: Basic Books.

Geertz, C. (1974). "From the native's point of view": On the nature of anthropological understanding. *Bulletin of the American Academy of Arts and Sciences, 28*(1), 26–45.

George, G., Haas, M. R., & Pentland, A. (2014). Big Data and management. *Academy of Management Journal, 57*(2), 321–6. Retrieved from https://journals.aom.org/doi/abs/10.5465/amj.2014.4002.

Gerstl-Pepin, C. I., & Gunzenhauser, M. G. (2002). Collaborative team ethnography and the paradoxes of interpretation. *International Journal of Qualitative Studies in Education, 15*(2), 137–54.

Gerstl-Pepin, C. I, & Patrizio, K. (2009). Learning from Dumbledore's Pensieve: metaphor as an aid in teaching reflexivity in qualitative research. *Qualitative Research, 9*(3), 299–308. Retrieved from http://journals.sagepub.com/doi/abs/10.1177/1468794109105029.

Giddens, A. (1991). *Modernity and Self-identity: Self and Society in the Late Modern Age*. Cambridge: Polity Press.

Giles, J. (2010). Data sifted from Facebook wiped after legal threats. *New Scientist*, https://www.newscientist.com/article/dn18721-data-sifted-from-facebook-wiped-after-legal-threats/.

Gillespie, A., & Cornish, F. (2010). Intersubjectivity: Towards a Dialogical Analysis. *Journal for the Theory of Social Behaviour, 40*(1), 19–46. Retrieved from https://onlinelibrary.wiley.com/doi/abs/10.1111/j.1468-5914.2009.00419.x.

Gillespie, T. (2018). *Custodians of the Internet: Platforms, Content Moderation, and the Hidden Decisions that Shape Social Media*. New Haven: Yale University Press.

Ginsberg, J., Mohebbi, M. H., Patel, R. S., Brammer, L., Smolinski, M. S., & Brilliant, L. (2009). Detecting influenza epidemics using search engine query data. *Nature, 457*(7232), 1012–14.

Giorgino, V. M. B. (2015). Contemplative methods meet social sciences: Back to human experience as it is. *Journal for the Theory of Social Behaviour, 45*(4), 461–83.

Giroux, H. A. (2015). Public intellectuals against the neoliberal university. In N. K. Denzin & M. D. Giardina (eds.), *Qualitative Inquiry—Past, Present, and Future: A Critical Reader* (pp. 194–221). London—New York: Routledge.

Given, J. (2006). Narrating the digital turn: Data deluge, technomethodology, and other likely tales. *Qualitative Sociology Review, 2*(1): 54–65.

Gloor, P. (2005). *Swarm Creativity: Competitive Advantage through Collaborative Innovation Networks*. Oxford: Oxford University Press.

Gloor, P., Fronzetti Colladon, A., de Oliveira, J. M., & Rovelli, P. (2019). Put your money where your mouth is: Using deep learning to identify consumer tribes from word usage. *International Journal of Information Management*(forthcoming), DOI:10.1016/j.ijinfomgt.2019.1003.1011. Retrieved from http://www.sciencedirect.com/science/article/pii/S0268401218313057.

Goffman, A. (2014). *On the Run: Fugitive Life in an American City*. Chicago: University of Chicago Press.

Goffman, E. (1963). *Behavior in Public Places: Notes on the Social Organization of Gatherings*. New York: Free Press.

Golden-Biddle, K., & Locke, K. D. (1997). *Composing Qualitative Research*. Thousand Oaks, Calif.: Sage Publications.

Golder, S. A., & Macy, M. W. (2011). Diurnal and seasonal mood vary with work, sleep, and daylength across diverse cultures. *Science, 333*(6051), 1878–81.

Golder, S. A., & Macy, M. W. (2014). Digital footprints: Opportunities and challenges for online social research. *Annual Review of Sociology, 40*, 129–52

Gorman, G. E. (2008). "They can't read, but they sure can count": Flawed rules of the journal rankings game. *Online Information Review, 32*(6), 705–8.

Goulden, M., Greiffenhagen, C., Crowcroft, J., McAuley, D., Mortier, R., Radenkovic, M., & Sathiaseelan, A. (2017). Wild interdisciplinarity: ethnography and computer science. *International Journal of Social Research Methodology, 20*(2), 137–50. Retrieved from http://dx.doi.org/10.1080/13645579.2016.1152022.

Granger, B. I. (1960). *Political Satire in the American Revolution, 1763–1783.* Ithaca: Cornell University Press.

Granovetter, M. S. (1973). The strength of weak ties. *American Journal of Sociology, 78*(6), 1360–80.

Gray, G. (2007). Health policy and politics: Networks, ideas and power. *Health Sociology Review, 16*(3/4), 348.

Gray, M. L., & Suri, S. (2019). *Ghost Work: How to Stop Silicon Valley from Building a New Global Underclass.* Boston: Eamon Dolan Books.

Greene, V. S. (2019). "Deplorable" satire: Alt-right memes, white genocide tweets, and redpilling normies. *Studies in American Humor, 5*(1), 31–69.

Greenwood, D. J., González Santos, J. L., & Cantón, J. (1991). *Industrial Democracy as Process: Participatory Action Research in the Fagor Cooperative Group of Mondragón.* Assen/Maastricht-Stockholm: Van Gorcum Arbetslivscentrum.

Gruber, T., Szmigin, I., Reppel, A. E., & Voss, R. (2008). Designing and conducting online interviews to investigate interesting consumer phenomena. *Qualitative Market Research: An International Journal, 11*(3), 256–74. Retrieved from https://www.emeraldinsight.com/doi/abs/10.1108/13522750810879002.

Guitton, M. J. (2012). Living in the hutt space: Immersive process in the Star Wars role-play community of second life. *Computers in Human Behavior, 28*(5), 1681–91.

Gunraj, D. N., Drumm-Hewitt, A. M., Dashow, E. M., Upadhyay, S. S. N., & Klin, C. M. (2016). Texting insincerely: The role of the period in text messaging. *Computers in Human Behavior, 55*, 1067–75.

Hadley, G. (2014). *English for Academic Purposes in Neoliberal Universities: A Critical Grounded Theory.* New York—London: Springer.

Haggart, B., & Jablonski, M. (2017). Internet freedom and copyright maximalism: Contradictory hypocrisy or complementary policies? *The Information Society, 33*(3), 103–18. Retrieved from https://doi.org/10.1080/01972243.2017.1294128.

Halavais, A. (2015). Bigger sociological imaginations: Framing big social data theory and methods. *Information, Communication & Society, 18*(5), 583–94. Retrieved from http://dx.doi.org/10.1080/1369118X.2015.1008543.

Halford, S., & Savage, M. (2017). Speaking sociologically with Big Data: Symphonic social science and the future for Big Data research. *Sociology, 51*(6), 1132–48. Retrieved from http://journals.sagepub.com/doi/abs/10.1177/0038038517698639.

Hammersley, M. (1990). What's wrong with ethnography? The myth of theoretical description. *Sociology, 24*(4), 597–615.

Hammersley, M. (1992). Deconstructing the qualitative–quantitative divide. In J. Brannen (ed.), *Mixing Methods: Qualitative and Quantitative Research.* London: Avebury.

Hammersley, M., & Atkinson, P. (1995). *Ethnography: Principles in Practice* (2nd ed.). London—New York: Routledge.

Hance, M. A., Blackhart, G., & Dew, M. (2018). Free to be me: The relationship between the true self, rejection sensitivity, and use of online dating sites. *The*

Journal of Social Psychology, 158(4), 421–9. Retrieved from https://doi.org/10.108 0/00224545.2017.1389684.

Hancock, R., Crain-Dorough, M., Parton, B., & Oescher, J. (2010). Understanding and using virtual ethnography in virtual environments. In B. K. Daniel (ed.), *Handbook of Research on Methods and Techniques for Studying Virtual Communities: Paradigms and Phenomena* (Vol. 1, pp. 457). Hershey: Information Science Reference.

Haraway, D. (1988). Situated knowledges: The science question in feminism and the privilege of partial perspective. *Feminist Studies, 14*(3), 575–99.

Hargittai, E., & Walejko, G. (2008). The participation divide: Content creation and sharing in the digital age. *Information, Community and Society, 11*(2), 239–56.

Hassard, J., & Kelemen, M. (2010). Paradigm plurality in case study research. In M. A. J., G. Durepos, & E. Wiebe (eds.), *Encyclopedia of Case Study Research* (Vol. 2, pp. 647–52). London-New Delhi-Thousand Oaks: Sage.

Hawi, N. S., & Samaha, M. (2017). The relations among social media addiction, self-esteem, and life satisfaction in university students. *Social Science Computer Review, 35*(5), 576–86.

Hayes, D., & Wynyard, R. (2016). The McDonaldization of higher education revisited. In J. E. Cote & A. Furlong (eds.), *Routledge Handbook of the Sociology of Higher Education* (pp. 74–84). London—New York: Routledge.

Helberger, N., Leurdijk, A., & de Munck, S. (2010). User generated diversity: some reflections on how to improve the quality of amateur productions. *Communications & Strategies, 77*(1), 55–77. Retrieved from http://dare.uva.nl/personal/pure/en/publications/user-generated-diversity-some-reflections-on-how-to-improve-the-quality-of-amateur-productions(8313f433-8aaa-49cb-81d1-feac308b58c7).

Hennig, M., Brandes, U., Pfeffer, J., & Mergel, I. (2012). *Studying Social Networks: A Guide to Empirical Research.* Frankfurt—New York: Campus Verlag.

Henwood, F., Wyatt, S., Hart, A., & Smith, J. (2003). "Ignorance is bliss sometimes": Constraints on the emergence of the "informed patient" in the changing landscapes of health information. *Sociology of health & illness, 25*(6), 589–607.

Hergueux, J., & Jacquemet, N. (2015). Social preferences in the online laboratory: A randomized experiment. *Experimental Economics, 18*(2), 251–83.

Hergueux, J., & Jemielniak, D. (2019). Should digital files be considered a commons? Copyright infringement in the eyes of lawyers. *The Information Society, 36*(4), DOI:10.1080/01972243.01972019.01616019.

Herring, S. C. (1996). Linguistic and critical research on computer-mediated communication: Some ethical and scholarly considerations. *The Information Society, 12*(2), 153–68.

Herring, S. C., Job-Sluder, K., Scheckler, R., & Barab, S. (2002). Searching for safety online: Managing" trolling" in a feminist forum. *The Information Society, 18*(5), 371–84.

Hetcher, S. A. (2009). Using social norms to regulate fan fiction and remix culture. *University of Pennsylvania Law Review, 157*(6), 1869–935.

Hewson, C. (2016). Research design and tools for online research. In N. G. Fielding, R. M. Lee, & G. Blank (eds.), *The SAGE Handbook of Online Research Methods* (pp. 57–75). Thousand Oaks—New Delhi—London: Sage.

Hill, B. M., & Monroy-Hernández, A. (2013). The remixing dilemma: The trade-off between generativity and originality. *American Behavioral Scientist, 57*(5), 643–63.

Hill, K. (2012). How Target figured out a teen girl was pregnant before her father did. *Forbes, February, 16,* https://www.forbes.com/sites/kashmirhill/2012/2002/2016/how-target-figured-out-a-teen-girl-was-pregnant-before-her-father-did/.

Hine, C. (2000). *Virtual Ethnography.* Thousand Oaks: Sage.

Hine, C. (2013). *The Internet. Understanding Qualitative Research.* Oxford: Oxford University Press.

Hine, C. (2015). Mixed methods and multimodal research and Internet technologies. In S. N. Hesse-Biber & R. B. Johnson (eds.), *The Oxford Handbook of Multimethod and Mixed Methods Research Inquiry* (pp. 503–21). Oxford: Oxford University Press.

Hobbs, M., Owen, S., & Gerber, L. (2017). Liquid love? Dating apps, sex, relationships and the digital transformation of intimacy. *Journal of Sociology, 53*(2), 271–84.

Hodkinson, P. (2015). Grounded theory and inductive research. In N. Gilbert & P. Stoneman (eds.), *Researching Social Life.* London—New Delhi—Thousand Oaks: Sage.

Hodkinson, P. (2017). Bedrooms and beyond: Youth, identity and privacy on social network sites. *New Media & Society, 19*(2), 272–88. Retrieved from https://journals.sagepub.com/doi/abs/10.1177/1461444815605454.

Hogler, R., & Gross, M. A. (2009). Journal rankings and academic research: Two discourses about the quality of faculty work. *Management Communication Quarterly, 23*(1), 107–26.

Hollway, W., & Jefferson, T. (2000). *Doing Qualitative Research Differently: Free Association, Narrative and the Interview Method.* London—New Delhi—Thousand Oaks: Sage.

Holmes, K. (2012). Perceived difficulty of friendship maintenance online: Geographic factors. *Advances in Applied Sociology, 2*(04), 309.

Höpfl, H. (1995). Organizational rhetoric and the threat of ambivalence. *Studies in Cultures, Organizations and Societies, 1*(2), 175–87.

Hornsey, M. J., Harris, E. A., & Fielding, K. S. (2018). The psychological roots of anti-vaccination attitudes: A 24-nation investigation. *Health Psychology, 37*(4), 307–15.

Houghton, K. J., Upadhyay, S. S. N., & Klin, C. M. (2018). Punctuation in text messages may convey abruptness. Period. *Computers in Human Behavior, 80*, 112–21.

Hsu, W. F. (2014). Digital ethnography toward augmented empiricism: A new methodological framework. *Journal of Digital Humanities, 3*(1), http://journalofdigitalhumanities.org/3-1/digital-ethnography-towardaugmented-empiricism-by-wendy-hsu/.

Huang, G. C., Unger, J. B., Soto, D., Fujimoto, K., Pentz, M. A., Jordan-Marsh, M., & Valente, T. W. (2014). Peer influences: The impact of online and offline friendship networks on adolescent smoking and alcohol use. *Journal of Adolescent Health, 54*(5), 508–14.

Huc-Hepher, S. (2015). Big Web data, small focus: An ethnosemiotic approach to culturally themed selective Web archiving *Big Data & Society, 2*(2), DOI:10.1177/2053951715595823.

Humphreys, L. (2018). *The Qualified Self: Social Media and the Accounting of Everyday Life*. Cambridge, MA: MIT Press.

Hunter, C., Jemielniak, D., & Postuła, A. (2010). Temporal and spatial shifts within playful work. *Journal of Organizational Change Management, 23*(1), 87–102.

Hynes, M. (2018). Shining a brighter light into the digital "black box": A call for stronger sociological (re) engagement with digital technology design, development and adoption debates. *Irish Journal of Sociology, 26*(1), 94–126.

Ihm, J. (2018). Social implications of children's smartphone addiction: The role of support networks and social engagement. *Journal of Behavioral Addictions, 7*(2): 473–81.

Imber, J. B. (2009). *Trusting Doctors: The Decline of Moral Authority in American Medicine*. Princeton: Princeton University Press.

Ingold, T. (2014). That's enough about ethnography! *HAU: Journal of Ethnographic Theory, 4*(1), 383–95. Retrieved from https://www.journals.uchicago.edu/doi/abs/10.14318/hau4.1.021.

Ioannidis, J. P. A. (2005). Why most published research findings are false. *PLOS Med, 2*(8), e124.

Jane, E. A. (2014). "Back to the kitchen, cunt": Speaking the unspeakable about online misogyny. *Continuum, 28*(4), 558–70. Retrieved from https://doi.org/10.1080/10304312.2014.924479. doi:10.1080/10304312.2014.924479

Janesick, V. J. (2016). *Contemplative Qualitative Inquiry: Practicing the Zen of Research*. London—New York: Routledge.

Jarrett, K. (2003). Labour of love: An archaeology of affect as power in e-commerce. *Journal of Sociology, 39*(4), 335–51.

Jasanoff, S., Markle, G. E., Peterson, J. C., & Pinch, T. (eds.). (2001). *Handbook of Science and Technology Studies*. London-New Delphi-Thousand Oaks, CA: Sage Publications.

Jean, N., Burke, M., Xie, M., Davis, W. M., Lobell, D. B., & Ermon, S. (2016). Combining satellite imagery and machine learning to predict poverty. *Science, 353*(6301), 790–4.

Jemielniak, D. (2006). The management science as a practical field: In support of action research. *The International Journal of Knowledge, Culture and Change Management 6*(3), 163–70.

Jemielniak, D. (2007). Managers as lazy, stupid careerists? Contestation and stereotypes among software engineers. *Journal of Organizational Change Management, 20*(4), 491–508.

Jemielniak, D. (2008a). Little Johnny and the Wizard of OS: The PC user as a fool hero. In M. Kostera (ed.), *Organizational Olympians: Heroes and Heroines of Organizational Myths*. London: Palgrave.

Jemielniak, D. (2008b). Software engineers or artists—programmers' identity choices. *Tamara Journal for Critical Organization Inquiry, 7*(1), 20–36.

Jemielniak, D. (2009). Time as symbolic currency in knowledge work. *Information and Organization, 19*, 277–93.

Jemielniak, D. (2013). Netnografia, czyli etnografia wirtualna—nowa forma badań etnograficznych. *Prakseologia, 154*, 97–116.

Jemielniak, D. (2014). *Common Knowledge? An Ethnography of Wikipedia*. Stanford, CA: Stanford University Press.

Jemielniak, D. (2015). Naturally emerging regulation and the danger of delegitimizing conventional leadership: Drawing on the example of Wikipedia. In H. Bradbury (ed.), *The SAGE Handbook of Action Research*. London, UK—New Delphi, India—Thousand Oaks, CA: Sage.

Jemielniak, D. (2016a). Breaking the glass ceiling on Wikipedia. *Feminist Review,* 113(1), 103–8.

Jemielniak, D. (2016b). Wikimedia movement governance: The limits of a-hierarchical organization. *Journal of Organizational Change Management, 29*(3), 361–78.

Jemielniak, D., & Aibar, E. (2016). Bridging the gap between Wikipedia and Academia. *Journal of the Association for Information Science and Technology, 67*(7), 1773–6.

Jemielniak, D., & Greenwood, D. J. (2015). Wake up or perish: Neo-liberalism, the social sciences, and salvaging the public university. *Cultural Studies* ↔ *Critical Methodologies, 15*(1), 72–82.

Jemielniak, D., & Jemielniak, J. (2002). Public and private space: The final frontier. In B. Czarniawska & R. Solli (eds.), *Organizing Metropolitan Space and Discourse*. Malmo: Liber.

Jemielniak, D., & Kostera, M. (2010). Narratives of irony and failure in ethnographic work. *Canadian Journal of Administrative Sciences, 27*(4), 335–47.

Jemielniak, D., Masukume, G., & Wilamowski, M. (2019). The most influential medical journals, according to Wikipedia: How quickly does new medical research propagate in a non-academic encyclopedia. *Journal of Medical Internet Research, 21*(1), e11429.

Jemielniak, D., & Przegalinska, A. (2020). *Collaborative Society*. Cambridge, MA: MIT Press.

Jemielniak, D., Przegalińska, A., & Stasik, A. (2018). Anecdotal evidence: Understanding organizational reality through organizational humorous tales. *Humor: International Journal of Humor Research, 31*(3), 539–61. Retrieved from https://www.degruyter.com/view/j/humr.2018.31.issue-3/humor-2017-0059/humor-2017-0059.xml.

Jemielniak, D., & Raburski, T. (2014). Liquid collaboration. In J. Kociatkiewicz & M. Kostera (eds.), *Liquid Organization: Zygmunt Bauman and Organization Theory*. London, UK—New York, NY: Palgrave.

Jemielniak, D., & Wilamowski, M. (2017). Cultural diversity of quality of information on Wikipedias. *Journal of the Association for Information Science and Technology, 68*(10), 2460–70.

Jenkins, H. (2006). *Convergence Culture: Where Old and New Media Collide*. New York: NYU Press.

Jenkins, H., Ford, S., & Green, J. (2018). *Spreadable Media: Creating Value and Meaning in a Networked Culture*. New York: NYU Press.

Jiang, Y. (2016). Cybernationalism. In G. Ritzer (ed.), *The Blackwell Encyclopedia of Sociology* (pp. doi:10.1002/9781405165518.wbeos9781405160721). New York: John Wiley & Sons.

Jick, T. D. (1979). Mixing qualitative and quantitative methods: Triangulation in action. *Administrative Science Quarterly, 24*(4), 602–11.

Jinasena, S. (2014). Social media impact on youth depression. *Sociology and Anthropology, 2*(7), 291–4.

John, N. A. (2017). *The Age of Sharing*. Cambridge, UK—Malden, MA: Polity.

Johnson, S. L., Faraj, S., & Kudaravalli, S. (2014). Emergence of power laws in online communities: The role of social mechanisms and preferential attachment. *Mis Quarterly, 38*(3), 795–808.

Jordan, T., & Taylor, P. A. (2004). *Hacktivism and Cyberwars: Rebels with a Cause?* London—New York: Routledge.

Joseph, K., Wei, W., Benigni, M., & Carley, K. M. (2016). A social-event based approach to sentiment analysis of identities and behaviors in text. *The Journal of Mathematical Sociology, 40*(3), 137–66. Retrieved from https://doi.org/10.1080/00 22250X.2016.1159206.

Julien, C. (2015). Bourdieu, social capital and online interaction. *Sociology, 49*(2), 356–73.

Jungherr, A., Schoen, H., Posegga, O., & Jürgens, P. (2017). Digital trace data in the study of public opinion: An indicator of attention toward politics rather than political support. *Social Science Computer Review, 35*(3), 336–56.

Kahn, W. A. (1989). Toward a sense of organizational humor: Implications for organizational diagnosis and change. *The Journal of Applied Behavioral Science, 25*(1), 45–63.

Kamińska, M. (2013). Masz anoreksję?chcesz mieć anoreksję?to blog dla Ciebie;). In M. Sokołowski (ed.), *Nowe media i wyzwania współczesności*. Toruń: Wydawnictwo Adam Marszałek.

Kamińska, M. (2014). Autoetnografia jako technika badań etnograficznych w Internecie. *Przegląd Socjologii Jakościowej, 10*(3), 170–83.

Kata, A. (2012). Anti-vaccine activists, Web 2.0, and the postmodern paradigm–An overview of tactics and tropes used online by the anti-vaccination movement. *Vaccine, 30*(25), 3778–89.

Katz, Y., & Shifman, L. (2017). Making sense? The structure and meanings of digital memetic nonsense. *Information, Communication & Society, 20*(6), 825–42.

Kaufmann, K. (2018). Navigating a new life: Syrian refugees and their smartphones in Vienna. *Information, Communication & Society, 21*(6), 882–98.

Kazmer, M. M., & Xie, B. (2008). Qualitative interviewing in Internet studies: Playing with the media, playing with the method. *Information, Communication & Society, 11*(2), 257–78. Retrieved from https://doi.org/10.1080/13691180801946333.

Keen, A. (2007). *The Cult of the Amateur: How Today's Internet Is Killing Our Culture*. New York: Broadway Business.

Kelty, C. M. (2004). Punt to culture. *Anthropological Quarterly, 77*(3), 547–58.

Khondker, H. H. (2011). Role of the new media in the Arab Spring. *Globalizations, 8*(5), 675–9.

Kidd, D., & McIntosh, K. (2016). Social media and social movements. *Sociology Compass, 10*(9), 785–94.

Kim, A. Y., & Escobedo-Land, A. (2015). OkCupid data for introductory statistics and data science courses. *Journal of Statistics Education, 23*(2), 1–25.

Kimmerle, J., Gerbing, K.-K., Cress, U., & Thiel, A. (2012). Exchange of complementary and alternative medical knowledge in sport-related Internet fora. *Sociology of Sport Journal, 29*(3), 348–64.

Kirkegaard, E. O., & Bjerrekær, J. D. (2016). The OKCupid dataset: A very large public dataset of dating site users. *Open Differential Psychology, 46*, 1–10.

Klein, N. (2000). *No Logo: No Space, No Choice, No Jobs: Taking Aim at the Brand Bullies* (1st ed.). Toronto: A.A. Knopf Canada.

Klumbytė, N. (2012). Soviet ethical citizenship: Morality, the state, and laughter in Lithuania, 1964–85. In N. Klumbytė & G. Sharafutdinova (eds.), *Soviet Society in the Era of Late Socialism.* New York: Lexington Books.

Knobel, M., & Lankshear, C. (2007). Online memes, affinities, and cultural production. In C. Lankshear, M. Knobel, C. Bigum, & M. A. Peters (eds.), *A New Literacies Sampler* (pp. 199–227). New York—Frankfurt: Peter Lang.

Knott, S. (2013). Design in the age of prosumption: The craft of design after the object. *Design and Culture, 5*(1), 45–67.

Konecki, K. (1990). Dependancy and worker flirting. In B. A. Turner (ed.), *Organizational Symbolism* (pp. 55–66). Berlin-New York: Gruyter.

Konecki, K. (2008a). Grounded theory and serendipity: Natural history of a research. *Qualitative Sociology Review, 4*(1), 171–88.

Konecki, K. (2008b). Triangulation and dealing with the realness of qualitative research. *Qualitative Sociology Review, 4*(3), 7–28.

Konieczny, P. (2009). Governance, organization, and democracy on the Internet: The iron law and the evolution of Wikipedia. *Sociological Forum, 24*(1), 162–92.

Konieczny, P. (2016). Teaching with Wikipedia in a 21st-century classroom: Perceptions of Wikipedia and its educational benefits. *Journal of the Association for Information Science and Technology, 67*(7), 1523–34. Retrieved from http://dx.doi.org/10.1002/asi.23616.

Konstan, J. A., Simon Rosser, B. R., Ross, M. W., Stanton, J., & Edwards, W. (2005). The story of subject naught: A cautionary but optimistic tale of Internet survey research. *Journal of Computer-Mediated Communication, 10*(2), doi.org/10.1111/j.1083-6101.2005.tb00248.x.

Kosinski, M., Stillwell, D., & Graepel, T. (2013). Private traits and attributes are predictable from digital records of human behavior. *Proceedings of the National Academy of Sciences, 110*(15), 5802–5.

Kosseff, J. (2016). The hazards of cyber-vigilantism. *Computer Law & Security Review, 32*(4), 642–9. Retrieved from http://www.sciencedirect.com/science/article/pii/S0267364916300863.

Kostakis, V. (2018). In defense of digital commoning. *Organization, 25*(6), 812–18. Retrieved from https://doi.org/10.1177/1350508417749887

Kozinets, R. V. (2002). The field behind the screen: Using netnography for marketing research in online communities. *Journal of Marketing Research, 39*(1), 61–72.

Kozinets, R. V. (2010). *Netnography: Doing Ethnographic Research Online.* Los Angeles, CA—London: Sage.

Kreiss, D. (2016). Seizing the moment: The presidential campaigns' use of Twitter during the 2012 electoral cycle. *New Media & Society, 18*(8), 1473–90.

Kreiss, D., Finn, M., & Turner, F. (2011). The limits of peer production: Some reminders from Max Weber for the network society. *New Media & Society, 13*(2), 243–59.

Kristofferson, K., White, K., & Peloza, J. (2014). The nature of slacktivism: How the social observability of an initial act of token support affects subsequent prosocial action. *Journal of Consumer Research, 40*(6), 1149–66.

Kunda, G. (1992). *Engineering Culture: Control and Commitment in a High-tech Corporation* (rev. ed.). Philadelphia, PA: Temple University Press.

Kuss, D. J., & Griffiths, M. D. (2017). Social networking sites and addiction: Ten lessons learned. *International Journal of Environmental Research and Public Health, 14*(311), doi:10.3390/ijerph14030311.

Kuwabara, K. (2015). Do reputation systems undermine trust? Divergent effects of enforcement type on generalized trust and trustworthiness. *American Journal of Sociology, 120*(5), 1390–428.

Labaree, R. V. (2002). The risk of "going observationalist": Negotiating the hidden dilemmas of being an insider participant observer. *Qualitative Research, 2*(1), 97–122.

Lageson, S. E. (2016). Digital punishment's tangled web. *Contexts, 15*(1), 22–7.

Lageson, S. E., & Maruna, S. (2018). Digital degradation: Stigma management in the Internet age. *Punishment & Society, 20*(1), 113–33.

Laidlaw, E. B. (2017). Online shaming and the right to privacy. *Laws, 6*(1), doi:10.3390/laws6010003.

Lakhani, K. R., & Wolf, R. (2003). Why hackers do what they do: Understanding motivation and effort in free/open source software projects. In J. Feller, B. Fitzgerald, S. A. Hissam, & K. R. Lakhani (eds.), *Perspectives on Free and Open Source Software*. Cambridge, MA: MIT Press.

Langer, R., & Beckman, S. C. (2005). Sensitive research topics: Netnography revisited. *Qualitative Market Research: An International Journal, 8*(2), 189–203.

Lantz, P. M., Viruell-Fuentes, E., Israel, B. A., Softley, D., & Guzman, R. (2001). Can communities and academia work together on public health research? Evaluation results from a community-based participatory research partnership in Detroit. *Journal of Urban Health, 78*(3), 495–507.

LaRose, R., & Tsai, H.-y. S. (2014). Completion rates and non-response error in online surveys: Comparing sweepstakes and pre-paid cash incentives in studies of online behavior. *Computers in Human Behavior, 34*, 110–19.

Lassiter, L. E. (2001). From" reading over the shoulders of natives" to" reading alongside natives," literally: toward a collaborative and reciprocal ethnography. *Journal of Anthropological Research, 57*(2), 137–49.

Latour, B. (1986). The powers of association. In J. Law (ed.), *Power, Action and Belief—A New Sociology of Knowledge?* London—Boston—Henley: Routledge & Kegan Paul.

Latour, B. (1987). *Science in Action*. Cambridge: Harvard University Press.

Latusek, D., & Cook, K. S. (2012). Trust in transitions. *Kyklos, 65*(4), 512–25.

Latusek, D., & Jemielniak, D. (2007). (Dis)trust in software projects: A thrice told tale. On dynamic relationships between software engineers, IT project managers, and customers. *The International Journal of Technology, Knowledge and Society, 3*(10), 117–25.

Latusek, D., & Jemielniak, D. (2008). Sources of uncertainty in project management: A "real life" account. *The International Journal of Technology, Knowledge and Society.* 4(5), 143–50.

Latzko-Toth, G., Bonneau, C., & Millettte, M. (2017). Small data, thick data: Thickening strategies for trace-based social media research. In L. Sloan &

A. Quan-Haase (eds.), *The SAGE Handbook of Social Media Research Methods*. Los Angeles—London—New Delhi: Sage.

Law, J. (2004). *After Method: Mess in Social Science Research*. London—New York: Routledge.

Lazer, D., Kennedy, R., King, G., & Vespignani, A. (2014). The parable of Google flu: Traps in Big Data analysis. *Science, 343*(6176), 1203–5.

Lazer, D., Pentland, A. S., Adamic, L., Aral, S., Barabasi, A. L., Brewer, D.,... Gutmann, M. (2009). Life in the network: The coming age of computational social science. *Science, 323*(5915), 721–3.

Lazer, D., & Radford, J. (2017). Data ex Machina: Introduction to Big Data. *Annual Review of Sociology, 43*(1), 19–39. Retrieved from http://www.annualreviews.org/doi/abs/10.1146/annurev-soc-060116-053457.

Leach, E. (1982). *Social Anthropology*. Oxford: Oxford University Press.

Leadbeater, C. (2008). *We-think: Mass Innovation. Not Mass Production*. London: Profile Books.

Leander, K. M., & McKim, K. K. (2003). Tracing the everyday "sitings" of adolescents on the Internet: A strategic adaptation of ethnography across online and offline spaces. *Education, Communication & Information, 3*(2), 211–40.

Leetaru, K. (2011). Culturomics 2.0: Forecasting large-scale human behavior using global news media tone in time and space. *First Monday, 16*(9), http://firstmonday.org/ojs/index.php/fm/article/view/3663/3040.

Leshinsky, R., & Schatz, L. (2018). "I don't think my landlord will find out": Airbnb and the challenges of enforcement. *Urban Policy and Research, 36*(4), 417–28.

Lessig, L. (2004). *Free Culture: How Big Media Uses Technology and the Law to Lock Down Culture and Control Creativity*. New York: Penguin Press.

Lessig, L. (2008). *Remix Making Art and Commerce Thrive in the Hybrid Economy*. Retrieved from http://www.archive.org/details/LawrenceLessigRemix

Lévy, P. (1997). Welcome to virtuality. *Digital Creativity, 8*(1), 3–10.

Lewandowsky, S., Ecker, U. K. H., & Cook, J. (2017). Beyond misinformation: understanding and coping with the "Post-Truth" era. *Journal of Applied Research in Memory and Cognition, 6*(4), 353–69. Retrieved from http://www.sciencedirect.com/science/article/pii/S2211368117300700.

Lichterman, P. (2017). Interpretive reflexivity in ethnography. *Ethnography, 18*(1), 35–45.

Light, D. W. (2007). Professional dominance in medicine. In G. Ritzer (ed.), *The Blackwell Encyclopedia of Sociology* (pp. 1–5). New York: Blackwell.

Lis, A., & Stasik, A. K. (2017). Hybrid forums, knowledge deficits and the multiple uncertainties of resource extraction: Negotiating the local governance of shale gas in Poland. *Energy Research & Social Science, 28*, 29–36.

Literat, I. (2017). The power of a pony: Youth literacies, participatory culture, and active meaning making. *Journal of Adolescent & Adult Literacy, 61*(1), 113–16. Retrieved from https://ila.onlinelibrary.wiley.com/doi/abs/10.1002/jaal.661.

Livingstone, S., & Das, R. (2013). The end of audiences? Theoretical echoes of reception amid the uncertainties of use. In J. Hartley, J. Burgess, & A. Bruns (eds.), *A Companion to New Media Dynamics* (pp. 104–22). Walden—Oxford—West Sussex: Wiley-Blackwell.

Llorente, A., Garcia-Herranz, M., Cebrian, M., & Moro, E. (2015). Social media fingerprints of unemployment. *PLoS ONE, 10*(5), e0128692.

Lo Iacono, V., Symonds, P., & Brown, D. H. (2016). Skype as a tool for qualitative research interviews. *Sociological Research Online, 21*(2), 1–15.

Lobo, L. (1990). Becoming a marginal native. *Anthropos, 85*, 125–38.

Lockie, S. (2017). Post-truth politics and the social sciences. *Environmental Sociology, 3*(1), 1–5. Retrieved from https://doi.org/10.1080/23251042.2016.1273444.

Lokot, T., & Diakopoulos, N. (2016). News bots: Automating news and information dissemination on Twitter. *Digital Journalism, 4*(6), 682–99.

Lotan, G., Graeff, E., Ananny, M., Gaffney, D., & Pearce, I. (2011). The Arab Spring. The revolutions were tweeted: Information flows during the 2011 Tunisian and Egyptian revolutions. *International Journal of Communication, 5*(31), 1375–405.

Lumsden, K., & Morgan, H. (2017). Media framing of trolling and online abuse: Silencing strategies, symbolic violence, and victim blaming. *Feminist Media Studies, 17*(6), 926–40. Retrieved from https://doi.org/10.1080/14680777.2017.1316755.

Lupton, D. (2012). *Digital Sociology: An Introduction*. Sydney: University of Sydney.

Lupton, D. (2014). Critical perspectives on digital health technologies. *Sociology Compass, 8*(12), 1344–59.

Lupton, D. (2016). *The Quantified Self: A Sociology of Self-tracking Cultures*. Cambridge, UK—Malden, MA: Polity.

Lyall, B., & Robards, B. (2018). Tool, toy and tutor: Subjective experiences of digital self-tracking. *Journal of Sociology, 54*(1), 108–24.

Lynch, O. H. (2009). Kitchen antics: The importance of humor and maintaining professionalism at work. *Journal of Applied Communication Research, 37*(4), 444–64.

MacIntyre, A. C. (1981). *After Virtue: A Study in Moral Theory*. Notre Dame, Ind.: University of Notre Dame Press.

Madden, R. (2017). *Being Ethnographic: A Guide to the Theory and Practice of Ethnography*. New Delhi—London—Thousand Oaks: Sage.

Malik, M. M., & Pfeffer, J. (2016). A macroscopic analysis of news content in Twitter. *Digital Journalism, 4*(8), 955–79. Retrieved from https://doi.org/10.1080/2167081 1.2015.1133249.

Malta, S., & Farquharson, K. (2014). The initiation and progression of late-life romantic relationships. *Journal of Sociology, 50*(3), 237–51.

March, E., Grieve, R., Marrington, J., & Jonason, P. K. (2017). Trolling on Tinder® (and other dating apps): Examining the role of the Dark Tetrad and impulsivity. *Personality and Individual Differences, 110*, 139–43. Retrieved from http://www.sciencedirect.com/science/article/pii/S0191886917300260.

Marcus, G. E. (1995). Ethnography in/of the world system: The emergence of multi-sited ethnography. *Annual Review of Anthropology, 24*, 95–117.

Markham, A. (2008). The methods, politics, and ethics of representation in online ethnography. In N. K. Denzin & Y. S. Lincoln (eds.), *Collecting and Interpreting Qualitative Materials* (Vol. 4, pp. 245–75). Los Angeles—London—New Delhi—Singapore: Sage.

Marres, N., & Weltevrede, E. (2013). Scraping the social? Issues in live social research. *Journal of Cultural Economy, 6*(3), 313–35. Retrieved from https://doi.org/10.1080/17530350.2013.772070.

Marsh, J. (2016). The relationship between online and offline play: Friendship and exclusion. In C. Richards & A. Burn (eds.), *Children's Games in the New Media Age* (pp. 123–46). London—New York: Routledge.

Marx, G. T. (2001). Murky conceptual waters: The public and private. *Ethics and Information Technology, 3,* 157–69.

Mason, J. (2006). Mixing methods in a qualitatively driven way. *Qualitative Research, 6*(1), 9–25.

Mason, M. (2009). *The Pirate's Dilemma: How Youth Culture Is Reinventing Capitalism.* New York: Free Press.

Massanari, A. L. (2015). *Participatory Culture, Community, and Play. Learning from Reddit.* Frankfurt—New York: Peter Lang.

Mastrandrea, R., Fournet, J., & Barrat, A. (2015). Contact patterns in a high school: A comparison between data collected using wearable sensors, contact diaries and friendship surveys. *PLoS ONE, 10*(9), e0136497.

Mattson, G. (2015). The modern career of "the oldest profession" and the social embeddedness of metaphors. *American Journal of Cultural Sociology, 3*(2), 191–223. Retrieved from https://doi.org/10.1057/ajcs.2015.4.

Maturo, A., Mori, L., & Moretti, V. (2016). An ambiguous health education: The quantified self and the medicalization of the mental sphere. *Italian Journal of Sociology of Education, 8*(3), 248–68.

Mauss, M. (1954/2001). *The Gift: Form and Reason for Exchange in Archaic Societies.* London: Routledge.

McCarthy, M. T. (2016). The big data divide and its consequences. *Sociology Compass, 10*(12), 1131–40. Retrieved from http://dx.doi.org/10.1111/soc4.12436.

McCarty, C., Lubbers, M. J., Vacca, R., & Molina, J. L. (2019). *Conducting Personal Network Research: A Practical Guide.* New York—London: Guilford Press.

McClean, S., & Moore, R. (2016). Folk healing, authenticity and fraud. In A. van Eck Duymaer van Twist (ed.), *Minority Religions and Fraud: In Good Faith* (pp. 91–112). London—New York: Routledge.

McDonald, K. (2015). From indymedia to anonymous: Rethinking action and identity in digital cultures. *Information, Communication & Society, 18*(8), 968–82.

McFarland, D. A., Lewis, K., & Goldberg, A. (2016). Sociology in the era of Big Data: The ascent of forensic social science. *The American Sociologist, 47*(1), 12–35. Retrieved from https://doi.org/10.1007/s12108-015-9291-8.

McLean, A. L., A. (eds.). (2007). *The Shadow Side of Fieldwork: Exploring the Blurred Borders between Ethnography and Life.* Oxford: Blackwell.

Meder, T. (2008). Internet. In D. Haase (ed.), *The Greenwood Encyclopedia of Folktales and Fairy Tales.* Westport-London: Greenwood Press.

Meho, L. I. (2006). E-mail interviewing in qualitative research: A methodological discussion. *Journal of the American Society for Information Science and Technology, 57*(10), 1284–95.

Mejias, U. (2010). The Twitter revolution must die. *International Journal of Learning and Media, 2*(4), 3–5.

Meyer, J. W., & Rowan, B. (1977). Institutionalized organizations: Formal structure as myth and ceremony. *The American Journal of Sociology, 83*(2), 340–63.

Michel, J.-B., Shen, Y. K., Aiden, A. P., Veres, A., Gray, M. K., Pickett, J. P.,... Orwant, J. (2010). Quantitative analysis of culture using millions of digitized books. *Science, 331*(6014), 176–82.

Milan, S. (2013). *Social Movements and Their Technologies. Wiring Social Change.* London—New York: Palgrave Macmillan.

Miller, D., & Slater, D. (2001). *The Internet: An Ethnographic Approach.* Oxford: Berg Publishers.

Miller, P. (2012). Wprowadzenie do obserwacji online: warianty i ograniczenia techniki badawczej. *Przegląd Socjologii Jakościowej, VIII*(1), 76–97.

Millington, B., & Millington, R. (2015). "The datafication of everything": Toward a sociology of sport and big data. *Sociology of Sport Journal, 32*(2), 140–60.

Milner, R. M. (2013a). Media lingua franca: Fixity, novelty, and vernacular creativity in Internet memes. *AoIR Selected Papers of Internet Research, 3*(14), https://spir. aoir.org/index.php/spir/article/view/806.

Milner, R. M. (2013b). Pop polyvocality: Internet memes, public participation, and the Occupy Wall Street movement. *International JOurnal of Communication Systems, 7*(34).

Mizruchi, M. S., & Stearns, L. B. (1988). A longitudinal study of the formation of interlocking directorates. *Administrative Science Quarterly, 33*, 194–210.

Mod, G. B. (2010). Reading romance: The impact Facebook rituals can have on a romantic relationship. *Journal of Comparative Research in Anthropology & Sociology, 1*(2), 61–77.

Moloney, M. E., & Love, T. P. (2018). Assessing online misogyny: Perspectives from sociology and feminist media studies. *Sociology Compass, 12*(5). 12:e12577.

Monroy-Hernandez, A., Hill, B. M., Gonzalez-Rivero, J., & boyd, d. (2011). Computers can't give credit: how automatic attribution falls short in an online remixing community. Paper presented at the Proceedings of the SIGCHI Conference on Human Factors in Computing Systems, Vancouver, BC, Canada.

Montgomery, J. D. (1992). Job search and network composition: Implications of the strength-of-weak-ties hypothesis. *American Sociological Review, 57*(5), 586–96.

Morozov, E. (2009). Iran: Downside to the "Twitter Revolution." *Dissent, 56*(4), 10–14.

Mouffe, C. (2008). *Polityczność.* Warszawa: Wydawnictwo Krytyki Politycznej.

Murthy, D. (2008). Digital ethnography An examination of the use of new technologies for social research. *Sociology, 42*(5), 837–55.

Nadai, E., & Maeder, C. (2005). Fuzzy fields. Multi-sited ethnography in sociological research. *Forum: Qualitative Social Research, 6*(3), http://www.qualitative-research.net/index.php/fqs/article/view/22/47.

Nagle, A. (2017). *Kill All Normies: Online Culture Wars from 4chan and Tumblr to Trump and the alt-right.* Alresford: John Hunt Publishing.

Nakayama, T. K. (2017). What's next for whiteness and the Internet. *Critical Studies in Media Communication, 34*(1), 68–72. Retrieved from http://dx.doi.org/10.1080/15295036.2016.1266684.

Narayan, K. (1993). How native is a "native" anthropologist? *American Anthropologist, 95*(3), 671–86.

Narli, N. (2018). Life, connectivity and integration of Syrian refugees in Turkey: Surviving through a smartphone. *Questions de communication, 33*(1), 269–86.

Retrieved from https://www.cairn.info/revue-questions-de-communication-2018-1-page-269.htm.

Nettleton, S., Burrows, R., & O'Malley, L. (2005). The mundane realities of the everyday lay use of the Internet for health, and their consequences for media convergence. *Sociology of Health & Illness, 27*(7), 972–92.

Neville, S., Adams, J., & Cook, C. (2016). Using Internet-based approaches to collect qualitative data from vulnerable groups: Reflections from the field. *Contemporary Nurse, 52*(6), 657–68.

Newett, L., Churchill, B., & Robards, B. (2018). Forming connections in the digital era: Tinder, a new tool in young Australian intimate life. *Journal of Sociology, 54*(3), 346–61. Retrieved from http://journals.sagepub.com/doi/abs/10.1177/1440783317728584.

Newman, M., Barabási A-L. & Watts, D. J. (2011). *The Structure and Dynamics of Networks*. Princeton: Princeton University Press.

Nicholl, H., Tracey, C., Begley, T., King, C., & Lynch, A. M. (2017). Internet use by parents of children with rare conditions: Findings from a study on parents' Web information needs. *Journal of medical Internet research, 19*(2), e51. Retrieved from http://www.ncbi.nlm.nih.gov/pmc/articles/PMC5350458/.

Nichols, T. (2017). *The Death of Expertise: The Campaign against Established Knowledge and Why It Matters*. Oxford: Oxford University Press.

Nicholson, B. (2012). Counting Culture; or, How to Read Victorian Newspapers from a Distance. *Journal of Victorian Culture, 17*(2), 238–46. Retrieved from http://dx.doi.org/10.1080/13555502.2012.683331.

Nie, N. H., & Hillygus, D. S. (2002). The impact of Internet use on sociability: Time-diary findings. *It & Society, 1*(1), 1–20.

Nissenbaum, A., & Shifman, L. (2017). Internet memes as contested cultural capital: The case of 4chan's/b/board. *New Media & Society, 19*(4), 483–501.

Nkomo, S. M. (2009). The seductive power of academic journal rankings: Challenges of searching for the otherwise. *Academy of Management Learning & Education, 8*(1), 106–21.

Nocera, J. L. A. (2002). Ethnography and hermeneutics in cybercultural research accessing IRC virtual communities. *Journal of Computer-Mediated Communication, 7*(2), 0 doi: 10.1111/j.1083-6101.2002.tb00146.x.

Norlock, K. J. (2017). Online shaming. *Social Philosophy Today, 33*, 187–197.

Nowak, A. W. (2013). Rozproszony ekspert a rozproszona baza danych–blogi sceptyczne, naukowe a struktury wiedzy. *Człowiek i Społeczeństwo, 36*(2), 257–75.

O'Connor, B., & Mackeogh, C. (2007). New media communities: Performing identity in an online women's magazine. *Irish Journal of Sociology, 16*(2), 97–116. Retrieved from http://journals.sagepub.com/doi/abs/10.1177/079160350701600206.

O'Hara, K., & Stevens, D. (2015). Echo chambers and online radicalism: Assessing the Internet's complicity in violent extremism. *Policy & Internet, 7*(4), 401–22. Retrieved from https://onlinelibrary.wiley.com/doi/abs/10.1002/poi3.88.

Olguín, D. O., Waber, B. N., Kim, T., Mohan, A., Ara, K., & Pentland, A. (2009). Sensible organizations: Technology and methodology for automatically measuring organizational behavior. *IEEE Transactions on Systems, Man, and Cybernetics, Part B (Cybernetics), 39*(1), 43–55.

Olssen, M. (2016). Neoliberal competition in higher education today: Research, accountability and impact. *British Journal of Sociology of Education, 37*(1), 129–48. Retrieved from https://doi.org/10.1080/01425692.2015.1100530.

Ong, W. J. (2002). *Orality and Literacy*. London: Routledge.

Onuch, O. (2015). EuroMaidan protests in Ukraine: Social media versus social networks. *Problems of Post-Communism, 62*(4), 217–35.

Oring, E. (2004). Risky business: Political jokes under repressive regimes. *Western Folklore, 63*(3), 209–36.

Ostertag, S. F., & Ortiz, D. G. (2017). Can social media use produce enduring social ties? Affordances and the case of Katrina bloggers. *Qualitative Sociology, 40*(1), 59–82.

Oxford English Dictionary. (2018). Gay. https://en.oxforddictionaries.com/definition/gay.

Özbilgin, M. F. (2009). From journal rankings to making sense of the world. *Academy of Management Learning & Education, 8*(1), 113–21.

Paccagnella, L. (1997). Getting the seats of your pants dirty: Strategies for ethnographic research on virtual communities. *Journal of Computer-Mediated Communication, 3*(1), 0 doi: 10.1111/j.1083-6101.1997.tb00065.x.

Palla, G., Barabási, A.-L., & Vicsek, T. (2007). Quantifying social group evolution. *Nature, 446*, 664.

Pantzar, M., Ruckenstein, M., & Mustonen, V. (2017). Social rhythms of the heart. *Health Sociology Review, 26*(1), 22–37. Retrieved from https://doi.org/10.1080/14461242.2016.1184580.

Pasquale, F. (2016). Two narratives of platform capitalism. *Yale Law & Policy Review, 35*, 309–19.

Payne, G., & Williams, M. (2005). Generalization in qualitative research. *Sociology, 39*(2), 295–314.

Pazaitis, A., Kostakis, V., & Bauwens, M. (2017). Digital economy and the rise of open cooperativism: The case of the Enspiral Network. *Transfer: European Review of Labour and Research, 23*(2), 177–92.

Pearce, C., & Artemesia. (2009). *Communities of Play: Emergent Cultures in Multiplayer Games and Virtual Worlds*. Cambridge, MA: MIT Press.

Pechenick, E. A., Danforth, C. M., & Dodds, P. S. (2015). Characterizing the Google Books corpus: Strong limits to inferences of socio-cultural and linguistic evolution. *PLoS ONE, 10*(10), e0137041. Retrieved from https://doi.org/10.1371/journal.pone.0137041.

Pendry, L. F., & Salvatore, J. (2015). Individual and social benefits of online discussion forums. *Computers in Human Behavior, 50*, 211–20.

Penner, L. (2015). "Dr Locock and his quack": Professionalizing medicine, textualizing identity in the 1840s–Kevin A. Morrison. In L. Penner & T. Sparks (eds.), *Victorian Medicine and Popular Culture* (pp. 23–40). London—New York: Routledge.

Petracci, M., Schwarz, P. K. N., Sánchez Antelo, V. I. M., & Mendes Diz, Ana M. (2017). Doctor–patient relationships amid changes in contemporary society: A view from the health communication field. *Health Sociology Review, 26*(3), 266–79. Retrieved from https://doi.org/10.1080/14461242.2017.1373031.

Pettigrew, A. M. (1990). Longitudinal field research on change: theory and practice. *Organization Science, 1*(3), 267–92.

Pietrowiak, K. (2014). Etnografia oparta na współpracy. Założenia, możliwości, ograniczenia. *Przegląd Socjologii Jakościowej, 10*(4), 18–36.

Ping, L. C., & Chee, T. S. (2009). Online discussion boards for focus group interviews: An exploratory study. *The Journal of Educational Enquiry, 2*(1), 50–60.

Piwek, L., Ellis, D. A., Andrews, S., & Joinson, A. (2016). The rise of consumer health wearables: promises and barriers. *PLoS Medicine, 13*(2), e1001953.

Possamai-Inesedy, A., & Nixon, A. (2017). A place to stand: Digital sociology and the Archimedean effect. *Journal of Sociology, 53*(4), 865–84. Retrieved from http://journals.sagepub.com/doi/abs/10.1177/1440783317744104.

Pouwelse, J. A., Garbacki, P., Epema, D., & Sips, H. (2008). Pirates and Samaritans: A decade of measurements on peer production and their implications for net neutrality and copyright. *Telecommunications Policy, 32*(11), 701–12.

Pragnell, C., & Gatzidis, C. (2011). Addiction in world of warcraft: A virtual ethnography study. In H. H. Yang & S. C.-Y. Yuen (eds.), *Handbook of Research on Practices and Outcomes in Virtual Worlds and Environments*. Hershey: Information Science Reference.

Preda, A. (2017). *Noise: Living and Trading in Electronic Finance*. Chicago: University of Chicago Press.

Prensky, M. (2001) Digital natives, digital immigrants. Part 1. *On the Horizon, 9*(5): 1–6.

Priedhorsky, R., Chen, J., Lam, S. T. K., Panciera, K., Terveen, L., & Riedl, J. (2007). Creating, destroying, and restoring value in Wikipedia. *Proceedings of the International ACM Conference on Supporting Group Work*, 259–68.

Prior, L. (2003). Belief, knowledge and expertise: The emergence of the lay expert in medical sociology. *Sociology of health & illness, 25*(3), 41–57. Retrieved from https://onlinelibrary.wiley.com/doi/abs/10.1111/1467-9566.00339.

Prus, R. C. (1996). *Symbolic Interaction and Ethnographic Research: Intersubjectivity and the Study of Human Lived Experience*. Albany, NY: SUNY Press.

Przegalińska, A. (2015a). Embodiment, engagement and the strength virtual communities: Avatars of second life in decay. *Tamara Journal for Critical Organization Inquiry, 13*(4), 48–62.

Przegalińska, A. (2015b). The Melon app, quantified self, and the Internet of Things. In G. Mazurek (ed.), *Management in Virtual Environments*. Warszawa: Poltext.

Przegalińska, A., Ciechanowski, L., Magnuski, M., & Gloor, P. (2018). Muse headband: Measuring tool or a collaborative gadget? In F. Grippa, J. Leitão, J. Gluesing, K. Riopelle, & P. Gloor (eds.), *Collaborative Innovation Networks: Building Adaptive and Resilient Organizations* (pp. 93–101). Cham: Springer International Publishing.

Purdam, K. (2014). Citizen social science and citizen data? Methodological and ethical challenges for social research. *Current Sociology, 62*(3), 374–92. Retrieved from http://journals.sagepub.com/doi/abs/10.1177/0011392114527997.

Putnam, L. L. (2009). Symbolic capital and academic fields: An alternative discourse on journal rankings. *Management Communication Quarterly, 23*(1), 127–34.

Rainie, L., & Wellman, B. (2012). *Networked: The New Social Operating System*. Cambridge, MA: MIT Press.

Randall, D., Harper, R., & Rouncefield, M. (2007). *Fieldwork for Design: Theory and Practice*. London: Springer-Verlag.

Raymond, E. S. (1999/2004). *The Cathedral and the Bazaar*. Beijing-Cambridge: O'Reilly.

Raza, S. A., Qazi, W., & Umer, A. (2017). Facebook is a source of social capital building among university students: Evidence from a developing country. *Journal of Educational Computing Research, 55*(3), 295–322.

Razaghpanah, A., Niaki, A. A., Vallina-Rodriguez, N., Sundaresan, S., Amann, J., & Gill, P. (2017). Studying TLS usage in Android apps. Paper presented at the Proceedings of the 13th International Conference on Emerging Networking Experiments and Technologies.

Reagle, J. M. (2010). *Good Faith Collaboration: The Culture of Wikipedia*. Cambridge, MA: MIT Press.

Reed, W. J. (2001). The Pareto, Zipf and other power laws. *Economics Letters, 74*(1), 15–19.

Rheingold, H. (1993). *The Virtual Community: Homesteading on the Electronic Frontier* (Vol. 1). Reading, MA.

Rheingold, H. (1994). *The Virtual Community: Surfing the Internet*. London: Minerva.

Rich, E., & Miah, A. (2017). Mobile, wearable and ingestible health technologies: towards a critical research agenda. *Health Sociology Review, 26*(1), 84–97.

Rieder, B. (2013). Studying Facebook via data extraction: The Netvizz application. Paper presented at the Proceedings of the 5th Annual ACM Web Science Conference.

Rintel, S. (2011). Obama? Norway killings? London riots? You can has a meme for that.... *The Conversation*, https://theconversation.com/obama-norway-killings-london-riots-you-can-has-a-meme-for-that-2328.

Riordan, M. A. (2017). Emojis as tools for emotion work: Communicating affect in text messages. *Journal of Language and Social Psychology, 36*(5), 549–67.

Riordan, M. A., Kreuz, R. J., & Blair, A. N. (2018). The digital divide: Conveying subtlety in online communication. *Journal of Computers in Education, 5*(1), 49–66. Retrieved from https://doi.org/10.1007/s40692-018-0100-6.

Ritzer, G. (2006). Who's a public intellectual? *The British Journal of Sociology, 57*(2), 209–13.

Ritzer, G. (2015). Automating prosumption: The decline of the prosumer and the rise of the prosuming machines. *Journal of Consumer Culture, 15*(3), 407–24.

Ritzer, G., & Jurgenson, N. (2010). Production, consumption, prosumption: The nature of capitalism in the age of the digital "prosumer." *Journal of Consumer Culture, 10*(1), 13–36.

Robins, G. (2015). *Doing Social Network Research: Network-based Research Design for Social Scientists*. London—Thousand Oaks—New Delhi: Sage.

Robnett, B., & Feliciano, C. (2011). Patterns of racial-ethnic exclusion by internet daters. *Social Forces, 89*(3), 807–28.

Robson, C. (2002). *Real World Research: A Resource for Social Scientists and Practitioner-Researchers*. Oxford-New York: Blackwell.

Rodak, O., & Mikołajewska-Zając, K. (2017). "Paradigm clash" in the digital labor literature: Reconciling critical theory and interpretive approach in empirical research. Paper presented at the Proceedings of the 8th International Conference on Social Media & Society, Toronto, ON, Canada.

Rogers, R. (2017). Foundations of digital methods: Query design. In M. T. Schäfer & K. van Es (eds.), *The Datafied Society: Studying Culture through Data* (pp. 75–94). Amsterdam: Amsterdam University Press.

Romer, P. M. (1990). Endogenous technological change. *Journal of Political Economy, 98*(5 part 2), S71–102.

Ronson, J. (2015). How one stupid tweet blew up Justine Sacco's life. *New York Times, 12*, https://www.nytimes.com/2015/2002/2015/magazine/how-one-stupid-tweet-ruined-justine-saccos-life.html.

Ronson, J. (2016). *So You've Been Publicly Shamed*. New York: Riverhead Books.

Rosenberg, A. (2010). Virtual world research ethics and the private/public distinction. *International Journal of Internet Research Ethics, 3*(1), 23–37.

Roy, D., Patel, R., DeCamp, P., Kubat, R., Fleischman, M., Roy, B.,...Guinness, J. (2006). The human speechome project. Paper presented at the International Workshop on Emergence and Evolution of Linguistic Communication.

Rufas, A., & Hine, C. (2018). Everyday connections between online and offline: Imagining others and constructing community through local online initiatives. *New Media & Society, 20*(10), 3879–3897. Retrieved from https://journals.sagepub.com/doi/abs/10.1177/1461444818762364.

Ruhleder, K. (2000). The virtual ethnographer: Fieldwork in distributed electronic environments. *Field Methods, 12*(3), 3–17.

Rusu, I.-A. (2016). Exchanging health advice in a virtual community: A story of tribalization. *Journal of Comparative Research in Anthropology & Sociology, 7*(2), 57–69.

Rutter, J., & Smith, G. (2005). Ethnographic presence in a nebulous setting. Virtual methods: Issues in social research on the Internet. In C. Hine (ed.), *Virtual Methods. Issues in Social Research on the Internet*. Oxford: Berg Publishers.

Rybas, N., & Gajjala, R. (2007). Developing cyberethnographic research methods for understanding digitally mediated identities. *Qualitative Social Research, 8*(3), http://www.qualitative-research.net/index.php/fqs/article/view/282/620.

Sade-Beck, L. (2008). Internet ethnography: Online and offline. *International Journal of Qualitative Methods, 3*(2), 45–51.

Sadilek, A., Caty, S., DiPrete, L., Mansour, R., Schenk, T., Bergtholdt, M.,... Gabrilovich, E. (2018). Machine-learned epidemiology: real-time detection of foodborne illness at scale. *npj Digital Medicine, 1*(1), 36. Retrieved from https://doi.org/10.1038/s41746-018-0045-1.

Salmons, J. (2012). *Cases in Online Interview Research*. Thousand Oaks—New Delhi—London: Sage.

Salmons, J. (2014). *Qualitative Online Interviews: Strategies, Design, and Skills*. Thousand Oaks—New Delhi—London: Sage Publications.

Sangster, A. (2015). You cannot judge a book by its cover: The problems with journal rankings. *Accounting Education, 24*(3), 175–86.

Sanjek, R. (ed.) (1990). *Fieldnotes: The Makings of Anthropology*. Ithaca: Cornell University Press.

Sarker, S., Xiao, X., & Beaulieu, T. (2013). Qualitative studies in information systems: A critical review and some guiding principles. *Mis Quarterly, 37*(4), iii–xviii.

Savage, M., & Burrows, R. (2009). Some further reflections on the coming crisis of empirical sociology. *Sociology, 43*(4), 762–72. Retrieved from http://journals.sagepub.com/doi/abs/10.1177/0038038509105420.

Sayers, J. (2018). *The Routledge Companion to Media Studies and Digital Humanities*. London—New York: Routledge.

Sbaffi, L., & Rowley, J. (2017). Trust and credibility in web-based health information: A review and agenda for future research. *Journal of medical Internet research, 19*(6), e218.

Schaffer, R., Kuczynski, K., & Skinner, D. (2008). Producing genetic knowledge and citizenship through the Internet: Mothers, pediatric genetics, and cybermedicine. *Sociology of Health & Illness, 30*(1), 145–59. Retrieved from https://onlinelibrary.wiley.com/doi/abs/10.1111/j.1467-9566.2007.01042.x.

Schonlau, M., & Couper, M. P. (2017). Options for conducting web surveys. *Statistical Science, 32*(2), 279–92.

Schor, J. B., & Attwood-Charles, W. (2017). The "sharing" economy: Labor, inequality, and social connection on for-profit platforms. *Sociology Compass, 11*(8), e12493.

Schroeder, R. (2014). Big Data and the brave new world of social media research. *Big Data & Society, 1*(2), 1–11.

Schroeder, R., & Axelsson, A. S. (eds.). (2006). *Avatars at Work and Play: Collaboration and Interaction in Shared Virtual Environments* (Vol. 34). Dordrecht: Springer.

Scott, J. (1988). Social network analysis. *Sociology, 22*(1), 109–27.

Scott, J. W. (1991). The evidence of experience. *Critical Inquiry, 17*(4), 773–97.

Scott, S., Hinton-Smith, T., Härmä, V., & Broome, K. (2012). The reluctant researcher: Shyness in the field. *Qualitative Research, 12*(6), 715–34.

Segerberg, A., & Bennett, W. L. (2011). Social media and the organization of collective action: Using Twitter to explore the ecologies of two climate change protests. *The Communication Review, 14*(3), 197–215.

Serrano, A., Arroyo, J., & Hassan, S. (2018). Participation inequality in Wikis: A temporal analysis using WikiChron. Paper presented at the Proceedings of the 14th International Symposium on Open Collaboration.

Shalizi, C. R., & Thomas, A. C. (2011). Homophily and contagion are generically confounded in observational social network studies. *Sociological Methods & Research, 40*(2), 211–39.

Shapka, J. D., Domene, J. F., Khan, S., & Yang, L. M. (2016). Online versus in-person interviews with adolescents: An exploration of data equivalence. *Computers in Human Behavior, 58*, 361–7. Retrieved from http://www.sciencedirect.com/science/article/pii/S0747563216300164.

Sharabi, L. L., & Caughlin, J. P. (2017). What predicts first date success? A longitudinal study of modality switching in online dating. *Personal Relationships, 24*(2), 370–91.

Sharma, V., Holmes, J. H., & Sarkar, I. N. (2016). Identifying complementary and alternative medicine usage information from Internet resources. *Methods of Information in Medicine, 55*(04), 322–32.

Shaw, A., & Hill, B. M. (2014). Laboratories of oligarchy? How the iron law extends to peer production. *Journal of Communication, 64*(2), 215–38. Retrieved from http://dx.doi.org/10.1111/jcom.12082.

Shifman, L. (2014a). The cultural logic of photo-based meme genres. *Journal of Visual Culture, 13*(3), 340–58.

Shifman, L. (2014b). *Memes in Digital Culture*. Cambridge, MA: MIT Press.

Shifman, L., & Blondheim, M. (2010). The medium is the joke: Online humor about and by networked computers. *New Media & Society, 12*(8), 1348–67.

Shifman, L., & Boxman Shabtai, L. (2014). Evasive targets: Deciphering polysemy in mediated humor. *Journal of Communication, 64*(5), 977–98.

Shifman, L., Levy, H., & Thelwall, M. (2014). Internet jokes: The secret agents of globalization? *Journal of Computer-Mediated Communication, 19*(4), 727–43.

Shirky, C. (2009). *Here Comes Everybody: The Power of Organizing without Organizations.* New York: Penguin.

Sismondo, S. (2010). *An Introduction to Science and Technology Studies.* Malden-Oxford: Wiley-Blackwell Chichester.

Sixsmith, J., & Murray, C. D. (2001). Ethical issues in the documentary data analysis of Internet posts and archives. *Qualitative health research, 11*(3), 423–32.

Skoric, M. M. (2012). What is slack about slacktivism? *Methodological and Conceptual Issues in Cyber Activism Research, 77*, 77–92.

Slane, A. (2018). Information brokers, fairness, and privacy in publicly accessible information. *Canadian Journal of Comparative & Contemporary Law, 4*, 249–192.

Smahel, D., Brown, B. B., & Blinka, L. (2012). Associations between online friendship and Internet addiction among adolescents and emerging adults. *Developmental Psychology, 48*(2), 381.

Smith, A., & Anderson, M. (2016). 5 facts about online dating. *Pew Research Center,* http://www.pewresearch.org/fact-tank/2016/02/29/5-facts-about-online-dating/.

Smith, N., Wickes, R., & Underwood, M. (2015). Managing a marginalised identity in pro-anorexia and fat acceptance cybercommunities. *Journal of Sociology, 51*(4), 950–67. Retrieved from http://journals.sagepub.com/doi/abs/10.1177/1440783313486220.

Solove, D. J. (2004). *The Digital Person: Technology and Privacy in the Information Age.* New York—London: NYU Press.

Solove, D. J. (2007). *The Future of Reputation: Gossip, Rumor, and Privacy on the Internet.* New Haven: Yale University Press.

Song, H., Zmyslinski-Seelig, A., Kim, J., Drent, A., Victor, A., Omori, K., & Allen, M. (2014). Does Facebook make you lonely?: A meta analysis. *Computers in Human Behavior, 36*, 446–52.

Sparkes-Vian, C. (2018). Digital propaganda: The tyranny of ignorance. *Critical Sociology*(preprint), 10.1177/0896920517754241. Retrieved from http://journals.sagepub.com/doi/abs/10.1177/0896920517754241.

Spencer, R. W., & Woods, T. J. (2010). The long tail of idea generation. *International Journal of Innovation Science, 2*(2), 53–63.

Sperschneider, W., & Bagger, K. (2003). Ethnographic fieldwork under industrial constraints: Toward design-in-context. *International journal of human-computer interaction, 15*(1), 41–50.

Spiller, K., Ball, K., Bandara, A., Meadows, M., McCormick, C., Nuseibeh, B., & Price, B. A. (2018). Data privacy: Users' thoughts on quantified self personal data. In B. Ajana (ed.), *Self-Tracking: Empirical and Philosophical Investigations* (pp. 111–24). Cham: Springer International Publishing.

Spillman, L. (2014). Mixed methods and the logic of qualitative inference. *Qualitative Sociology, 37*(2), 189–205.

Srnicek, N. (2017). *Platform Capitalism.* New York: John Wiley & Sons.

Stacey, J. (1999). Virtual truth with a vengeance. *Contemporary Sociology, 28*(1), 18–23.

Stake, R. E. (2005). Qualitative case studies. In N. K. Denzin & Y. S. Lincoln (eds.), *Handbook of Qualitative Research* (Vol. 3, pp. 443–66). Thousand Oaks: Sage.

Stallman, R. M. (2009). Viewpoint: Why open source misses the point of free software. *Communications of the ACM, 52*(6), 31–3. Retrieved from https://dl.acm.org/citation.cfm?id=1516058

Stallman, R. M., & Gay, J. (2009). *Free Software, Free Society: Selected Essays of Richard M. Stallman*. Paramount, CA: CreateSpace.

Stasik, A. (2018). Global controversies in local settings: anti-fracking activism in the era of Web 2.0. *Journal of Risk Research, 21*(12), 1562–78. Retrieved from https://doi.org/10.1080/13669877.2017.1313759.

Stebbins, R. A. (2001). *Exploratory Research in the Social Sciences* (Vol. 48). London—Thousand Oaks—New Delhi: Sage.

Steinberger, B. Z. (2017). Redefining employee in the gig economy: Shielding workers from the Uber model. *Fordham Journal of Corporate & Finance Law, 23*, 577–96.

Steinmetz, K. F. (2012). Message received: Virtual ethnography in online message boards. *International Journal of Qualitative Methods, 11*(1): 26–39.

Stephany, A. (2015). *The Business of Sharing: Making it in the New Sharing Economy*. London–New York: Palgrave-Macmillan.

Stroud, S. R., & Cox, W. (2018). The varieties of feminist counterspeech in the misogynistic online world. In J. R. Vickery & T. Everbach (eds.), *Mediating Misogyny: Gender, Technology, and Harassment* (pp. 293–310). Cham: Springer International Publishing.

Strumińska-Kutra, M. (2016). Engaged scholarship: Steering between the risks of paternalism, opportunism, and paralysis. *Organization, 23*(6), 864–83. Retrieved from https://journals.sagepub.com/doi/abs/10.1177/1350508416631163.

Sturges, P. (2015). Limits to freedom of expression? The problem of blasphemy. *IFLA Journal, 41*(2), 112–19. Retrieved from http://journals.sagepub.com/doi/abs/10.1177/0340035215584778.

Sudweeks, F., & Simoff, S. J. (1999). Complementary explorative data analysis: The reconciliation of quantitative and qualitative principles. In S. Jones (ed.), *Doing Internet Research: Critical Issues and Methods for Examining the Net*. Thousand Oaks—London—New Delhi: Sage.

Sugihartati, R. (2017). Youth fans of global popular culture: Between prosumer and free digital labourer. *Journal of Consumer Culture*, https://doi.org/10.1177/1469540517736522.

Surowiecki, J. (2004). *The Wisdom of Crowds*. New York: Anchor Books.

Sutton, J. (2011). An ethnographic account of doing survey research in prison: Descriptions, reflections, and suggestions from the field. *Qualitative Sociology Review, 7*(2), 45–63.

Sveningsson Elm, M. (2009). How do various notions of privacy influence decisions in qualitative internet research? In A. Markham & N. Baym (eds.), *Internet Inquiry: Conversations about Method* (pp. 69–87). London-New Delhi-Thousand Oaks: Sage.

Swan, M. (2013). The quantified self: Fundamental disruption in big data science and biological discovery. *Big Data, 1*(2), 85–99.

Sztompka, P. (1991). *Society in Action: The Theory of Social Becoming*. Chicago: University of Chicago Press.

Sztompka, P. (1993). Civilizational incompetence: The trap of post-communist societies. *Zeitschrift für Soziologie, 22*(2), 85–95. Retrieved from https://www.degruyter.com/view/j/zfsoz.1993.22.issue-2/zfsoz-1993-0201/zfsoz-1993-0201.xml.

Sztompka, P. (1999). *Trust: A Sociological Theory.* Cambridge, UK—New York, NY: Cambridge University Press.

Tay, L., Jebb, A. T., & Woo, S. E. (2017). Video capture of human behaviors: Toward a Big Data approach. *Current Opinion in Behavioral Sciences, 18*, 17–22.

Taycher, L. (2010). Books of the world, stand up and be counted! All 129,864,880 of you. *Google Books Search Blog,* https://booksearch.blogspot.com/2010/2008/books-of-world-stand-up-and-be-counted.html.

Terranova, T. (2004). *Network Culture: Cultural Politics for the Information Age.* New York: Pluto Press.

Thelwall, M. (2009). *Introduction to Webometrics: Quantitative Web Research for the Social Sciences* (Vol. 1). San Rafael, CA: Morgan & Claypool.

Thet, T. T., Na, J.-C., & Khoo, C. S. G. (2010). Aspect-based sentiment analysis of movie reviews on discussion boards. *Journal of Information Science, 36*(6), 823–48. Retrieved from http://journals.sagepub.com/doi/abs/10.1177/0165551510388123.

Thomas, D. R., Pastrana Portillo, S., Hutchings, A., Clayton, R. N., & Beresford, A. R. (2017). Ethical issues in research using datasets of illicit origin. *Proceedings of IMC '17,* https://www.repository.cam.ac.uk/handle/1810/267728.

Thomas, J. (1996). When cyber-research goes wrong: The ethics of the Rimm "Cyberporn" study. *The Information Society, 12*(2), 189–97.

Tourish, D., & Willmott, H. (2015). In defiance of folly: Journal rankings, mindless measures and the ABS guide. *Critical Perspectives on Accounting, 26*, 37–46.

Tousijn, W. (2006). Beyond decline: Consumerism, managerialism and the need for a new medical professionalism. *Health Sociology Review, 15*(5), 469–80.

Travers, M. (2009). New methods, old problems: A sceptical view of innovation in qualitative research. *Qualitative Research, 9*(2), 161–79.

Tsing, A. L. (2011). *Friction: An Ethnography of Global Connection.* Princeton: Princeton University Press.

Tsvetkova, M., García-Gavilanes, R., Floridi, L., & Yasseri, T. (2017). Even good bots fight: The case of Wikipedia. *PLoS ONE, 12*(2), e0171774.

Tushman, M. L., & Scanlan, T. J. (1981). Boundary spanning individuals: Their role in information transfer and their antecedents. *Academy of Management Journal, 24*(2), 289–305.

Underberg, N. M., & Zorn, E. (2013). *Digital Ethnography: Anthropology, Narrative, and New Media.* Austin: University of Texas Press.

Van de Rijt, A., Shor, E., Ward, C., & Skiena, S. (2013). Only 15 minutes? The social stratification of fame in printed media. *American Sociological Review, 78*(2), 266–89.

Van Dijck, J. (2009). Users like you? Theorizing agency in user-generated content. *Media, Culture, and Society, 31*(1), 41–58.

Van Dijck, J., & Nieborg, D. (2009). Wikinomics and its discontents: A critical analysis of Web 2.0 business manifestos. *New Media & Society, 11*(5), 855–74.

Van Dijck, J., Poell, T., & de Waal, M. (2018). *Platform Society.* Oxford: Oxford University Press.

Van Maanen, J. (1988/2011). *Tales of the Field: On Writing Ethnography* (2nd ed.). Chicago: University of Chicago Press.

Van Selm, M., & Jankowski, N. W. (2006). Conducting online surveys. *Quality and Quantity, 40*(3), 435–56. Retrieved from https://doi.org/10.1007/s11135-005-8081-8.

Varnhagen, C. K., Gushta, M., Daniels, J., Peters, T. C., Parmar, N., Law, D.,... Johnson, T. (2005). How informed is online informed consent? *Ethics and Behavior, 15*(1), 37–48.

Vergeer, M. (2015). Twitter and political campaigning. *Sociology Compass, 9*(9), 745–60. Retrieved from https://onlinelibrary.wiley.com/doi/abs/10.1111/soc4.12294.

Vessuri, H., Guédon, J.-C., & Cetto, A. M. (2014). Excellence or quality? Impact of the current competition regime on science and scientific publishing in Latin America and its implications for development. *Current Sociology, 62*(5), 647–65.

Vickery, J. R. (2014). The curious case of Confession Bear: The reappropriation of online macro-image memes. *Information, Communication & Society, 17*(3), 301–25. Retrieved from https://doi.org/10.1080/1369118X.2013.871056.

Vigen, T. (2015). *Spurious Correlations*. New York: Hachette Books.

Virno, P. (2008). Jokes and innovative action: For a logic of change. *Artforum, 46*(5), 251–8.

Von Hippel, E., & Von Krogh, G. (2003). Open source software and the" private-collective" innovation model: Issues for organization science. *Organization Science, 14*(2), 209–23.

Wakeford, N. (2003). The embedding of local culture in global communication: Independent internet cafes in London. *New Media & Society, 5*(3), 379–99.

Walker, A., & Panfil, V. R. (2017). Minor attraction: A queer criminological issue. *Critical Criminology, 25*(1), 37–53.

Walker, N. A. (1988). *A Very Serious Thing: Women's Humor and American Culture*. Minneapolis: University of Minnesota Press.

Walsh, D. (2004). Doing ethnography. In C. Seale (ed.), *Researching Society and Culture* (pp. 245–62). Newbury Park—London—New Delhi: Sage.

Walzer, S., & Oles, T. P. (2003). Accounting for divorce: Gender and uncoupling narratives. *Qualitative Sociology, 26*(3), 331–49.

Wang, D., Piazza, A., & Soule, S. A. (2018). Boundary-spanning in social movements: Antecedents and outcomes. *Annual Review of Sociology, 44*(1), 167–87. Retrieved from https://www.annualreviews.org/doi/abs/10.1146/annurev-soc-073117-041258.

Wang, T. (2013). Big data needs thick data. *Ethnography Matters, 13*, http://ethnographymatters.net/2013/2005/2013/big-data-needs-thick-data/.

Wang, Y., & Kosinski, M. (2018). Deep neural networks are more accurate than humans at detecting sexual orientation from facial images. *Journal of Personality and Social Psychology, 114*(2), 246–57.

Ward, J. (2017). What are you doing on Tinder? Impression management on a matchmaking mobile app. *Information, Communication & Society, 20*(11), 1644–59. Retrieved from https://doi.org/10.1080/1369118X.2016.1252412.

Warner, W. L., & Low, J. O. (1947). *The Social System of the Modern Factory: The Strike: A Social Analysis* (Vol. 4). New Haven: Yale University Press.

Washburn, J. (2006). *University, Inc.: The Corporate Corruption of Higher Education*. New York: Basic Books.

Weaver, S. (2010a). Liquid racism and the Danish Prophet Muhammad cartoons. *Current Sociology, 58*(5), 675–92.

Weaver, S. (2010b). The "Other" laughs back: Humour and resistance in anti-racist comedy. *Sociology, 44*(1), 31–48.

Weber, S. (2004). *The Success of Open Source*. Cambridge: Harvard University Press.

Weick, K. E. (1969/1979). *The Social Psychology of Organizing*. Reading, MA: Addison-Wesley Publications.

Wellman, B. (2004). The three ages of Internet studies: Ten, five and zero years ago. *New Media & Society, 6*(1), 123–9.

Wellman, B., & Berkowitz, S. D. (eds.). (1988). *Social Structures: A Network Approach*. Cambridge: Cambridge University Press.

Wen, Q., Gloor, P., Fronzetti Colladon, A., Tickoo, P., & Joshi, T. (2019). Finding top performers through email patterns analysis. *Journal of Information Science* (forthcoming), Retrieved from https://journals.sagepub.com/doi/abs/10.1177/0165551519849519.

Werbner, P., & Modood, T. (eds.). (2015). *Debating Cultural Hybridity: Multicultural Identities and the Politics of Anti-racism*. London: Zed Books.

White, D. S., & Le Cornu, A. (2011). Visitors and residents: A new typology for online engagement. *First Monday, 16*(9), DOI:10.5210/fm.v5216i5219.3171.

Whiteman, N. (2012). *Undoing Ethics. Rethinking Practice in Online Research*. New York-Dortrecht-Heidelberg-London: Springer.

Whyte, W. F. (1943/2012). *Street Corner Society: The Social Structure of an Italian Slum*. Chicago: University of Chicago Press.

Whyte, W. F., & Whyte, K. K. (1984). *Learning from the Field: A Guide from Experience*. Beverly Hills: Sage Publications.

Wiggins, B. E., & Bowers, G. B. (2015). Memes as genre: A structurational analysis of the memescape. *New Media & Society, 17*(11), 1886–1906.

Williams, M. L. (2007). Avatar watching: Participant observation in graphical online environments. *Qualitative Research, 7*(1), 5–24.

Williams, M. L., Burnap, P., & Sloan, L. (2017). Towards an ethical framework for publishing Twitter data in social research: Taking into account users' views, online context and algorithmic estimation. *Sociology, 51*(6), 1149–68.

Willis, P. (2013). *The Ethnographic Imagination*. New York: John Wiley & Sons.

Wittel, A. (2013). Counter-commodification: The economy of contribution in the digital commons. *Culture and Organization, 19*(4), 314–31.

Wojtala, M. (2018). Internet jako medium dla propagandy. *Młoda Humanistyka, 11*(1). Retrieved from http://www.humanistyka.com/index.php/MH/article/view/138.

Wolf, D. R. (1991). *The Rebels: A Brotherhood of Outlaw Bikers*. Toronto: University of Toronto Press.

Wolf, M. (1992). *A Thrice-told Tale: Feminism, Postmodernism, and Ethnographic Responsibility*. Stanford: Stanford University Press.

Wolfendale, J. (2007). My avatar, my self: Virtual harm and attachment. *Ethics and Information Technology, 9*, 111–19.

Wood, M. (1994). *Radical Satire and Print Culture, 1790–1822*. Oxford: Oxford University Press.

Wooldridge, T. (2014). The enigma of Ana: A psychoanalytic exploration of pro-anorexia internet forums. *Journal of Infant, Child, and Adolescent Psychotherapy, 13*(3), 202–16. Retrieved from https://doi.org/10.1080/15289168.2014.937978.

Woolgar, S. (1991). The turn to technology in social studies of science. *Science, Technology, & Human Values, 16*(1), 20–50.

Woźniak, A. (2016). Dyskurs wegański i wegetariański a szowinizm gatunkowy w memach internetowych. *Zoophilogica. Polish Journal of Animal Studies, 14*(2), 151–64.

Wu, S., & Ward, J. (2018). The mediation of gay men's lives: A review on gay dating app studies. *Sociology Compass, 12*(2), e12560.

Yang, Y. T., Delamater, P. L., Leslie, T. F., & Mello, M. M. (2016). Sociodemographic predictors of vaccination exemptions on the basis of personal belief in California. *American Journal of Public Health, 106*(1), 172–7. Retrieved from https://ajph.aphapublications.org/doi/abs/10.2105/AJPH.2015.302926.

Yeritsian, G. (2017). "Capitalism 2.0": Web 2.0 manifestoes and the new spirit of capitalism. *Critical Sociology, 44*(4–5), 703–17. Retrieved from https://doi.org/10.1177/0896920517691109.

Youyou, W., Kosinski, M., & Stillwell, D. (2015). Computer-based personality judgments are more accurate than those made by humans. *Proceedings of the National Academy of Sciences, 112*(4), 1036–40.

Ytre-Arne, B., & Das, R. (2019). An agenda in the interest of audiences: Facing the challenges of intrusive media technologies. *Television & New Media, 20*(2), 184–98.

Zannettou, S., Caulfield, T., Blackburn, J., De Cristofaro, E., Sirivianos, M., Stringhini, G., & Suarez-Tangil, G. (2018). On the origins of memes by means of fringe Web communities. *arXiv preprint*(arXiv:1805.12512).

Zhang, P., Li, M., Gao, L., Fan, Y., & Di, Z. (2014). Characterizing and modeling the dynamics of activity and popularity. *PLoS ONE, 9*(2), e89192.

Zimmer, M. (2018). Addressing conceptual gaps in Big Data research ethics: An application of contextual integrity. *Social Media+ Society, 4*(2), doi.org/10.1177/2056305118768300.

Zimmer, M. (2010). "But the data is already public": On the ethics of research in Facebook. *Ethics and Information Technology, 12*, 313–25.

Zittrain, J. (2008). *The Future of the Internet and How to Stop It*. New Haven: Yale University Press.

Zook, M., Barocas, S., Crawford, K., Keller, E., Gangadharan, S. P., Goodman, A.,… Narayanan, A. (2017). Ten simple rules for responsible big data research. *PLoS Computational Biology, 13*(3), e1005399.

Zukerfeld, M. (2017). The tale of the snake and the elephant: Intellectual property expansion under informational capitalism. *The Information Society, 33*(5), 243–60. Retrieved from https://doi.org/10.1080/01972243.2017.1354107.

Zukin, S., & Papadantonakis, M. (2017). Hackathons as co-optation ritual: Socializing Workers And Institutionalizing Innovation In The "New" Economy. In A. L. Kalleberg & S. P. Vallas (eds.), *Precarious Work* (pp. 157–81). Bingley: Emerald Publishing Limited.

Index